ATLA PUBLICATIONS SERIES
edited by Dr. Jack Ammerman

1. *The Literature of Islam: A Guide to Primary Sources in English Translation*, by Paula Youngman Skreslet and Rebecca Skreslet, 2006.
2. *A Broadening Conversation: Classic Readings in Theological Librarianship*, edited by Melody Layton McMahon and David R. Stewart, 2006.
3. *Donald G. Bloesch: A Research Bibliography*, by Paul E. Maher, 2007.

Donald G. Bloesch

A Research Bibliography

Paul E. Maher

ATLA Publications Series, No. 3

The Scarecrow Press, Inc.
Lanham, Maryland • Toronto • Plymouth, UK
and
American Theological Library Association
2007

SCARECROW PRESS, INC.

Published in the United States of America
by Scarecrow Press, Inc.
A wholly owned subsidiary of
The Rowman & Littlefield Publishing Group, Inc.
4501 Forbes Boulevard, Suite 200, Lanham, Maryland 20706
www.scarecrowpress.com

Estover Road
Plymouth PL6 7PY
United Kingdom

Copyright © 2007 by Paul E. Maher

British Library Cataloguing in Publication Information Available

Library of Congress Cataloging-in-Publication Data

Maher, Paul, 1951–
    Donald G. Bloesch : a research bibliography / Paul E. Maher.
        p. cm.—(ATLA publications series ; no. 3)
    Includes bibliographical references and index.
    ISBN-13: 978-0-8108-5989-0 (cloth : alk. paper)
    ISBN-10: 0-8108-5989-0 (cloth : alk. paper)
  1. Bloesch, Donald G., 1928—Bibliography. I. Title.
    Z8105.56.M24 2007
    [BX4827.B54]
    230'.044092–dc22   2007019276

∞™ The paper used in this publication meets the minimum requirements of
American National Standard for Information Sciences—Permanence of
Paper for Printed Library Materials, ANSI/NISO Z39.48-1992.
Manufactured in the United States of America.

In memory of my parents
Lewis Alexander Maher, 1904–1992
Ellen Irene Maher, 1920–2002

Contents

Foreword

I am most grateful to Paul Maher and the American Theological Library Association (ATLA) for making available this complete bibliography of my writings. A number of these books and articles have their origins in lectures in classes at the University of Dubuque Theological Seminary and conferences sponsored by churches, reformist groups, and educational institutions. This list of publications reveals my efforts to establish rapport with various traditions and movements without promoting syncretism or eclecticism. Among the ventures of faith that have commanded my attention are evangelical religious communities, the ecumenical dialogue, and renewal efforts within the mainline denominations. I have also engaged in conversations with churches and movements that are generally designated as sects and cults, most of which challenge the hegemony of the mainline churches. I am thinking here of such innovations as the Holiness revival, the Churches of Christ, the Seventh-Day Adventist Church, Dispensationalism, and the New Age movement. My principal partners in ecumenical conversations have been the Churches of the Protestant Reformation; the Free Churches, which have asserted their independence from state control; the Roman Catholic Church; and the Eastern Orthodox Churches.

Throughout my writing career, I have sought to build the case for an evangelical catholicism that rigorously upholds the authority and infallibility of the Bible and the overall reliability of church tradition, particularly as it is expressed in the creeds and confessions of the patristic church and the Reformation churches. Regrettably, the books and articles that I am presently working on cannot be included in this bibliography because it quite understandably records only those works that have actually been published. Although the decision has been made not to include foreign-language editions of my works, at least at this juncture in my writing vocation, it is well to note my interaction with eastern European and third-world churches. It is my hope that the data on these and some of my future publications will appear in a supplemental volume at a later date.

My future writings will focus on spirituality more than on academic theology, for I am convinced that the principal challenge facing the church of tomorrow is the practice of the Christian faith in a postmodern world. Throughout my research and writing, I continue to be in dialogue with the leading lights of Catholic and Orthodox mysticism as well as with the leaders and shapers of worldwide Protestantism, especially Reformed Protestantism. I see the hope of the church of tomorrow in a convergence of opinion on the salient doctrines and issues that have divided the churches in the past. A genuine reform of the church cannot take place without people of faith pressing for the unity of the churches based on truth rather than on an amalgamation of disparate views and practices that serve to hide rather than overcome our disunity.

It is said that the last ecumenical frontier is confronting the cleavage that exists between evangelical Protestants and ecumenists—those who seek to maintain continuity with the apostolic and patristic traditions that have shaped the history of Christianity. My work is dedicated to mitigating these tensions and breaking through the barriers between the churches, thereby preparing the way for a unified Christian witness in a postmodern and post-Christian world.

In the ecumenical vision I propose, I draw a firm distinction between an evangelical ecumenism bent on returning to the foundations of the faith and liberalism, which reduces ecumenicity to interfaith collaboration based on a common religious experience. Liberalism tries to erase the lines between religions but at the price of blurring the pivotal claims of each religion. When liberalism penetrates the bastions of Christianity, it invariably undercuts the apostolic dictum that Christ alone provides the way to salvation.

Again, I am indebted to my friend and former student Paul Maher for his painstaking research and his prodigious efforts to ensure accuracy. I also wish to express my appreciation to my wife Brenda for her work in tracing authors and publishers of articles and reviews contained in this volume.

Donald G. Bloesch
Emeritus Professor of Theology
University of Dubuque Theological Seminary

Acknowledgments

First and foremost, I extend my deepest appreciation to Professor and Mrs. Donald G. Bloesch for their encouragement throughout the course of this project and for their pointing me to key resources along the way. They have made many articles and papers available to me to which I would not otherwise have had access. I have been privileged to enjoy many hours of conversation with them on the telephone, via their hospitality at Bishop's Cafeteria in Dubuque and in their home. They are models of graciousness.

I offer my appreciation and admiration to Patrick McManus for having written "An Introduction to the Theology of Donald G. Bloesch," which appears in this volume.

I extend my warmest thanks and express my indebtedness also to Professor Joel Samuels, university archivist, and Mary Anne Knefel, university librarian, both of the University of Dubuque for providing unlimited access to the Bloesch archives, granting me hours from their busy schedules, and performing several online database searches.

I am grateful to Jack Ammerman, head librarian, Boston University School of Theology and series editor for the American Theological Library Association Bibliographic Series and to April Snider and Andrew Yoder of Scarecrow Press, for their patience and encouragement during the process of bringing this work to press.

I express my gratitude to many correspondents for answering questions about publication details, providing me with photocopies of articles, and so on. I am especially indebted to James Hafner, Library of Congress, Washington, D.C., for quite a number of difficult-to-find sources. In addition, I express my thanks to:

William Badke, associate librarian, Trinity Western University, Langley,
B.C.

Dr. Robert Q. Bailey, Spring Arbor University, Spring Arbor, Mich.

Rita Berk, library director, Moravian College and Moravian Theological
Seminary, Bethlehem, Pa.

Brenda Bickett, Middle Eastern and Islamic studies bibliographer,
Georgetown University, Washington, D.C.

Keith Bodner, Tyndale University College, Toronto, Ont.

Julie Bosak, office administrator, First Covenant Church, Omaha, Neb.

Marc Games, information services assistant, San Mateo Public Library,
San Mateo, Calif.

Francis Gardom, Trushare, London, England, U.K.

Jennine Goodart, head of interlibrary loan, Trinity International University, Deerfield, Ill.

Pat Gore, editor, *Vermont Catholic Tribune*, Burlington, Vt.

Douglas L. Gragg, Ph.D., head of public services and reference librarian, Pitts Theology Library, Emory University, Atlanta, Ga.

Matthew Hamilton, Moore Theological College Library, Newtown,
N.S.W., Australia

Susan Lehrman, assistant to the registrar, Tabor College, Hillsboro, Kan.

Dr. John Maher, Indiana Wesleyan University, Marion, Ind.

Erin Miller, administrative assistant, Mennonite Historical Library,
Goshen, Ind.

Rick Oliver, assistant director of library services, Assemblies of God
Theological Seminary, Springfield, Mo.

Elaine Fetyko Page, head of technical services, college archivist, A. C.
Buehler Library, Elmhurst College, Elmhurst, Ill.

Dr. David Parker, Indooroopilly, Qld., Australia

Elaine Philpott, Disciples of Christ Historical Society, Nashville, Tenn.

Brenda Quattlebaum, circulation manager, *The Baptist Record*, Jackson,
Miss.

John H. Rush, librarian, Emmaus Bible College, Dubuque, Iowa

Malc Seaman, The Church at Gun Hill, Pitsea, Basildon, Essex, England,
U.K.

Gary Shook, library director, Grace University Library, Omaha, Neb.

Matthew J. Smith, academic copywriter, InterVarsity Press, Downers
Grove, Ill.

John D. Thiesen, archivist and codirector of libraries, Mennonite Library and Archives, North Newton, Kas.

Gerald Turnbull, librarian, Vancouver School of Theology, Vancouver,
B.C.

Wayne Turner, coeditor, *Gospel Herald*, Beamsville, Ont.

Emily Van Dyke, Hall County Library System, Gainesville, Ga.

Joann Van Meter, rights coordinator, Standard Publishing, Cincinnati, Ohio

Chris Watson, *Santa Cruz Sentinel*, Santa Cruz, Calif.

Janet Wileman, international sales coordinator, InterVarsity Press, Nottingham, U.K.

In addition to the people mentioned above, I express my gratitude to the following libraries for making their collections open to the public:

Asbury Theological Seminary Library, Wilmore, Ky.
Associated Mennonite Biblical Seminary Library, Elkhart, Ind.
Ball State University Library, Muncie, Ind.
Billy Graham Center Library, Wheaton, Ill.
Calvin College Library, Grand Rapids, Mich.
Carnegie-Stout Public Library, Dubuque, Iowa
Christian Theological Seminary Library, Indianapolis, Ind.
Concordia Theological Seminary Library, Ft. Wayne, Ind.
Emmaus Bible College Library, Dubuque, Iowa
Galesburg Public Library, Galesburg, Ill.
Goshen College Library, Goshen, Ind.
Grace Theological Seminary Library, Winona Lake, Ind.
Illinois State University Library, Normal, Ill.
Illinois Wesleyan University Library, Bloomington, Ill.
Indiana Wesleyan University Library, Marion, Ind.
Lexington Theological Seminary Library, Lexington, Ky.
Lincoln Christian College and Seminary Library, Lincoln, Ill.
Loras College Library, Dubuque, Iowa
Louisville Presbyterian Theological Seminary Library, Louisville, Ky.
Mennonite Historical Library, Goshen, Ind.
Monmouth College Library, Monmouth, Ill.
Quincy University Library, Quincy, Ill.
Southern Baptist Theological Seminary Library, Louisville, Ky.
Southern Illinois University Library, Carbondale, Ill.
Taylor University Library, Ft. Wayne, Ind.
University of Dubuque Library, Dubuque, Iowa
University of Illinois Library, Urbana–Champaign, Ill.
University of Iowa Libraries, Iowa City, Iowa
Wartburg Theological Seminary Library, Dubuque, Iowa
Western Illinois University Library, Macomb, Ill.
Wheaton College Library, Wheaton, Ill.

Addenda, corrigenda, and gentle suggestions are welcomed via e-mail: pmah@mchsi.com.

An Introduction to the Theology of Donald G. Bloesch

Patrick M. McManus

> It is indeed refreshing to have the note of certainty struck when so much
> of theology seems to parade unbelief.[1]

It is fitting to begin this introduction to the theology of Donald G. Bloesch
with a brief remark by Karl Barth made upon his only visit to North
America. It is fitting not least of all because of his immense influence on
Bloesch's theology. In his 1962 lectures at Princeton Seminary, Barth char-
acterized an authentic "evangelical" theology:

> What the word "evangelical" will objectively designate is that theology
> which treats the *God of the Gospel*. "Evangelical" signifies the "catholic," ecu-
> menical . . . *continuity and unity* of this theology. Such theology intends to ap-
> prehend, to understand, and to speak of the God of the Gospel, in the midst
> of the variety of all other theologies and . . . in distinction from them. This is
> the God who reveals himself in the Gospel, who himself speaks to men and
> acts among and upon them. Wherever he becomes the object of human sci-
> ence, both its source and its norm, there is *evangelical* theology.[2]

Anyone well acquainted with the theology of Donald Bloesch understands how well he embodies Barth's description.

Donald George Bloesch was born in Bremen, Indiana, in 1928. His father, Herbert Bloesch, was a minister in the Evangelical Synod of North
America, which had its roots in Lutheran and Reformed Pietism. One of
his father's personal friends was Reinhold Niebuhr, who was ordained in
the same denomination as Donald's father. Donald remembers hearing
how his father drove Niebuhr around in a horse-drawn buggy when
Niebuhr was selling books for part-time employment. His maternal

grandparents in particular made sure that the young Bloesch was introduced to the Bible and to John Bunyan's *Pilgrim's Progress*. It was this pietistic heritage that shaped the theological thinking of the young Bloesch—a heritage that continues to inform his theology to this day.

In 1946, Bloesch entered Elmhurst College, at that time a preparatory pretheological school for students in the Evangelical and Reformed Church. Here he first encountered "liberal" theology, although not in the sophisticated form he would later meet at the University of Chicago. After graduation from Elmhurst, Bloesch entered Chicago Theological Seminary, where he completed a bachelor of divinity degree. He continued on in 1953 to pursue a PhD, the same year he was ordained in the United Church of Christ. After completing a dissertation under Bernard Meland on the apologetic theology of Reinhold Niebuhr,[3] Bloesch attained his doctorate in 1956. Previously, he had nearly completed a dissertation that Daniel Day Williams had agreed to supervise, but Williams left for another faculty, and Bloesch learned that he would need to begin a second dissertation.

After a period of postdoctoral study at Oxford University in England, Bloesch began his career as teacher of theology at the University of Dubuque Theological Seminary (UDTS) in the fall of 1957. Ironically, he was hired on a one-year contract, partly to offset the Barthian influence of Arthur Cochrane. The administration had assumed that his PhD from the University of Chicago Divinity School would reflect the liberalism of that environment. Thirty-five years later, in May of 1993, Bloesch, certainly no less a "Barthian" presence than Cochrane, officially retired from UDTS.[4] Although his official teaching career has come to an end, his longtime work for renewal within mainline Protestantism continues, as does his very productive writing career. He has just completed his magnum opus, a seven-volume systematic theology that was celebrated at UDTS in the spring of 2005. In the works are a fourth volume of his *Theological Notebook*, of which there are probably another nine in the UDTS library archives! A volume to be called *Spirituality Old and New* is forthcoming from InterVarsity Press, and a book on the paradox of holiness and a spiritual autobiography are also in the works.

Throughout his career he has been influenced by a diversity of theological luminaries but most significantly by John Calvin, Martin Luther, P. T. Forsyth, Karl Barth, and Emil Brunner. Throughout his corpus, Bloesch converses with the Christian tradition as broadly as any irenic ecumenical theologian, from Tertullian to Tillich, from Bernard of Clairvaux to Berdyaev. Thus, he rightly labels himself a "catholic evangelical" theologian. His ability to fuse an erudite theological sensibility with a profound Christian piety is an example for all who seek a career in theological education. His work reflects this connection and is grounded in his conviction that theology is done for the church, by the church, and, sometimes necessarily, against the church! His reach of influence is wide, and his works have been translated into numerous languages. His career has also had a wide ecumenical impact as he has been both officially and unofficially in contact with Roman Catholics, Lutherans, Presbyterians, and United Methodists at UDTS and abroad.

If I may, I would like to digress for just a moment. An introduction to the theology of Donald Bloesch would not be complete without mentioning his wife, Brenda Bloesch, née Brenda Mary Jackson, who has long taken on the arduous but rewarding task of copyediting all of Donald's written work (which is all done on a portable typewriter) and acting as a very capable and resourceful research assistant. She holds a PhD in French literature and is a vivacious and lively personality with a joie de vivre seldom found. She is a scholar in her own right with a spirited interest in theology. To spend time with her and Donald and to see them at work together is to witness true Christian charity in a very unique form. Well then, on to business.

The purpose of this introduction, as I see it, is not to provide a survey of Bloesch's theology but to whet the appetite of the readers and invite them into the pages of Bloesch's corpus themselves. I could do so by inviting readers to some of the more contentious areas of his theology, asking, for example, whether or not he is a universalist (which of course, like Barth before him, he is not!) or what exactly he means by "postmortem salvation"—two issues that are raised in his latest volume on eschatology.[5] As interesting as these questions might be, I will limit myself to examining and expositing two main areas of Bloesch's thought. At the heart of his entire theological contribution are the method of theological inquiry, which he characterizes as a method of Word and Spirit and the nature and function of Holy Scripture. These are both areas where Bloesch's contribution is at its most exciting but also where Bloesch incurs the most misinterpretation from his critics.

BLOESCH AND THEOLOGICAL METHOD

What Bloesch recognizes is that the result of much of modern theology, as it has developed in both its liberal and fundamentalist forms, is a wholesale reduction toward anthropology. On one level, this extensive anthropologization of theology generates a firm focus on methodological questions. For latter-day evangelicals, theological method is advanced in the service of clarifying the Bible and its propositions, which often seems to serve as an "answer book" for an individualistic faith in need of epistemological certainty and assurance. Methodology then is at the same time both a ground-clearing exercise and a pretheological discussion. On a deeper level, this intensification is due to modernity's assumption that reality is a given, which can be unearthed and grasped through proper means. Modern theology, according to Bloesch, can be read as one long and diverse conversation as to what the "proper" method is. For Bloesch, this anthropologization is not only a lost cause but a great aberration—and it was mainly Karl Barth, among others, who instructed him on this basic point.

For Bloesch, reality is not a given—neither historically, philosophically, nor existentially. Reality is given only in and to faith by God's act of faithful witness to himself in Jesus Christ as attested by Scripture. To begin with a priori epistemological criteria is to err on the side of immanentism, the foible of liberalism and evangelical scholasticism alike. Both liberalism and evangelical scholasticism are engaged in efforts to *correlate* realities and thus to subtract from the comprehensiveness of the reality of the gospel by connecting it with other independent realities. Bloesch's fundamental retort is that theology does not begin with a theory of meaning, a transcendental philosophy, or any comprehensive system of truth, but rather with the good news that God has acted in Jesus Christ for the sake of the world.

It was the Barthian turn in modern theology that provided Bloesch the formal structures within which he developed his account of the nature of the theological enterprise. Likewise, it was to Anselm that Barth turned to find "a vital key, if not the key, to an understanding of that whole process of thought that has impressed me . . . as the only one proper to theology."[6] The Barthian shift, then, is in direct and significant relationship to the equally labeled "shift" that the theological method of Anselm represents. For Barth, Anselm's *Proslogion* provided the conceptual tools needed to affirm that:

> Knowledge of God within the Christian Church is very well aware that it is established in its reality and to that extent also called into question by God's Word, through which alone it can be and have reality, and on the basis of which alone it can be fulfilled. But precisely because the knowledge of God cannot call itself in question in its effort to understand itself, it cannot ask whether it is real from some position outside itself.[7]

The conceptual key to which Barth refers is the notion that knowledge of God and humanity springs not from a priori presuppositions nor experiences, but from God's act of self-revelation in Jesus Christ. Therefore, our knowledge is a posteriori knowledge in that it is rooted in the faith that is awakened through God's action: revelation, faith, and *then* understanding. Bloesch, learning from Anselm via Barth, does not develop an epistemology in the traditional philosophic sense. Rather, all formal epistemological questions are subsumed under the rubric of revelation—knowledge is a dogmatic affair and neither principally nor essentially a philosophic one! However, far from disconnecting the rational faculties from theological discourse, as Bloesch has often been accused of doing, he adopts from Anselm the notion that the intelligam is only intelligible (but is really intelligible!) this side of the credo. That is, the intelligibility of Christianity is for Bloesch a function of its subject matter, a function of critical reflection. *Fides quaerens intellectum* offers a notion of theology as rational though not rationalistic—a very important distinction for Bloesch. Joseph Mangina's description of Barth on this score is undoubtedly apt for Bloesch as well: "The world of God is not a dark night in which all cats are grey, but a coherent world, indeed a world of powerful and urgent beauty; a world that can be described. The theologian's task is to explicate revelation, not to explain it, not to show how it is possible."[8] Reason, on Bloesch's reading, is through God's action, holy reason—to take up John Webster's phrase—sanctified by God because it corresponds *by* his activity *to* his activity.[9] Bloesch nowhere truncates reason's role within theological discourse but rather wholly affirms it *dogmatically*. For Bloesch, we simply do not know what reality looks like. We do not presuppose reason as a natural faculty that gives us access to reality and then go on to weigh revelation against that assumed reality. We begin *first* with God's act of revelation, as attested by the prophetic and apostolic witness to this act—the witness of Holy Scripture to Jesus Christ—and *then* describe reality in correspondence to *that* act. God's speech itself provides the very conditions that make reasoning about God viable or possible.

Given Bloesch's reaction against modernity and its methodologies, he tends to occupy a unique location on the margin of evangelical theology. This uniqueness is due in large part to his favorable reading of Barth, a move that has placed him at odds with many of that tradition. Consider the following:

> I see the gospel as an irreversible revelation from God that transcends every human formulation but is nonetheless inseparable from the New Testament kerygma or evangelical proclamation. The gospel cannot be uncovered by a historical analysis of biblical texts. . . . Nor can the gospel be reduced to universal ethical values or transcendental ideals. The gospel is the surprising movement of God into the human history recorded in the Bible culminating in the life, death and resurrection of Jesus Christ and the corresponding movement of God in the personal history of those who believe.[10]

This could not be said in both its scope and intent without the theological inspiration of Karl Barth, especially in the impression left by the second edition of his *Römerbrief*. The influence of Barth is likewise palpable throughout Bloesch's entire corpus. His basic moves in the province of method and authority follow the same lines of Barth's bold moves. His account of "faith seeking understanding," as we have shown, is in direct relationship to Barth and Anselm.[11] His ensuing account of theological rationality, the relationship between philosophy and theology, his doctrine of Scripture and his Christocentricity are all developed in relation to the influence of Karl Barth.

Yet it is an oversimplification to label Bloesch as merely "Barthian." Bloesch seeks to move beyond Barth, but only beyond him by going "through" him, on two main issues.[12] First, he sees Barth's account of salvation as overly objectivistic and seeks to fill out Barth's soteriology through being attentive to the life of holiness. As he himself testifies, "there is an unmistakable objectivistic bent in Barth's theology that tends to undercut the necessity for personal faith and repentance."[13] Even though the tradition that encompasses Bloesch's reading of Barth on the Christian life has itself come under recent criticism,[14] nevertheless it highlights Bloesch's concern for sustained theological reflection upon the Christian life, the life of holiness. Bloesch's sustained attention to the nature of the Christian life is a unique ecumenical example that a rigorous Reformed emphasis on divine activity need not preclude attention to the moral and ethical life, but rather properly demands and funds such attention.

Bloesch also endeavors to move beyond the mature Barth of the later volumes of *Church Dogmatics* by holding to a higher sacramental theology in which God's chosen vessels of witness and attestation to his divine act are effective *signs* of God's grace and not just acts of invocation on our part: "It seems that for Barth the infinite is capable of laying hold of the finite, but the finite is not capable of bearing or carrying the infinite."[15] For Bloesch,

Jesus Christ is the *Ursacrament* of the church, the visible sign of invisible grace, but he has chosen to act through the instruments of preaching and sacraments. A church grounded in Christ will have sacraments but not magic. It will have rituals but not ritualism. No sacrament or ritual has within itself the power to redeem, but when united with the Word of God, proclaimed and written, it may play a salutary role in making Christ's salvation concrete and efficacious.[16]

Or again:

The finite cannot of and in itself carry the infinite, but the infinite can use the finite to reveal itself. By the power of the Spirit the gospel can enter creaturely structures and thereby make them means of grace. . . . The Spirit is not inherent in these creaturely structures—Bible, church, and sacrament—but enters them from above again and again. . . . God is not bound to these means of grace, but we are bound to them, since they are provided by God to guide us.[17]

DONALD BLOESCH'S DIALECTIC OF WORD AND SPIRIT

Bloesch, standing firmly within the Reformed tradition, unfolds his ruling methodological theme of the dialectic between Word and Spirit. The main impetus for this dialectic is born from his concern to maintain a healthy tension between both the objectivity of revelation (Word) and the continuous action of the Spirit, notably the faith that it produces and bears out in the community of believers:

> When I speak of Word and Spirit, I am not thinking primarily of a book that receives its stamp of approval from the Spirit, though I affirm the decisive role of the Spirit in the inspiration and illumination of Scripture. I am thinking mainly of the living Word in its inseparable unity with Scripture and church proclamation as this is brought home to us by the Spirit in the awakening of faith.[18]

Consideration of other classic dialectics, such as immanent/transcendent, divine/human, continuity/discontinuity, objectivity/subjectivity, etc., can help us appropriate the use of the above dialectic. What Bloesch engages in is a dialectical method of theological argumentation, which he adopts most directly from Barth. Yet it is much more than simply a methodological tool. For Bloesch, as for Barth before him, theological method is a function of its subject matter. That is, content informs the form and method of argument. Dialectic is the method par excellence simply because we do not know God immediately or directly. Rather, knowledge of God is mediated and indirect but nevertheless real and true knowledge. We never *have* the truth but are consistently confronted by it through God's self-revelation, by Word and Spirit. For Bloesch, knowledge of God is always both objective and subjective. It is objective in that it is God's act of speech (Word) and subjective because *we* are awakened and sanctified to acknowledgment of that objectivity through the act of the Spirit. Yet the objective/subjective dichotomy does not devolve into either logical or existential absolutes: "To affirm a theology of Word and Spirit is to affirm that the experience of faith is correlative with God's self-revelation in Jesus Christ. Since faith is a work of the Spirit in the interiority of our being, the truth of the gospel is not only announced from without but also confirmed from within."[19] Bloesch's latter insistence that the Spirit is at work sanctifying from within is only made in light of the former. Bloesch's theology of Word and Spirit is never reduced to an interiority of Spirit nor to an objectivity of Word. Reduction to interiority is a danger he associates with classic mysticism and a type of Pentecostalism while reduction to objectivism is a danger he associates with Protestant scholasticism. Theology for Bloesch is always *theologia viatorum*, a theology for those along the way, and never *theologia comprehensorum*, theology for those who have arrived.[20]

Bloesch's concerns are developed in relation to two equally prominent dangers to theology—conservatism's rigid orthodoxy on the one hand and modern liberalism's anthropological theology on the other. The two dangers can, in fact, be understood as polarizing tendencies within the dialectic. Conservatism's fascination with the Word becomes a kind of objectivity and liberalism's emphasis on the Spirit a kind of subjectivity. Bloesch goes behind Protestant orthodoxy, as it developed through scholastics like Turretin or its later development in the Princeton theology of the nineteenth century, to the sources of the Reformed tradition. Convinced that these theologians were involved not so much in rehearing the Reformers as they were in developing an entirely modern/positivistic orthodox theology, Bloesch has sought to re-source the tradition. By emphasizing Word *and* Spirit, Bloesch understands himself to be reading that tradition more faithfully than did Protestant orthodoxy. This tension between Word and Spirit enables Bloesch to develop a theology of revelation that allows him to avoid the pitfalls of Protestant scholasticism. That scholasticism as it was refined—and reified!—in those like Benjamin Warfield and later in Carl Henry, rested on rationalism or some similar philosophical foundationalism. By following Barth in his doctrine of revelation, Bloesch understands the dialectic of Word and Spirit as being superlatively both a function and derivation of God's self act of revelation and communication in Christ. It is through this Christocentricity that Bloesch avoids the perils of Protestant scholasticism's static and inert doctrine of Scripture.

In relation to the hazards of liberalism, Bloesch's dialectic allows him to consider God's transcendence and his immanence together, or rather to consider God's immanence as a function of his transcendence. As God's Word, it is God's and not ours. Yet as God-in-the-flesh, his Spirit makes this Word alive to us as we are awakened to faithful knowing by the Spirit of the Word. Bloesch understands liberalism to have a tendency to obscure this basic notion of discontinuity between divine and human—the same discontinuity that Barth held in opposition to Harnack. The faultline of theological liberalism consists in its contention that theology is a positively mediating science between divine and human and thus a discipline of continuity and ultimately of immanence. For this reason, while Bloesch does negotiate between the two positions of conservatism and liberalism, he is anxious about the title "mediating theologian." He should not be thought to be engaging in any type of systematic correlation between the divine and human. The danger of such an approach became quite acute and palpable during the struggle in Germany when the "German Christians" really wanted to be good Christians but they wanted to be good Nazis as well.[21]

Yet although some still regard Bloesch as a centrist theologian, mediating between the Scylla of a rigid orthodoxy as in conservatism and the

Charybdis of subjectivism as in liberalism, he is engaged in something much more subversive than this.[22] Bloesch, following Barth before him, does not seek to mediate between the right and the left but rather recognizes that because both the left and the right are preoccupied with similar concerns, to "mediate" between the two is already to have given ground and to play by rules foreign to the gospel. That is, to affirm this type of contextual theology is to recognize *another* revelation than that of God-in-Christ. Bloesch, in a typically dialectical mode, seeks to usurp both poles by following Barth's language and conception of "event." It is the event of God-in-Christ that is both the pinnacle and foundation of our faith—God's self-revelation. But precisely because it is *God's* act and not ours, any philosophical foundationalism ignores God's freedom and is an abuse of our own.

Foundationalism, either in its liberal or scholastic forms, slights God's freedom because it dismisses knowledge as God's continuous and gracious gift—knowledge as a predicate of revelation. It is an abuse of our freedom simply because it is a dogmatic mislocation of authority. Authority upon the readings of both Protestant liberalism and scholasticism, despite their best efforts, issues in one type of internalism (immanentism) or another—that is, authority becomes largely an anthropological conception. Bloesch's appropriation of "event" language allows him to avoid developing an account of authority that is conceived of anthropologically. His is not the internalism of liberalism, which points to the authority of self, nor is it the internalism (in externalist guise) of Protestant scholasticism. The latter looks to the propositions of Scripture and their exactness, which we know to be incapable of error, for God's Word meets *our* basic criteria of factuality, coherence, and noncontradiction. To conceive of authority in such terms is, on Bloesch's reading, an exercise in sinful disobedience because it is not obedient to the freedom to which we are called. That is, the freedom of being bound to Christ and to witness to that freedom in our act of humble acknowledgment of God's gracious and free activity in the surprising sanctification of our reason. Rather, for Bloesch, authority is a theological category grounded in the act of God in Christ to which the accounts of both the prophets and apostles witness, to which both the Old and New Testaments testify. Scripture, in its act of witness, in its appropriation by God for his purpose of self-witness, is authoritative. We know this act, the authority of this Word, by the sanctifying work of God's Holy Spirit, by the Spirit that testifies to the Word. It is this account of authority that leads Bloesch to affirm with Barth that natural theology, in its varied garments, is a reversal of the movement of the subject–object relation and a usurpation of authority. God has come *to* us and has revealed himself *to* us in Jesus Christ. To affirm natural theology is to warrant a two-way street that we can equally make our way along via some discoverable knowledge ("general revelation")—in other words, we are in control. Bloesch holds that natural theology violates a proper ordering of the subject–object relationship and is thus ultimately idolatry—worshiping ourselves and not the subject deserving of our worship. For these same reasons, a positive relationship between philosophy and theology is suspect from the start. Although theological discourse can appropriate philosophical language, as it has and continues to do, Bloesch is adamant that theological realism need not meet any basic philosophical criteria to engage in its subject matter. As has already been stated, the subject matter justifies the language. But theology is free to employ and, in fact, cannot avoid using philosophical language and conceptions:

> We hold that Christian faith does not need to appeal for metaphysical support, but metaphysical speculation stands in need of the illumination and correction of faith. . . . In our view, the truth of the Gospel stands on its own foundation and is self-authenticating. . . . Just as faith is the ground of truly penetrating thought, so creative thought is the intellectual fruit of faith.[23]

It is not the issue of *whether* one uses philosophical description but of *how* that description is employed.

BLOESCH'S DOCTRINE OF HOLY SCRIPTURE

In the last section, I expound briefly on Bloesch's insistence upon a properly ordered account of Word and Spirit. Bloesch's theology of Word and Spirit, on a methodological level, has been developed largely as an alternative both to liberalism and evangelical rationalism. On another deeper and much more substantial level, however, Bloesch's theology is motivated by the conviction that God has acted in Jesus Christ for the reconciliation of all creation. He believes that this action occasions the subversion of all systematic and methodological attempts at comprehension. Consequently, Bloesch's principal concerns regarding theological authority and method are enclosed within consideration of God's act of self-revelation. Issues of method and authority are strictly secured to questions of the nature and function of divine revelation. It is just this conviction that supports and acts as the controlling center of his bibliology. It is Bloesch's unrelenting insistence on the freedom of God's sovereignty in revelation that drives his theology, both formally *and* materially. Because of this foundational contention, Bloesch maintains that while Scripture is certainly a very human and embedded text requiring social and anthropological definition,[24] by the activity of God, it is preeminently an instrument in God's economy of revelational and salvific activity:

> Theology will recover its integrity only when it bows before the reality of God's self-revelation in Jesus Christ communicated to us by the Spirit through Holy Scripture and the ongoing commentary on Scripture in the church. Theology is not "reflection on the praxis of the people of God" but reflection on the mystery of God's self-revelation to his people. Since Holy Scripture is the primary source and witness of this revelation, Scripture will be the fundamental guide and norm in any theology that claims to be faithful to the message of the apostolic church.[25]

Scripture is properly defined only in its relation to God and his activity. What Bloesch offers with weight that others, such as postliberals, tend to be light on is a concentrated stress upon God's revelation—his revelatory activity:

> The Word of God—the truth that proceeds out of the mouth of God—is living and dynamic. Too often in evangelical and conservative circles the Word is viewed as something static and frozen, waiting to be analyzed and dissected. But our ability to know the Word rests on the prior action of the Word. The Word himself must take the initiative and break through the barrier of human sin and finitude if we are to know the truth that regenerates and redeems.[26]

That is, for Bloesch, the doctrine of Scripture is not principally part of the "language" or "grammar" of the community but is subsumed primarily and fundamentally under the doctrine of God. The confession is that God, in his Triune nature, reveals himself and turns to his creation in Jesus Christ as witnessed by this word—only then is its "ecclesiality" a reality for reflection and comprehension. In this sense then, revelation comes to function for Bloesch as the controlling center of his concerns over Scripture.

At the outset, there are two imminent dangers Bloesch wishes to name and avoid: scriptural docetism and ebionitism. On the one hand, modern theology, concerned with protecting the revealed character of Scripture, tends to ignore the human locality of the text—the embedded particularity of this specific text as in fundamentalism. On the other, it has developed a methodology that—inadvertently or not—evades the question of divine activity as in modern liberalism. Bloesch describes the two poles as fundamentalism's concern to protect the transcendence of the text (through such doctrinal edifices as inerrancy, infallibility, etc.) and liberalism's concern over the immanence of the text and its existential import.[27]

Another way to parse the division for Bloesch is by using the labels "evangelical rationalism" and "religioethical experientialism." The first *equates* revelation with the Bible in its canonical form(s) in such a way that it "finds truth either by deducing conclusions from first principles set forth in Scripture or by deriving principles from the facts recorded in Scripture—the method of induction." The second option "makes human moral experience the supreme criterion in shaping theological understanding; the Bible is valued because it provides insights that elucidate the universal experience of transcendence."[28]

Modern theology, in both forms, can be faulted for obscuring the ontology of Scripture by regarding Scripture as functioning for the reading community primarily as epistemic criteria.[29] In fact, the failure of much of both evangelical and liberal bibliologies is precisely their overwhelming tendency toward considering Scripture primarily as epistemic criteria. This is a Protestant scholastic perversion of *sola Scriptura*. It is part and parcel of Bloesch's charge against evangelical rationalism:

> While trying to remain true to *sola Scriptura*, Protestant orthodoxy could at the same time seek rational and empirical supports for faith. The Bible and human reason came to function as dual authorities for the Christian. . . . Method in theological thinking bore the unmistakable imprint of Descartes and Leibniz: certainty came to be contingent on clarity and precision. The proofs for the existence of God, the plausibility of the biblical miracles and the trustworthiness of the biblical narratives were all elevated into prominence in theology.[30]

Bloesch's concern here lies at the heart of his theology. To describe Scripture in such a way reveals the methodological concerns largely presupposed on both ends of the spectrum in modern theology.

Specifically here, although Bloesch is on guard against liberalism and some forms of postliberalism, the main foe he has in mind in his constructive bibliology is evangelical rationalism. Most evangelicals would certainly insist that revelation is the controlling consideration regarding bibliology. Bloesch charges that their conception of revelation is subsumed within a larger framework of meaning, and therefore results in imposing a meaning on revelation that ultimately domesticates God's activity and transcendence because it freezes revelation into an epistemic code. The identifiable concern he has in mind in this regard is the doctrine of inerrancy. That inerrancy is problematic for Bloesch is certainly not unexpected given his proximity to Barth. Yet in his critique of inerrancy, Bloesch is very careful not to throw the baby out with the bath water:

> I am not comfortable with the term *inerrancy* when applied to Scripture because it has been co-opted by a rationalistic, empiricistic mentality that reduces truth to facticity. Yet I wish to maintain what is intended by this word—the abiding truthfulness and normativeness of the biblical witness. This truthfulness, however, is a property not of the human witness itself but of the Spirit who speaks in and through this witness. It is a property of the object and goal of this witness—Jesus Christ.[31]

Bloesch, although concerned about the intrusion of alien systems of meaning, is certainly willing to credit evangelicals with good intentions. Because the question of truth is a central concern for Bloesch, he is willing to grant that evangelical rationalists have at least offered an answer—even if they have gone amiss in their answer. This is why Bloesch considers liberalism, certain forms of postmodern theologies, pluralism, and mysticism as much more dangerous to the historic faith than evangelical rationalism. He states, "I have often observed that one of the banes of modern evangelicalism is rationalism, although it is always necessary to point out that this is a believing rationalism."[32] Nonetheless, Bloesch is adamant that evangelical rationalism is problematic. In his most recent volume on eschatology, Bloesch again strongly asserts his sympathetic distance from this form of rationalism.[33]

What Bloesch provides in response is an account of revelation and Scripture wherein God's action is basic and Scripture is defined principally and centrally with reference to that reality—and not in any historical or ideal sense:

> The presence of the living Word in Holy Scripture is not an ontological necessity but a free decision of the God who acts and speaks. It is not something to take for granted but something to hope for on the basis of God's promises. . . . The certainty that the Christian finds is not rational certainty of metaphysical truth but confidence in the power of Christ to redeem from sin and death.[34]

Bloesch's main point is that revelation is not an inherent quality of the text, but is rather a theological category pregnant with Christological meaning. Revelation is primarily a Christological category in that he, Jesus Christ, the Word made flesh, is revelation. Bloesch's insistence on this score, following Barth, is that Scripture is revelation in as much as it witnesses to this revelation, to Jesus Christ—yet it is never to Jesus Christ apart from the mediated reality of the textual witness.[35] That is, Scripture has an instrumental relationship to revelation wherein the connection is not one of direct identity but inseparability: "There is indeed an inseparable connection between the revealed Word of God or the 'mind of Christ' and the Bible. We can even speak of a unity or identity of witness and revelation, but it is an indirect identity, not a property of the witness but a matter of divine grace."[36] The necessary distinction (though not a "gap") between revelation and Scripture is organic for Bloesch to any account of divine agency and Scripture's relationship to that economy. What Bloesch offers is an account of Scripture that does not yield to the temptation of ostensive reference but does, of necessity, require transcendent reference to divine activity because Scripture itself witnesses in such a way. Or, more concretely, Bloesch's account moves freely in its dogmatic description of Scripture but does not anchor the text in its own irreducibility. Rather, the anchor is in God's irreducible activity of election, revelation, inspiration, and sanctification with respect to the scriptural word. Bloesch's response to the dangers of conservative and liberal bibliologies is to affirm, following Barth, that the being of Scripture "is" in its ever *becoming* the Word of God. Bloesch affirms that the

> Bible is intrinsically the Word of God in that it is encompassed by the "Word presence," the living reality of the Spirit of Christ. Because the sign participates in what it signifies, the Bible is included in the redemptive act of Christ and his Spirit works in the community of faith. The Bible in and of itself is not the Word of God—divine revelation—but is translucent to this revelation by virtue of the Spirit of God working within it.[37]

Bloesch's considerations here flow directly from his engagement with Barth on these issues. It is Bloesch's insistence on God's sovereign freedom in relation to creaturely reality, following Barth, that pushes him to make this distinction. Bruce McCormack has shown that for Barth, Scripture's ontology, its being as Word of God, is only so as it is vivified by the activity of God:

> The will of God, then, as expressed in the giving of the Bible to the church, is that it *be* Holy Scripture, the Word of God. And this will was and is realized in and through a union of God's Word with the human words of the prophets and apostles—a union that is not a hypostatic union but stands in a certain analogy to it. We would not falsify Barth's understanding if we were to describe the union in question as a "sacramental union."[38]

In an account such as Barth's, a "sacramental union" does not wedge a logical gap between revelation and its scriptural form but does issue a necessary distinction. Bloesch follows Barth in affirming that "while there is not an *identity* or *coalescence* between the written Word of God and the revealed Word (as in a major strand of Protestant orthodoxy), there is nevertheless a *correspondence* by virtue of the inspiring work of the Spirit."[39] Bloesch thus labels his "model" of Scripture and its authority a "sacramental" one directly in line with that of Barth's. However, it is sacramental only in its participation in the event of revelation by God's economy and not in the interpenetrating of divine and human essences that are established and fixed.

On this score, Bloesch would do well to clarify his position regarding Scripture's relation to the hypostatic union, even though he is clearly using such a relationship analogically.[40] He states in this connection, "It is permissible to say that the Bible as the Word of God has two natures—the human and the divine."[41] Such language can easily slide into an ontology of Scripture, which Bloesch is trying to avoid, whereby the Word of God (the Word made flesh) is an equivalent reality to the scriptural word.[42] Bloesch should heed the words of John Webster in this regard:

> No divine nature or properties are to be predicated of Scripture; its substance is that of a creaturely reality (even if it is a creaturely reality annexed to the self-presentation of God); and its relation to God is instrumental. In the case of the Bible, there can be no question of "a union of divine and human factors," but only of "the mystery of the human words *as* God's Word."[43]

Yet, given this critique, his overall intention is to guard against an account of Scripture that domesticates the transcendence, freedom, and mystery of God's sovereignty to the text qua its textuality. This is, for the large part, why Bloesch reacts so strongly against evangelical rationalism even more than against liberalism: Evangelical rationalism reduces God's revelation to an equation—a codification—of Scripture and revelation (a collapse of the Word into the word). Webster labels this "the hypertrophy of revelation" wherein revelation migrates from its "material dogmatic considerations" to unduly perform epistemological duties.[44]

According to Bloesch, the authority of Scripture is primarily a quality of God's activity in, through, and upon Scripture and not of the communal practice and performance of Scripture. This results fundamentally in the confession of God and only then leads to considerations of the sociality of that reality. That is, Bloesch offers a full theological ontology of Scripture whereby its being is wedded to its utility in the divine economy, not principally to its social and empirical functionality. Thus, the issue of what the church confesses becomes all the more clear. The truths of the church's claims are properly ordered in relation to the confession of and faith in the One who acts, not primarily in relation to the social reality of the "intratextuality" of those claims. Nevertheless, such an account does not of necessity negate that intratextuality. The social irreducibility of Christian community also need not be ignored on such a reading. If the community is to be clear in what it believes and confesses, the social reality of that community can ill afford to so inflate as to treat the "reality" it confesses as somehow ancillary.

In Bloesch's view, the act of reading Scripture is neither primarily a sociological nor an anthropological affair, even though it does not discount this necessary discourse. Rather, it is a soteriological affair engaged with the doctrine of inspiration. He follows Otto Weber in affirming that:

> The authority of Scripture can be secured neither objectively (in the sense of the classical doctrine of inspiration) nor subjectively (in the sense of our own experience), but rather that we will only be persuaded of it when God the

Holy Spirit, God in His freedom as the One who effects both our freedom and our bondage, reaches out to us through the scriptural Word.[45]

Bloesch, then, does not view inspiration as a quality of the text—or as evangelical rationalists would have it, the "autographic text"—but as a servant of God's salvific self-revelation: "The purpose of the inspiration of writers and writings is to serve God's self-revelation in Jesus Christ. By virtue of its divine inspiration the Bible is made a bearer of the Spirit of power, a sacramental sign of the presence of God."[46] Inspiration then is not to be separated and treated independently from soteriology. It is part of God's movement to us and for us: "Scripture is authoritative because it is penetrated and filled with the Holy Spirit. It is God-breathed, and the creative breath of God remains in and with Scripture. Yet the self-revelation of God is not inherent in the letter but is always an act of free grace."[47] Bloesch would no doubt agree with Webster that inspiration "indicates the inclusion of texts in the sanctifying work of the Spirit so that they may become fitting vessels of the treasure of the gospel."[48] Bloesch then offers us a sample of a *theological* hermeneutic or reading of Scripture, akin to precritical methods like Calvin's or Luther's. Take Bloesch's programmatic statement for example:

> I propose a christological hermeneutic by which we seek to move beyond historical criticism to the christological, as opposed to the existential significance of the text. . . . the Word of God is not procured by historical-grammatical examination of the text, nor by historical-critical research, nor by existential analysis, but is instead received in a commitment of faith. . . . The christological hermeneutic that I propose is in accord with the deepest insights of both Luther and Calvin. Both Reformers saw Christ as the ground and center of Scripture.[49]

Bloesch's doctrine of Scripture certainly does not end in the problematic quagmire of a docetic or *strictly* ontological account. Yet his ontology of Scripture, which is a functional ontology, is not a functional account such as we would find in postliberalism. Bloesch sets forth an ontology wherein God's purpose in Scripture by his activity *is* precisely its functionality—its ecclesiality, or performative function, is subsidiary to that primary functionality.

Positively, this means that, for Bloesch, theology is exhausted in its relation to Scripture. That is, theology's methodology is irreducibly defined in relation to its task of reading Scripture and not its employment of philosophical or extrascriptural schemas or considerations. This is not to deny the composite reality of Scripture and theology and the complex relations involved there. It is, however, to suggest that because hermeneutics is a dogmatic affair of the highest order, theology is to be judged by its transparency to Scripture, the qualified and vivified witness to the reality of God in Jesus

Christ.[50] Because God proceeds and speaks and thus precedes all human questioning, as Barth so clearly and consistently maintained, the hermeneutical problem *is* the being of God![51] No method is adequate. Again, Bloesch stands in line with Barth's assertion: "The question of the right hermeneutics cannot be decided in a discussion of exegetical *method*, but only in exegesis itself."[52] The separation between theology, exegesis, hermeneutics, and practical theology (ethics) is then an artificial one. Here, Bloesch's keen and nuanced appreciation of Pietism informs his consideration of the inseparability of reading Scripture and the Christian life of holiness. For Bloesch, a truly evangelical theology neither ignores the Christian life nor does it treat it as a separate or independent reality from that of dogmatics and exegesis. To know Jesus Christ is to be encountered and transformed by him through the powerful witness of his Spirit in and through the scriptural and preached Word. Reading and hearing Scripture is a matter of death and resurrection—learning what it means to die and to rise with Christ.

Bloesch, in his own unique way, offers us substantial considerations over method, authority, and Scripture to remedy the correlational and apologetical theology so pervasive on both sides of the theological divide. Evangelicalism will only profit from examining these contributions further—something I have sought to undertake here. Bloesch's contributions within evangelicalism carry much weight and should be mined by his fellow theologians, seminarians, pastors, and laypeople alike for generations to come. He is an evangelical churchman and theologian who continues prophetically to call Christ's church to individual and corporate renewal, reformation, and ecumenical peace and unity. For decades, he has rallied fellow believers against the torpidity and negligence of theological liberalism and against what he understands as the bane of evangelicalism—its adherence to Enlightenment rationality. Bloesch's most basic and fundamental response as an evangelical is that theology does not seek out foundations but acknowledges its one foundation—Jesus Christ, crucified and risen. Yet evangelicals will certainly be left with questions of unease. Both correlational and apologetic distrust come second nature to evangelicals. I can only maintain with Bloesch that it is not our job to make this message palatable—that task belongs to the Spirit of God alone—but in continuity with the pointing finger of the Baptist, in the power of that selfsame Spirit, we witness to the One who has come, who is risen from the dead, and who will come again.

NOTES

1. A note to Donald Bloesch from Old Testament scholar, Brevard Childs, September 12, 1971 (UDTS library archives).

2. Karl Barth, *Evangelical Theology: An Introduction* (New York: Holt, Rinehart, and Winston, 1963), 5f.

3. Only published recently as *Reinhold Niebuhr's Apologetics* (Eugene, Ore.: Wipf and Stock, 2002).

4. Although there is not a wealth of biographical material available, I would like to point the reader to Elmer Colyer's (a former student of Bloesch's and now professor at UDTS) introductory chapter to the festschrift he edited for Bloesch as an excellent introduction to his life and career. See Elmer M. Colyer, "Donald G. Bloesch and His Career," in *Evangelical Theology in Transition: Theologians in Dialogue with Donald Bloesch*, ed. Elmer M. Colyer (Downers Grove, Ill.: InterVarsity Press, 1999), 11–17. I would also like to point the reader to Bloesch's unfinished autobiography in the UDTS library archive. It is a valuable resource for those wishing to study Bloesch's theology in depth.

5. Donald G. Bloesch, *The Last Things: Resurrection, Judgment, Glory* (Downers Grove, Ill.: InterVarsity Press, 2004).

6. Karl Barth, *Anselm, Fides Quaerens Intellectum: Anselm's Proof of the Existence of God in the Context of His Theological Scheme*, repr. ed. (Pittsburgh: Pickwick, 1985), 11. Originally published as *Anselm: Fides Quaerens Intellectum* (Richmond, Va.: John Knox, 1960).

7. Karl Barth, *Church Dogmatics* (Edinburgh: T&T Clark, 1975), 4.

8. Joseph L. Mangina, *Karl Barth: Theologian of Christian Witness* (Aldershot, UK: Ashgate Press, 2004), 56.

9. John Webster, *Holiness* (Grand Rapids, Mich.: W. B. Eerdmans, 2003), 9–10. Webster demonstrates that Barth's account of theological rationality is in direct and radical opposition to modernity's philosophic and theological notions (be they idealistic, realistic, etc).

10. Donald G. Bloesch, *A Theology of Word and Spirit: Authority and Method in Theology* (Downers Grove, Ill.: InterVarsity Press, 1992), 13.

11. Ibid., 58.

12. Referring to Barth, Bloesch states, "We cannot simply remain with him but must strive to go through him and beyond him (this is what he would have wanted). But we definitely cannot ignore him!" From his "Karl Barth: Appreciation and Reservations" in *How Karl Barth Changed My Mind*, ed. Donald K. McKim, (Grand Rapids, Mich.: W. B. Eerdmans, 1986), 130.

13. Ibid., 128.

14. See both Joseph L. Mangina's *Karl Barth on the Christian Life: The Practical Knowledge of God* (New York: P. Lang, 2001) and John Webster's *Barth's Ethics of Reconciliation* (Cambridge, UK: Cambridge University Press, 1995).

15. Donald Bloesch, "The Legacy of Karl Barth," *TSF Bulletin* 9, no. 5 (May–June 1986), 9.

16. Donald G. Bloesch, *The Church: Sacraments, Worship, Ministry, Mission* (Downers Grove, Ill.: InterVarsity Press, 2002), 172.

17. Donald Bloesch, "A Response to Elmer Colyer," 1996. http://www.luthersem.edu/ctrf/JCTR/Vol01/Bloesch.htm

18. Bloesch, *Theology of Word and Spirit*, 14.

19. Ibid., 15.

20. Donald G. Bloesch, *Essentials of Evangelical Theology*, vol. 1 (San Francisco: Harper and Row, 1978), 19.

21. See Bloesch's response in his own festschrift, *Evangelical Theology in Transition*, 185.

22. I am thinking primarily of two readings, those of Stanley Grenz and Nancey Murphy. See Stanley Grenz, "'Fideistic Revelationalism': Donald Bloesch's Anti-rationalist Theological Method," in *Evangelical Theology in Transition*, 35–60; and Nancey C. Murphy, *Beyond Liberalism and Fundamentalism: How Modern and Postmodern Philosophy Set the Theological Agenda* (Valley Forge, Pa.: Trinity Press International, 1996). Grenz's conception of Bloesch's method as antirationalistic gives the impression that Bloesch is unconcerned with theological rationality. Nothing could be farther from the truth. On Murphy's reading, Bloesch is a foundationalist simply because he wishes to speak about the inspiration and infallibility of Holy Scripture as a norm for faith and practice. Her reading is far too overextended and neglects Bloesch's *dogmatic* account of Holy Scripture. My inkling is that any speech about the infallibility of Scripture is, for Murphy, foundationalism and a type of positivism. The tradition that wishes to affirm some sort of doctrine of inspiration and infallibility is far more nuanced and subtle and surely avoids Murphy's charge of foundationalism.

23. Donald G. Bloesch, *The Ground of Certainty: Toward an Evangelical Theology of Revelation*, repr. ed. (Eugene, Ore.: Wipf and Stock, 2002), 22.

24. Bloesch does offer substantive considerations regarding these issues. See Donald G. Bloesch, *Holy Scripture: Revelation, Inspiration and Interpretation* (Downers Grove, Ill.: InterVarsity Press, 1994), 141–70, 255–77.

25. Donald G. Bloesch, *God the Almighty: Power, Wisdom, Holiness, Love* (Downers Grove, Ill.: InterVarsity Press, 1995), 27–28.

26. Bloesch, *Holy Scripture*, 26.

27. Ibid., 18–21.

28. Ibid., 18.

29. William J. Abraham's recent genealogy of the "canon question" is helpful to us herein. Abraham's argument is that the understanding of canon and its authority has gradually become more and more concerned with defining itself in terms of providing epistemic criteria rather than operating as ecclesial canon. See his *Canon and Criterion in Christian Theology: From the Fathers to Feminism* (Oxford, UK: Clarendon, 1998).

30. Bloesch, *Holy Scripture*, 64.

31. Ibid., 27–28.

32. Donald G. Bloesch, *The Holy Spirit: Works and Gifts* (Downers Grove, Ill.: InterVarsity Press, 2000), 34.

33. Bloesch, *Last Things*, 191–95.

34. Ibid., 26f.

35. While Christology informs Bloesch's bibliology, it could do so more fully. For a suggestive essay along these lines, see John Webster's "'Eloquent and Radiant': The Prophetic Office of Christ and the Mission of the Church," in John Webster, *Barth's Moral Theology: Human Action in Barth's Thought* (Grand Rapids, Mich.: W. B. Eerdmans, 1998), 125–50.

36. Bloesch, *Holy Scripture*, 57.

37. Ibid., 27.

38. Bruce McCormack, "The Being of Holy Scripture Is in Its Becoming," in *Evangelicals and Scripture: Tradition, Authority, and Hermeneutics*, ed. Vincent Bacote, Laura C. Miguelez, and Dennis L. Okholm (Downers Grove, Ill.: InterVarsity Press, 2004), 69.

39. Bloesch, *Holy Scripture*, 58. Bloesch here prefers to speak of a *"conjunction* between the Word of God and sacred Scripture."

40. It is not Bloesch's intention to so collapse Christology into bibliology (the Word into the word). In fact, the whole objective of Bloesch's following Barth on this score is to avoid such an accounting. However, Bloesch must give more careful thought to the *instrumental* relationship between God's activity and Scripture—that is to a more thoroughly developed sacramental bibliology.

41. Bloesch, *Holy Scripture*, 70f.

42. *Nature*, specifically when we speak of the relations between the divine and the human, is a Christological term that should not be applied to Scripture. I am indebted on this point to John Webster's *Holy Scripture: A Dogmatic Sketch* (Cambridge, UK: Cambridge University Press, 2003), 23. Webster's work points at this juncture to G. C. Berkouwer's relevant and valuable discussion in his *Holy Scripture*, trans. and ed. Jack B. Rogers (Grand Rapids, Mich.: W. B. Eerdmans, 1975), 195–212.

43. Webster, *Holy Scripture*, 23. Webster is quoting Berkouwer, *Holy Scripture*, 203.

44. Ibid., 12.

45. Bloesch, *Holy Scripture*, 130. He is quoting Otto Weber, *Foundations of Dogmatics*, trans. Darrell L. Guder, 2 vols. (Grand Rapids, Mich.: W. B. Eerdmans; Mich.: W. B. 1981), 1:245.

46. Ibid., 120.

47. Ibid., 129.

48. Webster, *Holy Scripture*, 39.

49. Donald Bloesch, "A Christological Hermeneutic: Crisis and Conflict in Hermeneutics," in *The Use of the Bible in Theology: Evangelical Options*, ed. Robert K. Johnston (Atlanta: John Knox, 1985), 85.

50. I am indebted to Webster's recent *Holy Scripture* (123–35) for putting the matter this way.

51. See Eberhard Jüngel, *God's Being Is in Becoming: The Trinitarian Being of God in the Theology of Karl Barth: A Paraphrase*, trans. John Webster (Edinburgh: T&T Clark, 2001), 9–11.

52. Eberhard Busch, *Karl Barth: His Life from Letters and Autobiographical Texts*, trans. John Bowden (Grand Rapids: Eerdmans, 1994), 390. The quote is taken from a letter of Barth's to Gerhard Ebeling, December 7, 1952, in response to an invitation to a conference on the problem of theological method—an invitation that he refused.

Introduction to
the Bibliography

Chapter 1 of this bibliography attempts to provide a comprehensive list of all works by Donald G. Bloesch published in English and as many variant editions as possible. Presented chronologically, the list includes articles, books, book reviews written by Bloesch, and published letters. Within each year, items are listed alphabetically. Untitled works are given the name "[Review]" or "[Letter to the editor]" as appropriate and appear alphabetically by the name of the periodical in a separate sequence at each year's end. This overall arrangement makes it possible to trace the development of themes and ideas within Bloesch's work.

Certain typographical conventions are used in the structure of the citations in order to assist the reader and in the construction of the indexes. Titles of books and the names of journals are given in *italics*. Titles of articles in periodicals are given inside double quote marks ("") and end with a period. Chapters of books to which Bloesch has contributed are also included given in double quote marks but do not end in a period. The boldface word **Contents** refers to parts of a book while the boldface word **Headings** refers to parts of an article. When the contents of a book are given, the names of chapters are given in SMALL CAPS and further subdivisions are given in a normal size. This convention is used to help the reader distinguish the title of a chapter from a subheading within a chapter and carries over into the index of titles.

The notes in the entries are used to tie together the publication history of the various works, such as articles that were reprinted or became a chapter in a book, books that have been reprinted, and so on. These notes are based on information appearing in the articles and books themselves. The reader might be able to discern additional connections among the items via use of the title index or other tools. When two different items have an identical table of contents or the same headings, a note is used to tie together the two items and eliminate the need for repetition.

Unpublished correspondence, nonprint media (such as sound recordings), and archival material (such as typescripts), and so forth, have been excluded. Most publisher's promotional material has also been excluded unless it contains something of exceptional interest, such as an interview with Bloesch. It has not been possible to include translations from English into other languages even though Professor Bloesch's work has appeared in Chinese, Italian, Japanese, Korean, Polish, Russian, Serbo-Croatian, Spanish, and Turkish.

Chapter 2 of the bibliography includes book reviews of Bloesch's works, responses to specific articles, general critiques, theses and dissertations, and biographical citations. The book reviews are arranged first by title of the book reviewed and then by the author of the review. Unsigned or anonymous reviews are given alphabetically by name of the periodical in which they appeared and follow the list of signed reviews for each title.

Chapter 3 of the bibliography is comprised of several indexes. These indexes fall into two groups: several relating directly to chapter 1 and those relating to the bibliography as a whole. The first index consists of two checklists: an alphabetical listing of books where Bloesch is the author or primary editor and a checklist of those books to which he has contributed. The checklists are provided to assist acquisitions librarians or others who might wish to compare their holdings. The number following each citation refers to the entry in chapter 1 of the bibliography where a fuller description may be found. Following the checklists is an index of books reviewed by Bloesch listed by title. The final index relating directly to chapter 1 is an index of article titles, chapter titles of books, and headings within chapters and articles. A fuller explanation of the design of that index appears at the beginning of that index. An index of names comes next and includes names appearing in chapter 1 as well as reviewers, critics, and dissertation and thesis authors given in chapter 2. This list of names can be used to facilitate the exploration of the dialogue between Bloesch and other theologians. An index of periodicals follows next. The range of titles can be used to demonstrate the breadth of interaction between Bloesch and various points of view. Perhaps few other objective criteria are quite as revealing of his goal of being "both Catholic and Evangelical." Practically speaking, because no one library holds all the titles listed, the periodicals index is also intended to assist interlibrary loans. After the name of each periodical appears the International Standard Serial Number (ISSN), if available. These double sets of four-digit numerals are used to identify periodicals in many library catalogs and databases. Where no ISSN is available, a brief indication of place and publisher is given to help distinguish the name of each periodical from similar titles. After the identification of each periodical the citation numbers follow, indicating where each is listed in the bibliography.

The Bloesch Archives at the University of Dubuque have been of inestimable value in compiling this bibliography. In addition, the following indexes—although not a complete list of all indexes consulted—have been useful in gathering citations: *Australasian Religion Index, Bibliographia Internationalis Spiritualitatis, Book Review Index, Book Reviews of the Month, Catholic Periodical Index, Christian Periodical Index, Elenchus Bibliographicus Biblicus, Ephemerides Theologicae Lovanienses, Guide to Social Science and Religion in Periodical Literature, Humanities Index, Index to Book Reviews in Religion, International Index, Internationale Zeitschriften für Bibelwissenschaft und Genzgebiete, Magazine Index, Methodist Periodical Index, Methodist Reviews Index, 1918–1985, Mosher Subject Index to Select Periodical Literature, Readers' Guide to Periodical Literature, Religion Index One, Religion Index Two, Research in Ministry, Research Libraries' Information Network (RLIN), Restoration Serials Index, Southern Baptist Periodical Index, United Methodist Periodical Index*, and *World Cat (OCLC)*. In addition, the following files were also checked via *First Search*: *Article First, Arts & Humanities, ATLA Religion, Biography Index, BIP, Dissertations, Humanities Index*, and *Periodical Abstracts*.

In spite of the considerable availability of online materials and generally good state of indexing services, a very large number of smaller religious journals and denominational titles remain unindexed, especially retrospectively. Even few newspapers have very much in the way of retrospective indexes. In the case of Bloesch, this lack of indexes is especially important because he maintains dialogue with a large range of points of view, and they, in turn, respond to him.

Filing rules used throughout the bibliography are fairly straightforward: (1) Symbols and numerals file before letters. Thus, "*Faith & Renewal*" files before "*Faith and Mission*." (2) Spaces file before symbols or letters. Thus, "Be Wise as Serpents" files before "BEARING THE CROSS." (3) Hyphens function as "word separators" and so file as spaces. Thus, "Moral Re-Armament" files before "Moral Rearmament."

Except where noted by a double asterisk (**) all items appearing in this bibliography have been examined by the compiler. All bibliographic citations are numbered to make for succinct references between citations and to facilitate indexing. Numerals for citations that came to my attention at the last minute are given an alphabetical suffix (e.g., 425a, 425b). Although every attempt has been made to locate and verify as many citations as possible, some have surely escaped my attention, and a few were not included for lack of sufficient bibliographic data for identification. Although every reasonable care has been taken in the compilation of this bibliography, some error or inadvertent omission is almost inevitable in any work of this sort. Addenda, corrigenda, and gentle suggestions are welcomed via e-mail: pmah@mchsi.com.

Chapter 1

The Writings of Donald G. Bloesch

1947

1. "The Old Banjo." *Elm Leaves*, vol. 1 (May 1947), p. 18. **Notes**: Poem.
2. "Sweet Honey Bread." *Elm Leaves*, vol. 1 (May 1947), p. 18. **Notes**: Poem.
3. "The Tale of Jane O'Shea." *Elm Leaves*, vol. 1 (May 1947), p. 19. **Notes**: Poem.

1949

4. "Two Clashing Ideologies." *The Owl of Minerva*, vol. 5, no. 1 (February 1949), pp. 8–11.

1950

5. *A Philosophical Analysis of National Socialism.*—1950. 54 leaves; 28 cm. **Notes**: Thesis (BA)–Dept. of Philosophy, Elmhurst College, Elmhurst, Ill. **Contents**: IDEOLOGICAL BACKGROUND. Nationalism. Racism. Synthesis of National Socialism.—THE METAPHYSICAL RACE—RACIAL HONOR AND OPPORTUNISM—THE RACIAL NATION AND THE STATE—THE RELIGION OF THE RACE AND THE HERO—AN APPRAISAL. The Rationality of Nazism. The Spiritual Challenge of Nazism.

1951

6. "What Does It Mean to Be Free?" *The E. and R. Newsletter*, no. 1 (July 30, 1951), p. 1.

1952

7. "Theology and Philosophy." *Quest*, vol. 1 (Spring 1952), pp. 1–10.**

1953

8. *Emil Brunner's Approach to Non-Christian Religions.*—ii, 74 leaves; 28 cm. **Notes**: Thesis (BD)–Federated Theological Faculty in cooperation with the Chicago Theological Seminary, 1953. **Contents**: THE CRISIS IN THE HISTORY OF RELIGIONS. The Problem. From the Enlightenment to the New Titanism. The Contemporary Theological Reaction against the Enlightenment.—BRUNNER'S CONCEPTION OF THE "*ANALOGIA ENTIS*"—BRUNNER'S ANALYSIS OF THE WORLD RELIGIONS—AN EVALUATION OF BRUNNER'S METHODOLOGY—A CONSTRUCTIVE APPROACH TO NON-CHRISTIAN RELIGIONS.
9. "The Flight from God." *Witness*, vol. 1, no. 1 (February 1953), pp. 6–7.
10. "Theology and Psychotherapy." *Witness*, vol. 2, no. 1 (October 1953), pp. 7–10.

1956

11. *Reinhold Niebuhr's Re-evaluation of the Apologetic Task.*—1956. ii, 171 leaves. **Notes**: Thesis (Ph.D)–University of Chicago, Divinity School. Thesis number 3109. Published as item 419. **Contents**: INTRODUCTION. Two Types of Theology. Statement of Thesis.—NIEBUHR'S STRICTURE ON TRADITIONAL APOLOGETICS. Background of Niebuhr's Attack. Analysis of Syncretic Theology. Attitude towards Other Kinds of Apologetics.—NIEBUHR'S VINDICATION OF THE APOLOGETIC PRINCIPLE. General Revelation. Dialectical Theology. Existential Disruption.—APOLOGETICS AS A MEANS OF VALIDATING THE FAITH. The Negative Validation. The Positive Validation. Relation of Apologetics to Commitment.—A CRITIQUE OF NIEBUHR'S METHODOLOGY. The Authority of the Bible. Methodological Principles. Criticism of Niebuhr's Doctrine of Man. Criticism of Niebuhr's Conception of the Means of Grace. On the Apologetic Principle.—A NEW ROLE FOR APOLOGETICS. The Mission of the Church. Faith Seeking Understanding. Apologetics as a Subsidiary of Kerygmatic Theology. Apologetics as an Aid in Witnessing.—EPILOGUE.

1959

12. "The Bible, Plato, and the Reformers." *Interpretation*, vol. 13, no. 2 (April 1959), pp. 219–21. **Notes**: Review of: *The Rise and Fall of the Individual* / W. P. Witcutt.—New York: Macmillan, 1958.
13. "The Christian and the Drift towards War." *Theology and Life*, vol. 2, no. 4 (November 1959), pp. 318–26. **Headings**: War Is Evil—Alternatives to War—Nuclear War—The Church and the Cold War—A Radical Stand and Strategy.

14. "Creation as Event." *The Christian Century*, vol. 76, no. 37 (September 16, 1959), pp. 1055–56. **Notes**: Review of: *The Doctrine of Creation* / Karl Barth.—Edinburgh: T. and T. Clark, 1958. (*Church Dogmatics*; vol. 3, part 1).
15. [Review] *Religion in Life*, vol. 29, no. 1 (Winter 1959–1960), pp. 154–55. **Notes**: Reviews of: *Fundamentalism and the Church* / A. Gabriel Hebert.—Philadelphia: Westminster, 1957; and *"Fundamentalism" and the Word of God: Some Evangelical Principles* / J. I. Packer.—Grand Rapids, Mich.: W. B. Eerdmans, 1958. Also published: item 16.
16. [Review] *Theology and Life*, vol. 2, no. 3 (August 1959), pp. 248–50. **Notes**: Reviews of: *Fundamentalism and the Church* / A. Gabriel Hebert.—Philadelphia: Westminster, 1957; and *"Fundamentalism" and the Word of God: Some Evangelical Principles* / J. I. Packer.—Grand Rapids, Mich.: W. B. Eerdmans, 1958. Also published: item 15.

1960

17. "Biblical Religion vs. Culture Religion." *The Seminarian*, vol. 4, no. 1 (February 15, 1960), pp. 7–8. **Notes**: Also published: item 18.
18. "Biblical Religion vs. Culture Religion." *Theology and Life*, vol. 3, no. 3 (August 1960), pp. 175–76. **Notes**: Also published: item 17.
19. "Billy Graham: A Theological Appraisal." *Theology and Life*, vol. 3, no. 2 (May 1960), pp. 136–43. **Headings**: Graham's Message—Lacking in Social Interest—The Bible in Graham's Preaching—Rising above Fundamentalism.
20. "Defender of Free Grace." *The Christian Century*, vol. 77, no. 11 (March 16, 1960), p. 318. **Notes**: Reviews of: *Autobiography of St. Thérèse of Lisieux* / newly translated by Ronald Knox; with a foreword by Vernon Johnson.—New York: Kenedy, 1958; and *The Hidden Face: A Study of St. Thérèse of Lisieux* / Ida F. Görres; translation by Richard and Clara Winston.—New York: Pantheon, 1959.
21. "Dr. Evans, an Appreciation." *The Seminarian*, vol. 4, no. 2 (May 13, 1960), p. 3. **Notes**: Concerning Dr. Richard Evans.
22. "Love Illuminated." *The Christian Century*, vol. 77, no. 50 (December 14, 1960), p. 1470. **Notes**: Review of: *The Four Loves* / C. S. Lewis.—New York: Harcourt, Brace, 1960.
23. "Nothing Ventured." *The Christian Century*, vol. 77, no. 42 (October 19, 1960), pp. 1217–18. **Notes**: Review of: *Reasons for Faith* / John H. Gerstner.—New York: Harper, 1960.
24. [Review] *Interpretation*, vol. 14, no. 2 (April 1960), p. 230. **Notes**: Review of: *Sex and Love in the Bible* / William Graham Cole.—London: Hodder and Stoughton, 1960.
25. [Review] *The Presbyterian Outlook*, vol. 142, no. 13 (March 28, 1960), p. 15. **Notes**: Review of: *The Objective Society* / Everett Knight.—New York: G. Braziller, 1960.
26. [Review] *Theology and Life*, vol. 3, no. 2 (May 1960), pp. 150–51. **Notes**: Review of: *In His Service: The Servant Lord and His Servant People* / Lewis S. Mudge.—Philadelphia: Westminster, 1959.

27. [Review] *Theology and Life*, vol. 3, no. 4 (November 1960), pp. 331–32. **Notes**: Review of: *Reasons for Faith* / John H. Gerstner.—New York: Harper, 1960.

1961

28. "Critics Answered." *The Christian Century*, vol. 78, no. 47 (November 22, 1961), pp. 1400–1401. **Notes**: Letter to the editor. A rejoinder to the October 4 criticism of DGB's August 9 review of Paul Minear's *Images of the Church*.
29. "Syncretism: Its Cultural Forms and Its Influence." *Dubuque Christian American*, vol. 36, no. 2 (May, 1961), p. 2.
30. "Vain Hope for Victory." *The Pulpit*, vol. 32, no. 11 (November 1961), pp. 9–11 (329–31). **Notes**: At head of title: The State Must Not Play God. Sermon on Psalms 33:16–19.
31. "World-Relatedness." *The Christian Century*, vol. 78, no. 32 (August 9, 1961), pp. 958–59. **Notes**: Review of: *Images of the Church in the New Testament* / Paul S. Minear.—Philadelphia: Westminster, 1960.
32. [Review] *Interpretation*, vol. 15, no. 1 (January 1961), pp. 106–7. **Notes**: Review of: *The Providence of God* / Georgia Harkness.—New York: Abingdon, 1960.
33. [Review] *The Presbyterian Outlook*, vol. 143, no. 45 (December 11, 1961), p. 15. **Notes**: Review of: *The Word of God in the World Today: Contemporary Problems in the Light of Scripture* / Hilda Graef.—1st ed.—Garden City, N.Y.: Hanover House, 1960.

1962

34. "The Christian Life in the Plan of Salvation." *Theology and Life*, vol. 5, no. 4 (November 1962), pp. 299–308. **Headings**: The Mystery of Salvation—The Plan of Salvation in Theological History—A Biblical, Dynamic View of Salvation—Another Look at the Paradox.
35. *The Theological Seminary of the University of Dubuque Presents the Inaugural Address of Donald Bloesch, Ph.D., Associate Professor of Theology, Entitled, "The Christian Life in the Plan of Salvation": February 7, 1962.* (Dubuque, Iowa: The University of Dubuque, 1962), 11 pp.; 23 cm. **Notes**: Variant issue: item 36.
36. *The Theological Seminary of the University of Dubuque Presents the Inaugural Address of Donald Bloesch, Ph.D., Associate Professor of Theology, Entitled, "The Christian Life in the Plan of Salvation": February 7, 1962. The Installation Address of C. Howard Wallace, D.Theol., Associate Professor of Biblical Theology, Entitled, "The Historical-Critical Method in the Work of Interpreting the Scriptures."* (Dubuque, Iowa: The University, 1962), 25 pp.; 23 cm. **Notes**: Variant issue: item 35. DGB's address is on pp. 3–11.
37. [Review] *The Presbyterian Outlook*, vol. 144, no. 40 (November 5, 1962), p. 15. **Notes**: Review of: *A Kierkegaard Critique: An International Selection of Essays Interpreting Kierkegaard* / by F. J. Billeskov . . . [et al.]; edited by Howard A. Johnson and Niels Thulstrup.—1st ed.—New York: Harper, 1962.

1963

38. "Virgin Birth Defended." *The Christian Century*, vol. 80, no. 16 (April 17, 1963), pp. 493–94. **Notes**: Review of: *The Virgin Birth* / Thomas Boslooper.—Philadelphia: Westminster, 1962.

1964

39. *Centers of Christian Renewal.*—Philadelphia: United Church, 1964. 173 pp.; 21 cm. **Contents**: THE EVANGELICAL COMMUNITIES—THE LEE ABBEY COMMUNITY—KOINONIA FARM—THE COMMUNITY OF TAIZÉ—THE AGAPE COMMUNITY—ST. JULIAN'S COMMUNITY—THE IONA COMMUNITY—THE ECUMENICAL SISTERHOOD OF MARY—BETHANY FELLOWSHIP—THE RELIGIOUS COMMUNITY AND THE CHURCH.
40. "A Name for Your Church." *United Church Herald*, vol. 7, no. 10 (May 15, 1964), pp. 18–19.
41. [Review] *The Pulpit*, vol. 35, no. 3 (March 1964), pp. 27–28 (91–92). **Notes**: Review of: *The Restored Relationship: A Study in Justification and Reconciliation* / Arthur B. Crabtree.—Valley Forge, Pa.: Judson, 1963.

1965

42. "The Divine Sacrifice." *Theology and Life*, vol. 8, no. 3 (Fall 1965), pp. 192–202. **Headings**: The Foundation of Salvation—The Plight of Man—The Message of the Cross—The Two Poles of Salvation.
43. "Spiritual Ecumenism." *The Christian Century*, vol. 82, no. 47 (November 24, 1965), pp. 1450–51. **Notes**: Review of: *Protestantism in an Ecumenical Age: Its Root, Its Right, Its Task* / Otto Piper.—Philadelphia: Fortress, 1965.
44. [Review] *The Presbyterian Outlook*, vol. 147, no. 14 (April 5, 1965), p. 15. **Notes**: Review of: *How the Church Can Minister to the World without Losing Itself* / Langdon Gilkey.—1st ed.—New York: Harper and Row, 1964.
45. [Review] *Theology and Life*, vol. 8, no. 3 (Fall 1965), pp. 238–40. **Notes**: Review of: *Christ's Church: Evangelical, Catholic, and Reformed* / Bela Vassady.—Grand Rapids, Mich.: W. B. Eerdmans, 1965.

1966

46. "The Charismatic Revival: A Theological Critique." *Religion in Life*, vol. 35, no. 3 (Summer 1966), pp. 364–80. **Headings**: The Theological Thrust of This Revival—The Gift of Tongues in Paul's Theology—The View in Acts and Mark—The Psychological Interpretation of Tongues—A Theological Appraisal.
47. "The Confession and the Sacraments." *Monday Morning*, vol. 31, no. 6 (March 14, 1966), pp. 6–8. **Notes**: Regarding the *Confession of 1967* of the United Presbyterian Church in the U.S.A.

48. "Gambling Views Disappoint Him." *The Des Moines Register* (October 25, 1966), p. 6. **Notes**: Letter to the editor.
49. "Necessary Belief?" *United Church Herald*, vol. 9, no. 12 (June 15, 1966), p. 6. **Notes**: Letter to the editor regarding the Virgin Birth.
50. "Prophetic Preaching and Civil Rights." *The Pulpit*, vol. 37, no. 2 (February 1966), pp. 7–9 (39–41). **Notes**: At head of title: What Are We Preaching–The Gospel or the Great Society? **Headings**: Preaching on Racial Justice—The Nature of Prophetic Preaching—Prophetic and Evangelical Preaching.
51. "The Secular Theology of Harvey Cox." *The Dubuque Seminary Journal*, vol. 1, no. 2 (Fall 1966), pp. 1–4.
52. "A Theology of Christian Commitment." *Theology and Life*, vol. 9, no. 4 (Winter 1966), pp. 335–44. **Notes**: Expanded as part of item 66. **Headings**: Christ and Culture—Need Again for Diastasis—Beyond Neo-Orthodoxy—The Need for Christian Life—Godliness in the World—The Coming Kingdom—Word and Life.
53. [Review] *Christian Advocate*, vol. 10, no. 1 (January 13, 1966), p. 20. **Notes**: Review of: *Ultimate Concern: Tillich in Dialogue* / [edited by] D. MacKenzie Brown.—1st ed.—New York: Harper and Row, 1965.
54. [Review] *Christian Advocate*, vol. 10, no. 19 (October 6, 1966), p. 19. **Notes**: Reviews of: *On the Boundary: An Autobiographical Sketch* / Paul Tillich.—New York: Scribner, 1966; and *The Future of Religions* / Paul Tillich; edited by Jerald C. Brauer.—1st ed.—New York: Harper and Row, c1966.
55. [Review] *The Presbyterian Outlook*, vol. 148, no. 7 (February 14, 1966), p. 15. **Notes**: Review of: *Secular Salvations* / Ernest B. Koenker.—Philadelphia: Fortress, 1965.

1967

56. "Catholic Theology Today." *Christianity Today*, vol. 12, no. 3 (November 10, 1967, pp. 38–39 (142–43). **Notes**: Cf. item 89. Review of: *Theological Investigations. Vol. IV* / Karl Rahner; translated with an introduction by Cornelius Ernst.—Baltimore: Helicon, 1966.
57. *The Christian Life and Salvation*.—Grand Rapids, Mich.: W. B. Eerdmans, c1967. 164 pp.; 23 cm. **Notes**: Foreword by John A. Mackay. Another edition: item 316. **Contents**: THE PLAN OF SALVATION—THE VARIOUS MEANINGS OF SALVATION—THE DIVINE SACRIFICE—BEARING THE CROSS—THE CROWN OF GLORY—THE CHRISTIAN PILGRIMAGE—THE PARADOX OF SALVATION.
58. "The Constitution on Divine Revelation." *Journal of Ecumenical Studies*, vol. 4, no. 3 (Summer 1967), pp. 550–51.
59. "The Crisis of Piety." *The Covenant Quarterly*, vol. 25, no. 1 (February 1967), pp. 3–11. **Notes**: Reprinted as part of item 66. **Headings**: The Meaning of Piety—The Crisis of Piety—Toward the Recovery of Piety—Learning from Pietism—A Theology of Devotion.
60. "An Exposé of the New Factory Farms." *The Catholic Worker*, vol. 33, no. 11 (November 1967), p. 2. **Notes**: Reprinted: cf. item 69 and item 70.

61. "The Pilgrimage of Faith." *Encounter*, vol. 28, no. 1 (Winter 1967), pp. 47–62. **Notes**: reprinted as part of item 66. **Headings**: Two Types of Theology—The Witness of the Reformers—The Quest for Signs—Faith versus Sight.
62. [Review] *Christian Advocate*, vol. 11, no. 25 (December 28, 1967), p. 16. **Notes**: Review of: *Salvation in History* / Oscar Cullmann; [English translation drafted by Sidney G. Sowers and afterward completed by the editorial staff of the SCM Press].—1st American ed.—New York: Harper and Row, 1967.
63. [Review] *The Presbyterian Outlook*, vol. 149, no. 11 (March 13, 1967), p. 15. **Notes**: Review of: *Christ the Center* / Dietrich Bonhoeffer; introduced by Edwin H. Robertson and translated by John Bowden.—1st ed.—New York: Harper and Row, 1966.

1968

64. *The Christian Witness in a Secular Age: An Evaluation of Nine Contemporary Theologians.*—Minneapolis: Augsburg, c1968. 160 pp.; 22 cm. **Notes**: Reprinted: item 412. **Contents**: INTRODUCTION, THE SECULARIZATION OF WESTERN CULTURE—REAPPRAISING THE CHRISTIAN WITNESS—KARL BARTH—EMIL BRUNNER—RUDOLF BULTMANN—REINHOLD NIEBUHR—PAUL TILLICH—DIETRICH BONHOEFFER—JOHN ROBINSON—HARVEY COX—THOMAS ALTIZER—BEYOND APOLOGETICS, A RESTATEMENT OF THE CHRISTIAN WITNESS.
65. "Church Funds for Revolution?" *Christianity Today*, vol. 12, no. 15 (April 26, 1968), pp. 27–28 (747–48). (editorials) **Notes**: On the Ecumenical Institute in Chicago.
66. *The Crisis of Piety: Essays towards a Theology of the Christian Life.*—Grand Rapids, Mich.: W. B. Eerdmans, c1968. 168 pp.; 23 cm. **Notes**: Second edition: item 293. The chapter entitled "The Crisis of Piety" is a reprint of item 59; the chapter entitled "The Pilgrimage of Faith" is a reprint of item 61; the chapter entitled "A Theology of Christian Commitment" is an expansion of item 52. **Contents**: INTRODUCTION, THE NEED FOR SPIRITUAL RENEWAL—THEOLOGY AT THE CROSSROADS—THE CRISIS OF PIETY—THE MISSION OF THE CHURCH: SPIRITUAL OR SECULAR?—TOWARD THE RECOVERY OF THE DEVOTIONAL LIFE—THE MEANING OF CONVERSION—TWO TYPES OF SPIRITUALITY—A THEOLOGY OF CHRISTIAN COMMITMENT—THE PILGRIMAGE OF FAITH.
67. "Ecumenical Studies." *Journal of the American Academy of Religion*, vol. 36, no. 3 (September 1968), pp. 287–89. **Notes**: Reviews of: *The Way to Unity after the Council* / Augustin Cardinal Bea; translation by Gerard Noel.—New York: Herder and Herder, 1967; and *Our Dialogue with Rome: The Second Vatican Council and After* / George B. Caird.—London; New York: Oxford University Press, 1967.
68. "Evangelical Spirituality" in *Christian Spirituality East & West* / Jordan Aumann, Thomas Hopko, Donald G. Bloesch.—Chicago: Priory, c1968, pp. 165–202. **Headings**: FOUNDATIONS OF EVANGELICAL SPIRITUALITY. The Holy and the Profane. The Two Kingdoms. Justification and Sanctification.—THE MEANS OF GRACE AND THE LIFE OF GRACE. Word and Sacraments. Inner-worldly Asceticism.

The Role of Prayer.—OUR HOLY VOCATION. The Meaning of Sainthood. The Priority of Evangelism.

69. "An Exposé of the New Factory Farms." *NCSAW Report* (February 1968), p. 4. **Notes**: Reprint of item 60.

70. "Intensive Farming: Serious Moral Problems Are Raised by the New Animal Food Factories." *Lutheran Forum*, vol. 2, no. 7 (July 1968), pp. 4–6. **Notes**: Parts previously appeared as item 60.

71. "The Meaning of Conversion." *Christianity Today*, vol. 12, no. 17 (May 24, 1968), pp. 8–10 (824–26).

72. "Thielicke's Ethics: A Review Article." *Lutheran Quarterly*, vol. 20, no. 3 (August 1968), pp. 309–13. **Notes**: Review of: *Theological Ethics* / Helmut Thielicke; edited by William H. Lazareth.—Philadelphia: Fortress, 1966.

73. *This Immoral War*.—[Dubuque, Iowa: University of Dubuque, 1968] 11 pp. pamphlet. **Contents**: WHY WE PROTEST—CRIMINAL METHODS IN WARFARE—THE DETERIORATION OF WARFARE—THE EMERGING NATIONALISM.

74. "What's Wrong with the Liturgical Movement?" *Christianity Today*, vol. 12, no. 7 (January 5, 1968), pp. 6–7 (326–27).

75. [Review] *Journal of Ecumenical Studies*, vol. 5, no. 2 (Spring 1968), pp. 391–92. **Notes**: Review of: *The Sacraments: An Ecumenical Dilemma* / edited by Hans Küng.– New York: Paulist, 1967.

76. [Review] *Religion in Life*, vol. 37, no. 2 (Summer 1968), pp. 308–9. **Notes**: Review of: *Glossolalia: Tongue Speaking in Biblical, Historical, and Psychological Perspective* / Frank Stagg, E. Glenn Hinson, and Wayne Oates.—Nashville: Abingdon, 1967.

1969

77. "Can Gospel Preaching Save the Day?" *Eternity*, vol. 20, no. 7 (July 1969), pp. 6–8, 33. **Subheading**: Examples of Luther and Calvin.

78. "Fractured Theology." *The Reformed Journal*, vol. 19, no. 2 (February 1969), pp. 14–16. **Notes**: On the polarity between conservative/liberal, etc. **Headings**: The Contemporary Debate—The Full Gospel—Putting the Cart before the Horse—Ultimate and Penultimate.

79. "Historicist Theology." *Christianity Today*, vol. 13, no. 20 (July 4, 1969), pp. 16–17 (904–5). **Notes**: Review of: *Systematic Theology: A Historicist Perspective* / Gordon D. Kaufman.—New York: Scribner, 1969.

80. "Martyred for Christ." *Presbyterian Life*, vol. 22, no. 15 (August 1, 1969), pp. 34–35. **Notes**: Review of: *The Life and Death of Dietrich Bonhoeffer* / Mary Bosanquet.—1st ed.—New York: Harper and Row, 1969.

81. "The Need for Biblical Preaching." *The Reformed Journal*, vol. 19, no. 1 (January 1969), pp. 11–14. **Notes**: Reprinted as part of item 92. **Headings**: The Famine of the Word of God—The Hallmarks of Biblical Preaching—Our Need for God's Word and Spirit.

82. "Syncretism and Social Involvement." *Eternity*, vol. 20, no. 10 (October 1969), pp. 44–45. **Notes**: Review of: *The Protest of a Troubled Protestant* / Harold O. J. Brown.—New Rochelle, N.Y.: Arlington House, 1969.

83. "Why People Are Leaving the Churches." *Religion in Life*, vol. 38, no. 1 (Spring 1969), pp. 92–101. **Headings**: Transformation of the Sermon—Rethinking the Church's Mission—The New Apostasy—Conversion and Social Reform.
84. [Letter to the Editor] *Christianity Today*, vol. 13, no. 14 (April 11, 1969), p. 19 (633). **Notes**: Regarding "The Church and Political Action" by Malcolm Nygren, which appeared in vol. 13, no. 12 (March 14, 1969), pp. 9–10, 12 (529–30, 532).
85. [Letter to the Editor] *The Telegraph Herald*, vol. 133, no. 227 (September 26, 1969), p. 4. **Notes**: Regarding the condition of and funding for the Dubuque County Jail.
86. [Review] *Encounter*, vol. 30, no. 3 (Summer 1969), pp. 272–74. **Notes**: Review of: *The Reality of Faith: A Way between Protestant Orthodoxy and Existentialist Theology* / H. M. Kuitert; translated by Lewis B. Smedes.—Grand Rapids, Mich.: W. B. Eerdmans, 1968.
87. [Review] *The Presbyterian Outlook*, vol. 151, no. 13 (March 31, 1969), p. 15. **Notes**: Review of: *Is the Last Supper Finished?: Secular Light on a Sacred Meal* / Arthur A. Vogel; with a preface by Bernard Cooke.—New York: Sheed and Ward, 1968.
88. [Review] *Religion in Life*, vol. 38, no. 3 (Autumn 1969), pp. 454–55. **Notes**: Reviews of: *The Search for a Usable Future* / Martin E. Marty.—1st ed.—New York: Harper and Row, 1968; and *The Whole Man: Studies in Christian Anthropology* / Ronald G. Smith.—Philadelphia: Westminster, 1969.

1970

89. "A Catholic Theologian Speaks." *Christianity Today*, vol. 14, no. 20 (July 3, 1970), pp. 26–28 (914–16). **Notes**: Cf. item 56. Review of: *Theological Investigations. Vol. VI* / Karl Rahner; translated with an introduction by Cornelius Ernst.—Baltimore: Helicon Press, 1966.
90. "Evangelical Confession." *Dialog*, vol. 9, no. 1 (Winter 1970), pp. 26–34. **Headings**: The Need for Confession—Confession in Theological History—A Reappraisal of Confession.
91. "Is Christianity a Comedy?" *Eternity*, vol. 21, no. 4 (April 1970), pp. 59–60. **Notes**: At head of title: The Celebration of Life. Review of: *The Feast of Fools: A Theological Essay on Festivity and Fantasy* / Harvey Cox.—Cambridge: Harvard University, 1969.
92. *The Reform of the Church.*—Grand Rapids, Mich.: W. B. Eerdmans, c1970. 199 pp.; 23 cm. **Notes**: Foreword by Franklin H. Littell. Reprinted: item 382. The chapter entitled "The Need for Biblical Preaching" first appeared as item 81. **Contents**: THE NEED FOR BIBLICAL PREACHING—LITURGICAL RENEWAL—THE CRISIS OF BAPTISM—THE CENTRALITY OF THE EUCHARIST—EVANGELICAL CONFESSION—CHURCH DISCIPLINE—A NEW KIND OF CONFIRMATION—NEW FORMS OF THE CHURCH—THE CHARISMATIC GIFTS—DIVINE HEALING—EVANGELISM IN A SECULAR AGE—SPIRITUAL DISCIPLINES—THE NEED FOR SOCIAL RELEVANCE—CHRISTIAN UNITY.

93. "True and False Ecumenism: Growing Disenchantment with the Ecumenical Movement." *Christianity Today*, vol. 14, no. 21 (July 17, 1970), pp. 3–5 (931–33). **Headings**: Questionable Kinds of Ecumenism—Evangelical Ecumenism—Bonhoeffer's Legacy—A Prognosis.

94. [Review] *Encounter*, vol. 31, no. 3 (Summer 1970), pp. 283–84. **Notes**: Review of: *Power without Glory: A Study in Ecumenical Politics* / Ian Henderson.—Richmond, Va.: John Knox, 1969.

95. [Review] *Religious Education*, vol. 65, no. 3 (May–June 1970), pp. 279–80. **Notes**: Review of: *In Pursuit of Dietrich Bonhoeffer* / William Kuhns; with a foreword by Eberhard Bethge.—Dayton, Ohio: Pflaum, 1967.

1971

96. "Burying the Gospel, Part I." *Christianity Today*, vol. 15, no. 25 (September 24, 1971), pp. 8–11 (1132–35). **Notes**: Revised and expanded as part of item 129. Part II is in item 97 **Headings**: Social Activism—Psychological Analysis—Liturgical Innovation.

97. "Burying the Gospel, Part II." *Christianity Today*, vol. 16, no. 1 (October 8, 1971), pp. 12–14. **Notes**: Revised and expanded as part of item 129. Part I is in item 96. **Headings**: Cultural Preaching—Church Mergers—Crisis in the Church.

98. "'Christian' Radical?" *The Christian Century*, vol. 88, no. 44 (November 3, 1971), p. 1296. **Notes**: Review of: *Schweitzer: Prophet of Radical Theology* / Jackson Lee Ice.—Philadelphia: Westminster, 1971.

99. "Decision and Risk." *The Christian Century*, vol. 88, no. 4 (January 27, 1971), pp. 133–35. **Notes**: Reviews of: *Put Your Arms around the City* / James W. Angell.—Old Tappan, N.J.: Revell, 1970; and *Habitation of Dragons: A Book of Hope about Living as a Christian* / Keith Miller.—Waco, Tex.: Word, 1970.

100. *The Ground of Certainty: Toward an Evangelical Theology of Revelation.*—Grand Rapids, Mich.: W. B. Eerdmans, c1971. 212 pp.; 21 cm. **Notes**: Reprinted: item 343 and item 416. **Contents**: THE CONTEMPORARY DEBATE IN THEOLOGY—THE THEOLOGICAL ENCOUNTER WITH PHILOSOPHY—A NEW ROLE FOR PHILOSOPHY OF RELIGION—THE GROUND OF CERTAINTY—THEOLOGY AND PHILOSOPHY—THE PROBLEM OF EVIL—THE MEANING OF TRUTH—FAITH AND MYSTICISM—PHILOSOPHY, MYTH, AND CULTURE RELIGION—FAITH AND REASON.

101. "Heaven's Warning to Earth's Pride." *Eternity*, vol. 22, no. 5 (May 1971), pp. 12–13, 45–47. **Subheading**: Institutional Idolatry.

102. "The Meaning of Salvation." *Good News*, vol. 4, no. 4 (April–June 1971), pp. 53–57. **Notes**: At head of title: Ecumenical Perspective. Revised and expanded as "What Kind of Bread Do We Give Them?" item 117.

103. "The Misunderstanding of Prayer." *The Christian Century*, vol. 88, no. 51 (December 22, 1971), pp. 1492–94. **Headings**: Recent Reinterpretations—Dissolution of Prayer—Rediscovering Biblical Prayer.

104. *Servants of Christ: Deaconesses in Renewal* / edited with an introduction by Donald G. Bloesch.—Minneapolis: Bethany Fellowship, c1971. 181 pp.: ill.; 21

cm. **Contents**: THE ORIGIN OF THE MODERN DIACONATE FOR WOMEN / Frederick S. Weiser—DEACONESSES IN THE ANGLICAN COMMUNION / Elizabeth Souttar—THE SISTERS OF REUILLY / Ansgar Christensen—THE CHANGING DIACONATE IN NORTH AMERICA / Louise Burroughs—A ROMAN CATHOLIC SISTER LOOKS AT LUTHERAN DEACONESSES / Mary Louise Norpel.

105. [Review] *Eternity*, vol. 22, no. 4 (April 1971), p. 50. **Notes**: Review of: *To Will & to Do: An Ethical Research for Christians* / Jacques Ellul; translated by C. Edward Hopkin.—Philadelphia: Pilgrim, 1969.

1972

106. "Child Communion as a Means of Cheap Grace." *Monday Morning*, vol. 37, no. 5 (March 6, 1972), pp. 3–5. **Notes**: Reprinted as: "Unrestricted Communion," item 111.

107. "The Ideological Temptation." *Listening*, vol. 7, no. 1 (Winter 1972), pp. 45–54. **Headings**: Two Types of Ideology—Infiltration of Ideology into the Church—Combating Ideology—Conclusion, The Christian Contribution.

108. "The New Evangelicalism." *Religion in Life*, vol. 41, no. 3 (Autumn 1972), pp. 327–39. **Notes**: Reprinted as part of item 114. **Headings**: Salient Notes—Differences from Neo-Orthodoxy—Weaknesses in the New Evangelicalism—Prognosis.

109. "New Wind Rising." *Christianity Today*, vol. 16, no. 9 (February 4, 1972), p. 17 (409). **Notes**: Review of: *Theology of the Liberating Word* / compiled by Frederick Herzog.—Nashville: Abingdon, 1971.

110. "Salvation as Justice." *The Christian Century*, vol. 89, no. 26 (July 5–12, 1972), pp. 751–52. **Notes**: Review of: *The Message of Liberation in Our Age* / Johannes Verkuyl; translated by Dale Cooper.—Grand Rapids, Mich.: W. B. Eerdmans, 1972.

111. "Unrestricted Communion." *The Presbyterian Journal*, vol. 30, no. 50 (April 12, 1972), pp. 12–13. **Notes**: Reprint of: "Child Communion as a Means of Cheap Grace," item 106.

112. [Review] *Journal of Ecumenical Studies*, vol. 9, no. 1 (Winter 1972), pp. 133–34. **Notes**: Review of: *The Gospel and Unity* / edited by Vilmos Vajta.—Minneapolis: Augsburg, 1971.

1973

113. "Catholic Ferment." *The Christian Century*, vol. 90, no. 6 (February 7, 1973), pp. 184–86. **Notes**: Review of: *Revolution in Rome* / David F. Wells.—Downers Grove, Ill.: InterVarsity, 1972.

114. *The Evangelical Renaissance.*—Grand Rapids, Mich.: W. B. Eerdmans, c1973. 165 pp.; 21 cm. **Notes**: Reprinted: item 120. The chapter entitled, "The New Evangelicalism" originally appeared as item 108. **Contents**: INTRODUCTION: THE RESURGENCE OF EVANGELICALISM—THE NEW EVANGELICALISM—THE

HALLMARKS OF EVANGELICALISM—A REASSESSMENT OF KARL BARTH—THE LEGACY OF PIETISM.

115. "Key 73: Pathway to Renewal?" *The Christian Century*, vol. 90, no. 1 (January 3, 1973), pp. 9–11. **Headings**: Theological Stance—Some Reservations—The Soul of Ecumenism.

116. "The Missing Dimension." *The Reformed Review*, vol. 26, no. 3 (Spring 1973), pp. 162–68, 179–88. **Notes**: Reprinted as part of item 129. **Headings**: The Secularizing of Theology—Two Misunderstandings—The Biblical View—The Church's Spiritual Mandate.

117. "What Kind of Bread Do We Give Them?" *Eternity*, vol. 24, no. 3 (March 1973), pp. 37–40, 49. **Notes**: Revised and expanded version of: "The Meaning of Salvation," item 102. **Headings**: Man's Deepest Need—Spiritual Goal Paramount—No Other Answer—A More Terrible Famine.

118. "The Wind of the Spirit: Thoughts on a Doctrinal Controversy." *The Reformed Journal*, vol. 23, no. 8 (October 1973), pp. 11–16.

119. [Review] *Journal of Ecumenical Studies*, vol. 10, no. 4 (Fall 1973), pp. 801–3. **Notes**: Review of: *The Christian Tradition. Vol. I, The Emergence of the Catholic Tradition (100-600)* / Jaroslav Pelikan.—Chicago: University of Chicago Press, 1971.

1974

120. *The Evangelical Renaissance.*—London: Hodder and Stoughton, 1974. 170 pp.; 18 cm. **Notes**: For contents cf. item 114, of which this is a reprint. The difference in pagination is due to half-titles for the indexes.

121. "Hardness of Heart." *Cross Talk*, vol. 3, no. 3, part 10 (September, October, November 1974). **Headings**: The Nature of Sin—Solution to the Sin Problem.

122. "Ramm Reaffirms Our Great Heritage." *Eternity*, vol. 25, no. 1 (January 1974), p. 36. **Notes**: Review of: *The Evangelical Heritage* / Bernard Ramm.—Waco, Tex.: Word, 1973.

123. "Rethinking Mission." *The Christian Century*, vol. 91, no. 7 (February 20, 1974), pp. 211–12. **Notes**: Reviews of: *Liberal Christianity at the Crossroads* / John B. Cobb Jr.—Philadelphia: Westminster, 1973; and *Frontiers for the Church Today* / Robert McAfee Brown.—New York: Oxford University Press, 1973.

124. "Rethinking the Church's Mission" in *Vocation and Victory: An International Symposium Presented in Honour of Erik Wickberg, LL.D., General of the Salvation Army, Knight Commander of the Order of Vasa Bestowed by His Late Majesty Gustaf VI Adolf King of Sweden* / edited by J. W. Winterhager and Arnold Brown.—Bâle, Switzerland: Brunnen, 1974, pp. 251–62. **Notes**: Reprinted as part of item 129. **Headings**: The Full Gospel—The Priority of Evangelism—Social Concern in the Church's Mission—How Christians Can Change the World.

125. *Wellsprings of Renewal: Promise in Christian Communal Life.*—Grand Rapids, Mich.: W. B. Eerdmans, c1974. 124 pp.: ill.; 21 cm. **Contents**: INTRODUCTION, THE COMMUNITY PHENOMENON—TWO PATTERNS OF DISCIPLESHIP—THE PROTEST OF THE REFORMATION—ATTEMPTS TO RECOVER COMMUNITY LIFE—THE COMMU-

NITY REVIVAL IN EUROPE—NEW EXPERIMENTS IN AMERICA AND ASIA—TOWARD A
NEW FORM OF COMMUNITY LIFE.

126. "Whatever Became of Neo-Orthodoxy?" *Christianity Today*, vol. 19, no. 5 (December 6, 1974), pp. 7–12 (239–44). **Headings**: Its Weaknesses—Its Strengths—Relevance Today.

127. [Review] *The Reformed Journal*, vol. 24, no. 2 (February 1974), p. 23. **Notes**: Reviews of: *Concepts of Deity* / H. P. Owen.—New York: Herder and Herder, 1971; and *The Freedom of God: A Study of Election and Pulpit* / James Daane.— Grand Rapids, Mich.: W. B. Eerdmans, 1973.

1975

128. "The Basic Issue." *Decision*, vol. 16, no. 11 (November 1975), p. 4. **Notes**: At head of title: Why Did Jesus Suffer and Die? That Is the Determining Question.

129. *The Invaded Church.*—Waco, Tex.: Word, c1975. 133 pp.; 23 cm. **Notes**: The chapter "Burying the Gospel" is a revised and expanded edition of item 96 and item 97; "A Church Divided" is a revised and expanded edition of item 135 and item 137; "The Missing Dimension" first appeared as item 116; "How Christians Can Change the World" first appeared as part of item 124. **Contents**: A CHURCH DIVIDED—BURYING THE GOSPEL—THE CHURCH AND SOCIAL INVOLVEMENT—THE MISSING DIMENSION—HOW CHRISTIANS CAN CHANGE THE WORLD.

130. *Light a Fire: Gospel Songs for Today.*—St. Louis, Mo.: Eden, c1975. [84] pp.; 23 cm. **Contents**: God the Almighty—Jesus Thank You for Your Kindness—Our Savior's Wondrous Love—Jesus Is My Sole Defense—God of the Earth and Sea—Renew Me by Thy Holy Spirit—By His Loving-Kindness—Blessed Jesus Thou Hast Won—Sing a Song of Praise—Through the Power of God the Holy Spirit—O Christ Our Glorious Redeemer—Standing on the Solid Rock—Christ Our Conquering Savior—Praised Be His Name—O Jesus Lamb of God—The Saints March On—Jesus Reigns o'er Earth and Heaven— Heavenly Light Shine down on Me—Here's My Heart—Tell the Story—Jesus Loves Me—Jesus Savior, Holy King—Jesus Is Mighty to Save!—Give Praise to Him Above—I Will Sing of Christ's Salvation—O Jesus I Love Thee Most of All—In Dark Gethsemane—Hallelujah Dearest Savior—The Light Shines in the Darkness—Christ Thou Holy One—O Savior Hear My Prayerful Cry—Through the Grace of Jesus—Jesus Has Come to Save His Own—In This Time of Racial Strife—Jesus Is Our Captain—Give to Christ the Glory— Cling Ever to Jesus—There at the Cross—Jesus the Savior Has Died for Our Sins—We Are Traveling on to Zion—Through the Might of Christ Our Savior—Dearest Savior Hear Our Prayer—O Come Thou Holy Son of God— Christ Our Conquering Redeemer—Glory to Our King and Savior—We Are Warriors of Christ—Praise Be to Jesus Forever—Glorious Savior Hear My Prayer—Prepare to Meet Your Glorious Savior—There Is Heavenly Sunlight—In This Vale—What a Privilege to Follow—Light a Fire—Walking

through This Valley—When I'm Sad and Deep in Gloom—Holy God Prepare
Me Now—Christ Thou Holy Lamb of God—Wonderful, Bountiful Savior—
Gracious God I Sing Thy Praises—Blest Redeemer Pilot Me—When in Time
of Trouble—Give Praise to the Christ Child—Shout and Sing You Men of
Zion—God Showed His Love—Jesus Refuge of the Burdened—We Are Trav-
eling unto Our Home—Thank the Lord for All His Loving-Kindness—Sing
His Praise—Jesus Knows Our Every Failing—Come Lord Jesus and De-
liver—The Church of God Goes Forth—God Is Our Comfort—By His Spirit.

131. "Moltmann's Crucified God." *Communio*, vol. 2, no. 4 (Winter 1975), pp.
413–14. **Notes**: "Reprinted with permission of *Christianity Today.*" Review of:
*The Crucified God: The Cross of Christ as the Foundation and Criticism of Christ-
ian Theology* / Jürgen Moltmann.—London: SCM, 1974.

132. "New Enlightenment." *The Christian Century*, vol. 92, no. 12 (April 2, 1975),
p. 339. **Notes**: Reviews of: *Atheism: The Case against God* / George H. Smith.—
1st paperback ed.—Buffalo, N.Y.: Prometheus, 1979; and *Without Burnt Offer-
ings: Ceremonies of Humanism* / Algernon D. Black.—New York: Viking, 1974.

133. "A New Tribalism." *Christianity Today*, vol. 19, no. 8 (January 17, 1975), p. 32
(394). **Notes**: Review of: *The Restless Heart: Breaking the Cycle of Social Identity*
/ Robert C. Harvey.—Grand Rapids, Mich.: W. B. Eerdmans, 1973.

134. "To Build Bridges." *The Christian Century*, vol. 92, no. 4 (January 29, 1975), pp.
89–91. **Notes**: Review of: *Models of the Church* / Avery Dulles.—1st ed.—Garden City, N.Y.: Doubleday, 1974.

135. "What Troubles Christendom?" *His*, vol. 35, no. 5 (February 1975), pp. 18–21.
Notes: Revised and expanded as part of item 129. Continued by: "Where the
Church Touches the World," item 137. **Headings**: The Two Mentalities—
Evangelism—Voice of God.

136. "What's behind the Manson Cult?" *Christianity Today*, vol. 20, no. 5 (December 5, 1975), p. 35 (271). **Notes**: Review of: *Our Savage God: The Perverse Use of
Eastern Thought* / R. C. Zaehner.—New York: Sheed and Ward, 1974.

137. "Where the Church Touches the World." *His*, vol. 35, no. 6 (March 1975), pp.
12–14. **Notes**: Revised and expanded as part of item 129. Continues: "What
Troubles Christendom?" item 135. **Headings**: Justice—Inner Mission—Unity.

138. [Review] *Eternity*, vol. 26, no. 11 (November 1975), pp. 51–52. **Notes**: Review
of: *The Evangelical Faith. Vol. 1, Prolegomena, The Relation of Theology to Modern
Thought Forms* / Helmut Thielicke; translated and edited by Geoffrey W.
Bromiley.—Grand Rapids, Mich.: W. B. Eerdmans, 1974.

1976

139. "An Evangelical Views the New Catholicism." *Communio*, vol. 3, no. 3 (Fall
1976), pp. 215–30. **Notes**: "The New Catholicism has more in common with
'culture-Protestantism' than with the historic Catholic faith."

140. *Jesus Is Victor!: Karl Barth's Doctrine of Salvation.*—Nashville: Abingdon,
c1976. 176 pp.; 19 cm. **Notes**: Reprinted: item 402. **Contents**: THE CHALLENGE
OF BARTH—BARTH'S CONTINUING RELEVANCE—THE OBJECTIVISTIC SLANT—

Reinterpreting the Atonement—Universal Salvation?—Two Conflicting Orientations—Barth in Retrospect.

141. "Options in Current Theology." *Christianity Today*, vol. 20, no. 14 (April 9, 1976), pp. 39–40 (735–36). **Notes**: Review of: *Thinking about God* / John Macquarrie.—1st American ed.—New York: Harper and Row, 1975.

142. "Prayer and Mysticism (1): Two Types of Spirituality." *The Reformed Journal*, vol. 26, no. 3 (March 1976), pp. 23–26. **Notes**: Revised as part of item 185.

143. "Prayer and Mysticism (2): Divergent Views on Prayer." *The Reformed Journal*, vol. 26, no. 4 (April 1976), pp. 22–25. **Notes**: Revised as part of item 185.

144. "Prayer and Mysticism (3): Towards Renewed Evangelical Prayer." *The Reformed Journal*, vol. 26, no. 5 (May–June 1976), pp. 20–22. **Notes**: Revised as part of item 185.

145. "A Righteous Nation." *Cross Talk*, vol. 5, no. 1, part 1 (March–April–May 1976). **Headings**: Two Kinds of Righteousness—Hallmarks of a Righteous Nation—The Mission of the Church.

146. "True Spirituality." *Christianity Today*, vol. 21, no. 2 (October 22, 1976), pp. 44–45 (106–7). **Notes**: Review of: *The Inward Pilgrimage: Spiritual Classics from Augustine to Bonhoeffer* / Bernhard Christensen.—Minneapolis: Augsburg, 1976.

147. "Wind of the Spirit." *The Review of Books and Religion*, vol. 5, no. 5 (Mid-February 1976), p. 11. **Notes**: Reviews of: *Aspects of Pentecostal-Charismatic Origins* / edited by Vinson Synan.—Plainfield, N.J.: Logos International, 1975; and *Jesus and the Spirit: A Study of the Religious and Charismatic Experience of Jesus and the First Christians as Reflected in the New Testament* / James D. G. Dunn.—Philadelphia: Westminster, 1975.

148. [Review] *Christian Scholar's Review*, vol. 6, no. 1 (1976), pp. 81–83. **Notes**: Review of: *The Evangelicals: What They Believe, Who They Are, Where They Are Changing* / edited by David F. Wells and John D. Woodbridge.—Nashville: Abingdon, 1975.

149. [Review] *Eternity*, vol. 27, no. 9 (September 1976), pp. 53–54. **Notes**: Review of: *The New Demons* / Jacques Ellul; translated by C. Edward Hopkin.—New York: Seabury, 1975.

1977

150. "The Basic Issue" in *Christ Is Victor* / edited by W. Glyn Evans.—Valley Forge, Pa.: Judson, 1977, pp. 27–30.

151. "Biblical Piety vs. Religiosity." *Religion in Life*, vol. 46, no. 4 (Winter 1977), pp. 488–96. **Headings**: The Strange World within the Bible—True and False Prophecy—Biblical vs. Cultural Religion.

152. "Breakthrough into Freedom." *The Presbyterian Journal*, vol. 36, no. 29 (November 16, 1977), pp. 7–8, 19–20.

153. "Christian Humanism." *Christianity Today*, vol. 21, no. 15 (May 6, 1977), pp. 50–51 (894–95). **Notes**: Review of: *On Being a Christian* / Hans Küng; translated by Edward Quinn.—Garden City, N.Y.: Doubleday, 1976.

154. "The Church: Catholic and Apostolic." *Christianity Today*, vol. 22, no. 5 (December 9, 1977), pp. [46]–47 ([372]–73). **Notes**: Review of: *The Church* / G. C. Berkouwer; translated by James E. Davison.—Grand Rapids, Mich.: W. B. Eerdmans, 1976.

155. "Creative Transcendence." *The Reformed Journal*, vol. 27, no. 12 (December 1977), p. 30. **Notes**: The volume is labeled "28" on the cover, but is actually 27 given the chronological sequence. Review of: *Historical Transcendence and the Reality of God: A Christological Critique* / Ray Sherman Anderson; with a foreword by D. M. MacKinnon.—1st American ed.—Grand Rapids, Mich.: W. B. Eerdmans, 1975.

156. "Defender of Evangelicalism." *The New Review of Books and Religion*, vol. 1, no. 10 (June 1977), p. 6. **Notes**: Review of: *The Evangelical Faith. Vol. 2, The Doctrine of God and of Christ* / Helmut Thielicke; translated and edited by Geoffrey W. Bromiley.—Grand Rapids, Mich.: W. B. Eerdmans, 1977.

157. "The Mystical Side of Luther." *Christianity Today*, vol. 21, no. 20 (July 29, 1977), p. 30 (1130). **Notes**: Review of: *Luther and the Mystics: A Re-examination of Luther's Spiritual Experience and His Relationship to the Mystics* / Bengt R. Hoffman.—Minneapolis: Augsburg, 1976.

158. "The Pilgrimage of Karl Barth." *Christianity Today*, vol. 22, no. 2 (October 21, 1977), pp. 35–36 (101–2). **Notes**: Review of: *Karl Barth, His Life from Letters and Autobiographical Texts* / Eberhard Busch; translated by John Bowden.—Philadelphia: Fortress, 1976.

159. [Review] *Eternity*, vol. 28, no. 1 (January 1977), pp. 56–58. **Notes**: Review of: *Catholicism Confronts Modernity: A Protestant View* / Langdon Gilkey.—New York: Seabury, 1975.

1978

160. "A Bleak Outlook." *The Christian Century*, vol. 95, no. 27 (August 30–September 6, 1978), pp. 801–2. **Notes**: Review of: *The Betrayal of the West* / Jacques Ellul; translated by Matthew J. O'Connell.—New York: Seabury, 1978.

161. "A Call to Spirituality" in *The Orthodox Evangelicals* / edited by Robert E. Webber and Donald Bloesch.—Nashville: Nelson, 1978, pp. 146–65. **Headings**: The Problem in Spirituality—Hallmarks of Evangelical Spirituality—Need for Catholic Continuity—Pathways to Evangelical–Catholic Unity.

162. *Essentials of Evangelical Theology. Vol. 1, God, Authority, Salvation.*—1st ed.—San Francisco: Harper and Row, c1978. xii, 265 pp.; 25 cm. **Notes**: Vol. 2: item 172. Reprinted: item 214, item 215, and item 378; excerpted: item 176, item 231, and item 432. **Contents**: THE MEANING OF *EVANGELICAL*. Evangelicalism and Catholicism. Evangelicalism and Liberalism. A Systematic Evangelical Theology? The Bane of Modern Evangelicalism.—THE SOVEREIGNTY OF GOD. Creator and Lord. Omnipotent Will. Holy Love. The Holy Trinity. *Soli Deo Gloria*. Erosion of the Biblical View of God.—THE PRIMACY OF SCRIPTURE. Its Divine Authority. Scriptural Primacy. Infallibility and Inerrancy. The Hermeneutical Task. Misconceptions in Modern Evangelicalism.—TOTAL DEPRAVITY. The Grandeur and Misery of Mankind. Total and Universal Corruption. The

Meaning of Sin. Manifestations and Consequences of Sin. The Story of the Fall. Modern Optimism.—THE DEITY OF JESUS CHRIST. The Struggle with Liberalism. The New Testament Witness. Jesus Christ—True God and True Man. Areas of Tension within the Christian Family. Two Types of Christological Heresy. Kenotic Christology. The Contemporary Scene.—THE SUBSTITUTIONARY ATONEMENT. The Biblical Understanding. Differing Views on the Atonement. Three Aspects of the Atonement. Objective and Subjective Atonement. Particular and Universal Atonement. The Obligation of the Christian. Misunderstandings in Modern Theology.—SALVATION BY GRACE. The Gift of Grace in Biblical Perspective. An Age-Old Controversy. The Paradox of Salvation. The Means of Grace. Current Questions.—FAITH ALONE. The Meaning of Faith. Justification by Faith. The Certainty of Faith. Modern Misconceptions.

163. *The Orthodox Evangelicals: Who They Are and What They Are Saying* / edited by Robert E. Webber, Donald Bloesch.—Nashville: Nelson, c1978. 239 pp.; 20 cm. **Contents**: THE CHICAGO CALL: AN APPEAL TO EVANGELICALS—BEHIND THE SCENES: A PERSONAL ACCOUNT / Robert Webber—A CALL TO HISTORIC ROOTS AND CONTINUITY / Richard Lovelace—A CALL TO BIBLICAL FIDELITY / Roger Nicole—A CALL TO CREEDAL IDENTITY / Morris Inch—A CALL TO HOLISTIC SALVATION / Lane Dennis—A CALL TO SACRAMENTAL INTEGRITY / Thomas Howard—A CALL TO SPIRITUALITY / Donald Bloesch—A CALL TO CHURCH AUTHORITY / Jon Braun—A CALL TO CHURCH UNITY / F. Burton Nelson—RESERVATIONS ABOUT CATHOLIC RENEWAL IN EVANGELICALISM / David F. Wells—A ROMAN CATHOLIC APPRAISAL OF THE CHICAGO CALL / Benedict T. Viviano—AN ANNOTATED BIBLIOGRAPHY FOR FURTHER READING / Jan Dennis.

164. "A Subversive Act." *The Christian Century*, vol. 95, no. 6 (February 22, 1978), pp. 195–96. **Notes**: Review of: *Thy Will Be Done: Praying the Our Father as Subversive Activity* / Michael H. Crosby.—Maryknoll, N.Y.: Orbis, 1977.

165. "Tensions in the Church." *Christianity Today*, vol. 22, no. 14 (April 21, 1978), pp. 36–39 (920–23). **Notes**: Review of: *The Church in the Power of the Spirit: A Contribution to Messianic Ecclesiology* / Jürgen Moltmann.—London: SCM, 1977.

166. "Toward a Catholic Evangelical Understanding of the Lord's Supper." *Spirituality Today*, vol. 30, no. 3 (September 1978), pp. 236–49. **Headings**: A Means of Grace—The Real Presence—Eucharistic Sacrifice—Opportunity for Rededication—Means of Church Discipline—Eucharist and Ministry—Sacerdotalism and Secularism.

167. [Review] *New Oxford Review*, vol. 45, no. 5 (May 1978), pp. 21–22. **Notes**: Review of: *Final Testimonies* / Karl Barth; edited by Eberhard Busch; translated by Geoffrey W. Bromiley.—Grand Rapids, Mich.: W. B. Eerdmans, 1977.

168. [Review] *The Reformed Review*, vol. 31, no. 2 (Winter 1978), pp. 93–95. **Notes**: Review of: *God, Revelation, and Authority. Vols. 1–2* / Carl F. H. Henry.—Waco, Tex.: Word, 1976.

1979

169. "A Catholic Examination of the Basics." *Christianity Today*, vol. 23, no. 25 (November 2, 1979), p. 50 (1483). **Notes**: Review of: *Foundations of Christian*

Faith: An Introduction to the Idea of Christianity / Karl Rahner; translated by William V. Dych.—New York: Seabury, 1978.

170. "Crisis in Biblical Authority." *Theology Today*, vol. 35, no. 4 (January 1979), pp. 455–62. **Notes**: Also available as an electronic resource via: theologytoday.pt-sem.edu (accessed February 14, 2007).

171. "Donald G. Bloesch Replies." *New Oxford Review*, vol. 46, no. 4 (May 1979), pp. 10–11. **Notes**: A response to Canon Francis W. Read's article in the same issue, entitled "Ecumenical Overtones of The Chicago Call."

172. *Essentials of Evangelical Theology. Vol. 2, Life, Ministry, and Hope.*—1st ed.—San Francisco: Harper and Row, c1979. xii, 315 pp.; 25 cm. **Notes**: Vol. 1: item 162. Reprinted: item 214, item 215, and item 378. **Contents**: THE NEW BIRTH. The Meaning of Regeneration. The New Birth and Experience. Baptism by Water and the Spirit. Continual Conversion. Erroneous Interpretations.—SCRIPTURAL HOLINESS. The Call to Holiness. Justification and Sanctification. Christian Perfection. Holiness in the World. The Life of Prayer. Worldly Christianity.—THE CRUCIALITY OF PREACHING. Preaching as a Means of Grace. Preaching the Whole Counsel of God. Reformed Worship. Biblical versus Cultural Preaching.—THE PRIESTHOOD OF ALL BELIEVERS. Priesthood in the Bible. The Gifts of the Holy Spirit. Historical Development. The Ministry of the Word and Sacraments. Toward a Catholic Balance.—TWO KINGDOMS. The Biblical Testimony. Development in Catholic Thought. Reformation and Post-Reformation Perspectives. Modern Discussion. A Theological Reappraisal.—THE CHURCH'S SPIRITUAL MISSION. The New Testament Perspective. Witness of the Church Tradition. Reinterpreting the Church's Mission. Evangelism and Social Concern.—THE PERSONAL RETURN OF CHRIST. Current Issues in Eschatology. The Second Advent. The Resurrection of the Dead. The Millennium.—HEAVEN AND HELL. Promise and Warning. The Historical Controversy. Universalism and Particularism in Karl Barth. The Twofold Outcome.—HOW DISTINCTIVE IS EVANGELICALISM? Confusion in Terminology. Supreme Authority of the Word of God. The Transcendent God. The Radical Pervasiveness of Sin. The Uniqueness of Jesus Christ. The Free Gift of Salvation. Inward Religion.—TOWARD THE RECOVERY OF BIBLICAL FAITH. The Outlook for Evangelicalism. The Need to Reappraise Biblical Authority. The Need to Rediscover Evangelical Distinctives. The Need to Recover Catholic Substance. Toward a Catholic Evangelicalism.

173. "Process Theology in Reformed Perspective." *Listening*, vol. 14, no. 3 (Fall 1979), pp. 185–95. **Notes**: Revised: item 174.

174. "Process Theology in Reformed Perspective." *The Reformed Journal*, vol. 29, no. 10 (October 1979), pp. 19–24. **Notes**: Revision of item 173.

175. "A Response to 'Theological Education and Liberation Theology' by Frederick Herzog, et al." *Theological Education*, vol. 16, no. 1 (Autumn 1979), pp. 16–19.

176. "Scriptural Primacy" in *Issues in Sexual Ethics* / edited by Martin Duffy; contributing editors, Gerald M. Sanders, Leslie C. Wicker.—Souderton, Pa.: United Church People for Biblical Witness, 1979, pp. 27–35. **Notes**: Excerpted from vol. 1 of *Essentials of Evangelical Theology* (cf. item 162), pp. 51–87. **Headings**: Its Divine Authority—Scriptural Primacy—Infallibility

and Inerrancy—The Hermeneutical Task—Misconceptions in Modern Evangelicalism.

177. [Review] *Eternity*, vol. 30, no. 3 (March 1979), pp. 50, 52. **Notes**: Review of: *The Grammar of Faith* / Paul L. Holmer.—1st ed.—San Francisco: Harper and Row, 1978.

178. [Review] *Theology Today*, vol. 36, no. 3 (October 1979), pp. 452–53. **Notes**: Not same as item 212. Review of: *Historical Theology: An Introduction* / Geoffrey W. Bromiley.—Grand Rapids, Mich.: W. B. Eerdmans, 1978. Also available as an electronic resource via: theologytoday.ptsem.edu (accessed February 14, 2007).

179. [Review] *TSF News and Reviews*, vol. 3, no. 2 (November 1979), p. 11. **Notes**: Review of: *Understanding Pietism* / Dale W. Brown.—Grand Rapids, Mich.: W. B. Eerdmans, 1978.

1980

180. "Hartshorne, Barth, and Process Theology." *The Reformed Journal*, vol. 30, no. 5 (May 1980), pp. 31–32. **Notes**: Review of: *Becoming and Being: The Doctrine of God in Charles Hartshorne and Karl Barth* / Colin E. Gunton.—Oxford; New York: Oxford University Press, 1978.

181. "How the 20th Century Is Eroding the Christian Message." *Pastoral Renewal*, vol. 5, no. 5 (November 1980), pp. 38d–38e. **Notes**: Review of: *The Secularist Heresy: The Erosion of the Gospel in the Twentieth Century* / Harry Blamires.—Ann Arbor, Mich.: Servant, 1980, c1956.

182. "Liturgical Sexism: A New Dispute." *Eternity*, vol. 31, no. 6 (June 1980), p. 13.

183. "Postmodern Orthodoxy." *Christianity Today*, vol. 24, no. 6 (March 21, 1980), p. 37 (393). **Notes**: Reprinted as: "A Theologian Rediscovers the Roots of Faith," item 188. Review of: *Agenda for Theology* / Thomas C. Oden.—1st ed.—San Francisco: Harper and Row, 1979.

184. "Rationalism." *The Christian Century*, vol. 97, no. 13 (April 9, 1980), pp. 414–15. **Notes**: Review of: *God, Revelation, and Authority. Vols. 3–4* / Carl F. H. Henry.—Waco, Tex.: Word, 1979.

185. *The Struggle of Prayer.*—1st ed.—San Francisco: Harper and Row, c1980. ix, 180 pp.; 22 cm. **Notes**: Another edition: item 298; excerpted: item 220. The chapter "Prayer and Mysticism" is a revision of item 142, item 143, and item 144. **Contents**: THE CRISIS OF PRAYER. The New Religious Situation. The Misunderstanding of Prayer. Toward the Recovery of Biblical Prayer. Reappraising Mental Prayer.—THE SCRIPTURAL BASIS OF PRAYER. The Living and Almighty God. The Decisive Role of Jesus Christ. The Outpouring of the Holy Spirit. Public and Private Prayer. Unanswered Prayer.—DIALOGUE WITH GOD. Dialogic Encounter. Approaching the Throne of God. Time and Length of Prayer. Waiting and Striving in Prayer.—HEARTFELT SUPPLICATION. The Essence of Prayer. Other Elements in True Prayer. Striving with God. Perseverance in Prayer. Evangelical versus Magical Prayer. Intercessory Prayer. Effectual Prayer.—PRAYER AND MYSTICISM. Confronting the Mystics. Two Patterns of Spirituality. Divergent Views on Prayer. Possibility of Convergence?—PRAYER

AND ACTION. The Labor of Prayer. Action and Contemplation. Various Types of Discipleship. An Age of Activism.—THE GOAL OF PRAYER. Two Understandings. Ultimate and Penultimate Goals. Constant Communion with God. Personal and Social Religion. The Coming of the Kingdom.

186. "The Sword of the Spirit: The Meaning of Inspiration." *The Reformed Review*, vol. 33, no. 2 (Winter 1980), pp. 65–72. **Notes**: Also published: item 187. **Headings**: The Present Controversy—The Salvific Sword.

187. "The Sword of the Spirit: The Meaning of Inspiration." *Themelios*, vol. 5, no. 3 (May 1980), pp. 14–19. **Notes**: Also published: item 186, q.v. for headings.

188. "A Theologian Rediscovers the Roots of Faith." *Pastoral Renewal*, vol. 5, no. 5 (November 1980), pp. 38c–38d. **Notes**: Reprint of "Postmodern Orthodoxy," item 183, q.v. for additional note.

189. "To Reconcile the Biblically Oriented." *The Christian Century*, vol. 97, no. 24 (July 16–23, 1980), pp. 733–35. **Notes**: A response to the article, "The Challenge of Conservative Theology" by Peter Schmiechen, which appeared in *The Christian Century*, vol. 97, no. 13 (April 9, 1980), pp. 402–6.

190. "What Think Ye of Christ? A Test." *Christianity Today*, vol. 24, no. 15 (September 5, 1980), p. 25 (955). **Notes**: Reprinted: item 209.

1981

191. "The Challenge Facing the Churches" in *Christianity Confronts Modernity: A Theological and Pastoral Inquiry by Protestant Evangelicals and Roman Catholics* / edited by Peter Williamson and Kevin Perrotta.—Ann Arbor, Mich.: Servant, 1981, pp. 205–23. **Notes**: A response by Peter Hocken follows, pp. 224–28, and by Richard Lovelace, pp. 229–37. Variant issue: item 192. **Headings**: The Church in Crisis—Erosion of Biblical Authority—The God Problem—Reinterpreting Salvation—Reappraising the Mission of the Church—An Emerging Confessional Situation—Need for a New Evangelical Alliance.

192. "The Challenge Facing the Churches" in *Christianity Confronts Modernity: A Theological and Pastoral Inquiry by Protestant Evangelicals and Roman Catholics* / edited by Peter Williamson and Kevin Perrotta.—Edinburgh, Scotland: Handsel, 1981, pp. 205–23. **Notes**: Variant issue of item 191, q.v. for notes and headings.

193. "A Discussion of Hans Küng's, *Does God Exist?*" *Dialog*, vol. 20, no. 4 (Fall 1981), pp. 317–21. **Notes**: A response by Richard Jensen follows DGB's article. **Headings**: The Gospel in an Age of Nihilism—His Basic Argument—Where Küng Can Be Appreciated—Some Critical Questions.

194. *Faith & Its Counterfeits*.—Downers Grove, Ill.: InterVarsity, c1981. 122 pp.; 21 cm. **Contents**: RELIGION THAT GLORIFIES GOD—LEGALISM—FORMALISM—HUMANITARIANISM—ENTHUSIASM—ECLECTICISM—HEROISM—TOWARD THE RECOVERY OF TRUE RELIGION.

195. "Is Concern over Heresy Outdated?" *Eternity*, vol. 32, no. 11 (November 1981), pp. 16–17. **Notes**: Also published: item 216.

196. "Karl Barth and the Life of the Church." *Center Journal*, vol. 1, no. 1 (Winter 1981), pp. 65–77. **Headings**: Barth as a Church Theologian—Word and Sacraments—The Mission of the Church—The Role of Confessions—Concluding Appraisal.

197. "Karl Barth Speaks Again on Piety and Morality, Logos and Praxis." *The Review of Books and Religion*, vol. 10, no. 3 (Mid-November 1981), p. 9. **Notes**: Review of: *Ethics* / Karl Barth; edited by Dietrich Braun; translated by Geoffrey W. Bromiley.—New York: Seabury, 1981.

198. "Peril and Opportunity in the Church Today." *Center Journal*, vol. 1, no. 1 (Winter 1981), pp. 14–17. **Notes**: Also published: item 199 and item 218.

199. "Peril and Opportunity in the Church Today." *Living Faith*, vol. 2, no. 3 (Fall 1981), pp. 3–5. Also published: item 198 and item 218.

200. "Reflections on Intercommunion." *Living Faith*, vol. 1, no. 4 (Winter 1981), pp. 13–17.

201. "The Reformers Shed the Shackles of Legalism: A Primer in Pauline Theology." *Christianity Today*, vol. 25, no. 18 (October 23, 1981), pp. 18–20 (1367–69). **Headings**: An Enduring Biblical Theme—Luther's Evangelical Discovery—Two Kinds of Righteousness—The Cruciality of the Cross—The Decisive Role of Faith—Doctrinal Confusion Today.

202. "Rethinking Monotheism." *The Reformed Journal*, vol. 31, no. 11 (November–December 1981), pp. 29–30. **Notes**: Review of: *The Trinity and the Kingdom: The Doctrine of God* / Jürgen Moltmann; translated by Margaret Kohl.—1st American ed.—San Francisco: Harper and Row, 1981.

203. "Soteriology in Contemporary Christian Thought." *Interpretation*, vol. 35, no. 2 (April 1981), pp. 132–44. **Headings**: Neo-Orthodoxy—Existentialist Theology—Liberation Theology—Process Theology—Other Theological Currents—A Summary Evaluation.

204. "Suffering of Farm Animals." *The Des Moines Register* (Sunday, October 25, 1981). **Notes**: Letter to the editor.

205. "Systematic Theology." *University of Dubuque Theological Seminary Alumni Bulletin*, vol. 6, no. 3 (Summer 1981), pp. 8–9. Revised as "Encountering Systematics as an Evangelical," item 213.

206. "Traditional Roles Defended." *Christianity Today*, vol. 25, no. 7 (April 24, 1981), p. 56 (621). **Notes**: Vol. "26" appears on the issue itself, but from the date, etc., it is clear that vol. "25" is intended. Review of: *Man and Woman in Christ: An Examination of the Roles of Men and Women in the Light of Scripture and the Social Sciences* / Stephen B. Clark.—Ann Arbor, Mich.: Servant, 1980.

207. "What Kind of People?" *A.D. United Church of Christ*, vol. 10, no. 5 (May 1981), pp. 18, 20. **Notes**: At head of title: Evangelicals.

208. "What Kind of People?" *A.D. United Presbyterian*, vol. 10, no. 5 (May 1981), pp. 18, 20. **Notes**: At head of title: Evangelicals.

209. "What Think Ye of Christ? A Test" in *New England Sunday School Association Teachers' Conference, October 16 and 17, 1981, Grace Chapel, Lexington, Massachusetts: Outlines of Sessions for Local Church Youth Ministry Conducted by Rev. Richard O'Hara . . . .*—[S.l.: M. Linker, 1981 or 1982] **Notes**: Reprint of item 190.**

210. [Review] *Eternity*, vol. 32, nos. 7–8 (July–August 1981), pp. 33–34. **Notes**: About the *Junaluska Affirmation of Scriptural Christianity for United Methodists.* Review of: *Essentials of Wesleyan Theology: A Contemporary Affirmation* / Paul A. Mickey.—Grand Rapids, Mich.: Zondervan, 1980.

211. [Review] *Interpretation*, vol. 35, no. 1 (January 1981), pp. 102–3. **Notes**: Review of: *A Critical Faith: A Case for Religion* / Gerd Theissen.—1st American ed.—Philadelphia: Fortress, 1979.

212. [Review] *Living Faith*, vol. 2, no. 3 (Fall 1981), pp. 27–28. **Notes**: Not same as: item 178. Review of: *Historical Theology: An Introduction* / Geoffrey W. Bromiley.—Grand Rapids, Mich.: W. B. Eerdmans, 1978.

1982

213. "Encountering Systematics as an Evangelical." *Catalyst*, vol. 8, no. 2 (February 1982), pp. 1–3. **Notes**: Revision of "Systematic Theology," item 205.
214. *Essentials of Evangelical Theology*.—1st HarperCollins pbk. ed.—[San Francisco]: HarperSanFrancisco [sic], 1982. 2 v.; 24 cm. **Notes**: For contents cf. item 162 and item 172, of which this is a reprint.
215. *Essentials of Evangelical Theology*.—1st Harper and Row [sic] pbk. ed.—San Francisco: Harper and Row, 1982. 2 v.; 24 cm. **Notes**: Vol. 1 has at base of spine: RD 386; vol. 2 has at base of spine: RD 387. For contents cf. item 162 and item 172, of which this is a reprint.
216. "Is Concern over Heresy Outdated?" *Good News*, vol. 16, no. 2 (September–October 1982), pp. 67–70. **Notes**: Also published: item 195.
217. *Is the Bible Sexist?: Beyond Feminism and Patriarchalism*.—Westchester, Ill.: Crossway, c1982. 139 pp.; 21 cm. **Notes**: Reprinted: item 401. **Contents**: THE PRESENT CONTROVERSY—THE MAN–WOMAN RELATIONSHIP IN THE BIBLE—WOMEN MINISTERS?—REVISING THE LANGUAGE ABOUT GOD—A BIBLICAL ALTERNATIVE.
218. "Peril and Opportunity in the Church Today." *The Presbyterian Layman*, vol. 15, no. 2 (March–April 1982), pp. 11–12. **Notes**: Also published: item 198 and item 199. **Headings**: The Church Must Resist—God's Word Must Take Precedence—The Church Must Not Become Captive.
219. "Secular Humanism—Not the Only Enemy." *Eternity*, vol. 33, no. 1 (January 1982), p. 22. **Headings**: Nationalism—Technological Materialism—Mysticism—Nihilism.
220. "The Struggle of Prayer." *Presbyterian Communiqué* (Summer/Fall 1982), pp. 24–25, 31. **Notes**: Reprinted by permission of Harper and Row. Excerpt of item 185. **Headings**: The Living and Almighty God—Omnipresent—Omniscient—Omnipotent—Transcendent—Holy—Sovereign Freedom—Love.
221. [Review] *New Oxford Review*, vol. 49, no. 3 (April 1982), p. 24. **Notes**: Review of: *The Fundamentalist Phenomenon: The Resurgence of Conservative Christianity* / edited by Jerry Falwell; with Ed Dobson and Ed Hindson.—Garden City, N.Y.: Doubleday, 1981.
222. [Review] *TSF Bulletin*, vol. 6, no. 2 (November–December 1982), p. 23. **Notes**: Review of: *The Atoning Gospel* / James E. Tull.—Macon, Ga.: Mercer University Press, 1982. Also published: item 234.

1983

223. "Apocalyptic and Lost [sic] Things." *The Review of Books and Religion*, vol. 12, no. 1 (Mid-September 1983), p. [6]. **Notes**: Review of: *The Open Heaven: A Study of Apocalyptic in Judaism and Early Christianity* / Christopher Rowland.—New York: Crossroad, 1982.

224. "But Should We Be Ordained?" *Eternity*, vol. 34, no. 7 [*sic*] (July–August 1983), p. 38. **Notes**: Review of: *Ordination, A Biblical-Historical View* / Marjorie Warkentin.—Grand Rapids, Mich.: W. B. Eerdmans, 1982.

225. "The Catholic Bishops on War and Peace." *Center Journal*, vol. 3, no. 1 (Winter 1983), pp. 163–76.

226. "Donald Bloesch Responds." *Evangelical Newsletter*, vol. 10, no. 20 (October 28, 1983), p. 3. **Notes**: A reply to Clark Pinnock's article "Evangelical Trends: Post-Liberal, Neo-Classical and Name It/Claim It," which appeared in the same issue.

227. "'Evangelical': Integral to Christian Identity? An Exchange between Donald Bloesch and Vernard Eller." *TSF Bulletin*, vol. 7, no. 2 (November–December 1983), pp. 5–10.

228. *The Future of Evangelical Christianity: A Call for Unity amid Diversity.*—1st ed.—Garden City, N.Y.: Doubleday, 1983. x, 202 pp.; 22 cm. **Notes**: Another edition: item 294; excerpted: item 251. **Contents:** THE PROBLEM OF EVANGELICAL IDENTITY. Evangelicalism in Crisis. Current Misunderstandings. Redefining "Evangelical." Evangelicalism, Orthodoxy, and Fundamentalism.—THE NEW CONSERVATISM. Fundamentalism. Neoevangelicalism. Confessionalist Evangelicalism. Charismatic Religion. Neo-Orthodoxy. Catholic Evangelicalism. The Road Ahead.—EVANGELICAL DISUNITY. The Present Situation. The Scandal of Disunity. The Ideological Temptation. Types of Ideology. The Need to Resist Ideology. The Growing Church Conflict.—PATHWAYS TO EVANGELICAL OBLIVION. Restorationism. Separatism. Accommodationism. Revisionist versus Confessional Theology.—TOWARD THE RECOVERY OF EVANGELICAL FAITH. Reclaiming Historical Roots. New Statements on Biblical Authority. Breakthroughs in Theological Methodology. Fresh Confessions of Faith. A Viable Doctrine of the Church. A Biblical, Evangelical Spirituality. Rediscovering Ethical Imperatives. Overcoming Polarization on the Women's Issue. Renewal through Biblical Preaching. A Biblical and Relevant Eschatology. Promise of Renewal.

229. "Many Barth Letters." *The Review of Books and Religion*, vol. 11, no. 8 (Mid-May 1983), p. 9. **Notes**: Reviews of: *Letters, 1961–1968* / Karl Barth; edited by Jürgen Fangmeier and Hinrich Stoevesandt; translated and edited by Geoffrey W. Bromiley.—Grand Rapids, Mich.: W. B. Eerdmans, 1981; and *Karl Barth–Rudolf Bultmann Letters, 1922–1966* / edited by Bernd Jaspert; translated and edited by Geoffrey W. Bromiley.—Grand Rapids, Mich.: W. B. Eerdmans, 1981.

230. "Pietism" in *Beacon Dictionary of Theology* / edited by Richard S. Taylor; associate editors, J. Kenneth Grider and Willard H. Taylor.—Kansas City, Mo.: Beacon Hill, 1983, pp. 400–02.

231. "The Primacy of Scripture" in *The Authoritative Word: Essays on the Nature of Scripture* / edited by Donald K. McKim.—Grand Rapids, Mich.: W. B. Eerdmans, 1983, pp. 117–53. **Notes**: Excerpted from vol. 1 of *Essentials of Evangelical Theology* (cf. item 162), pp. 51–87. Cf. item 176 for headings.

232. [Review] *The Christian Century*, vol. 100, no. 34 (November 16, 1983), pp. 1057–58. **Notes**: Review of: *Models of Revelation* / Avery Dulles.—1st ed.—Garden City, N.Y.: Doubleday, 1983.

233. [Review] *Christianity Today*, vol. 27, no. 19 (December 16, 1983), pp. 55–56. **Notes**: Review of: *After Fundamentalism: The Future of Evangelical Theology* /

Bernard Ramm.—1st ed.—San Francisco: Harper and Row, 1983. A review by Robert K. Johnston of the same book immediately precedes DGB's.

234. [Review] *Interpretation*, vol. 37, no. 1 (January 1983), pp. 106–7. **Notes**: Review of: *The Atoning Gospel* / James E. Tull.—Macon, Ga.: Mercer University Press, 1982. Also published: item 222.

235. [Review] *New Oxford Review*, vol. 50, no. 4 (May 1983), pp. 31–32. **Notes**: Review of: *By What Authority: The Rise of Personality Cults in American Christianity* / Richard Quebedeaux.—1st ed.—San Francisco: Harper and Row, 1982.

236. [Review] *The Presbyterian Outlook*, vol. 165, no. 7 (February 14, 1983), p. 14. **Notes**: Cf. item 239. Review of: *The Faith of the Church: A Reformed Perspective on Its Historical Development* / M. Eugene Osterhaven.—Grand Rapids, Mich.: W. B. Eerdmans, 1982.

237. [Review] *Spirituality Today*, vol. 35, no. 4 (Winter 1983), pp. 369–70. **Notes**: Review of: *Here Am I!: A Believer's Reflection* / Adrio König; translated from Afrikaans.—Pretoria: University of South Africa, 1978.

238. [Review] *TSF Bulletin*, vol. 6, no. 3 (January–February 1983), pp. 23–24. **Notes**: Review of: *The Analogical Imagination: Christian Theology and the Culture of Pluralism* / David Tracy.—New York: Crossroad, 1981.

239. [Review] *TSF Bulletin*, vol. 6, no. 5 (May–June 1983), p. 28. **Notes**: Cf. item 236. Review of: *The Faith of the Church: A Reformed Perspective on Its Historical Development* / M. Eugene Osterhaven.—Grand Rapids, Mich.: W. B. Eerdmans, 1982.

240. [Review] *Zygon*, vol. 18, no. 4 (December 1983), pp. 480–82. **Notes**: Review of: *Creation, Science, and Theology: Essays in Response to Karl Barth* / W. A. Whitehouse; edited by Ann Loades.—Grand Rapids, Mich.: W. B. Eerdmans, 1981.

1984

241. "Cause for Rejoicing." *Pastoral Renewal*, vol. 9, no. 5 (December 1984), pp. 79–80. **Notes**: The title refers to the Incarnation. **Heading**: The Gift of Illumination.

242. "Christ and Culture, Do They Connect? Some Theologians Stand against Our Culture, Others See It as a Stepping Stone to Christianity." *Christianity Today*, vol. 28, no. 10 (July 13, 1984), pp. 54–58. **Notes**: Reviews of: *Basic Questions in Theology: Collected Essays* / Wolfhart Pannenberg; translated by George H. Kehm.—Philadelphia: Westminster, 1983; and *In Search of Humanity: A Theological and Philosophical Approach* / John Macquarrie.—New York: Crossroad, c1983; and *Reality and Evangelical Theology* / T. F. Torrance.—1st ed.—Philadelphia: Westminster, c1982; and *Contours of a World View* / Arthur F. Holmes.—Grand Rapids, Mich.: W. B. Eerdmans, c1983; and *Living Faith: Belief and Doubt in a Perilous World* / Jacques Ellul; translated by Peter Heinegg.—1st ed.—San Francisco: Harper and Row, c1983.

243. "Concerns and Hopes for the United Church of Christ." *Living Faith*, vol. 5, nos. 1–2 (Spring–Summer 1984), pp. 41–45, 60. **Headings**: My Background—My Concerns—A Call for Renewal.

244. "Conversion" in *Evangelical Dictionary of Theology* / edited by Walter A. Elwell.—Grand Rapids, Mich.: Baker, 1984, pp. 272–73. **Notes**: Reprinted: item 265; abridged: item 317; 2nd edition: item 397.
245. *Crumbling Foundations: Death and Rebirth in an Age of Upheaval.*—Grand Rapids, Mich.: Academie, Zondervan, c1984. 168 pp.; 21 cm. **Contents**: DEATH AND RESURRECTION. The End of an Era. Radical Faith.—THE PHENOMENON OF SECULARISM. The Advance of Secularism. The German Christians and Current Parallels. A New Godlessness.—THE DARKENING HORIZON. The Church in Retreat. The Attack on Ethics. Christians under Persecution. The Subversion of Education.—THE MAIN THREATS TODAY. Technological Humanism. The Trend toward Collectivism. The Rise of Nihilism. Rebirth of the Gods.—THE CHURCH IN DISARRAY. Dissipation of Faith. A New Sacralism. Promise and Peril.—NEW MODELS FOR THE CHURCH. A New Kind of Saint. Twentieth-Century Saints.—THE CHALLENGE FACING CHURCHES AND SEMINARIES. An Emerging Confessional Situation. Recovery of Evangelical Faith. Diastasis or Correlation?—HUMAN FOLLY AND DIVINE GRACE. The Indefectibility of the Church. The Outpouring of the Holy Spirit. An Apocalyptic Age. Rediscovering the Spiritual Gifts. The Hope of the Church.—DISCIPLESHIP UNDER THE CROSS. The Call to Obedience. The Forms of Our Obedience. Discipleship as a Sign of Redemption.
246. "Descent into Hell (Hades)" in *Evangelical Dictionary of Theology* / edited by Walter A. Elwell.—Grand Rapids, Mich.: Baker, 1984, pp. 313–15. **Notes**: Reprinted: item 266; abridged: item 318; 2nd edition: item 398.
247. "The Dubuque Declaration." **Notes**: Although issued as a corporate statement of the Biblical Witness Fellowship, DGB was responsible for much of the text. The Declaration has been published in each issue of *The Witness* since 1984 and is also available as an electronic resource via: www.biblicalwitness.org/introduction.htm (accessed February 14, 2007).
248. "Fate, Fatalism" in *Evangelical Dictionary of Theology* / edited by Walter A. Elwell.—Grand Rapids, Mich.: Baker, 1984, pp. 407–8. **Notes**: Reprinted: item 268; abridged: item 320; 2nd edition: item 399.
249. "Forsyth, Peter Taylor, 1848–1921" in *Evangelical Dictionary of Theology* / edited by Walter A. Elwell.—Grand Rapids, Mich.: Baker, 1984, pp. 422–23. **Notes**: Reprinted: item 270; abridged: item 324; 2nd edition: item 400.
250. "In Defense of Biblical Authority." *The Reformed Journal*, vol. 34, no. 9 (September 1984), pp. 28–30. **Notes**: Review of: *Scripture and Truth* / edited by D. A. Carson and John D. Woodbridge.—Grand Rapids, Mich.: Zondervan, 1983.
251. "The Integrity of the Gospel." *Pastoral Renewal*, vol. 8, no. 7 (February 1984), pp. 94, 96. **Notes**: "Excerpted from *The Future of Evangelical Christianity*," item 228.
252. "Living God or Ideological Construct?" *The Reformed Journal*, vol. 34, no. 6 (June 1984), pp. 29–31. **Notes**: Reviews of: *Sexism and God-Talk: Toward a Feminist Theology* / Rosemary Radford Ruether.—Boston: Beacon, 1983; and *Metaphorical Theology: Models of God in Religious Language* / Sallie McFague.—Philadelphia: Fortress, 1982.
253. "Moral Rearmament [*sic*]" in *Evangelical Dictionary of Theology* / edited by Walter A. Elwell.—Grand Rapids, Mich.: Baker, 1984, pp. 733–34. **Notes**: Reprinted: item 271; abridged: item 328; 2nd edition: item 403.

254. "The Need for a Confessing Church Today." *The Reformed Journal*, vol. 34, no. 11 (November 1984), pp. 10–15. **Headings**: Meaning of a Confessing Church—Types of Confession—Hallmarks of a True Confession—A Confessing Church vs. a Cultural Church—The Work of a Confession.

255. "Prayer" in *Evangelical Dictionary of Theology* / edited by Walter A. Elwell.—Grand Rapids, Mich.: Baker, 1984, pp. 866–68. **Notes**: Reprinted: item 272; abridged: item 329; 2nd edition: item 405. **Headings**: Heiler's Typology—Hallmarks of Christian Prayer—The Paradox of Prayer.

256. "Sanctity." *Pastoral Renewal*, vol. 9, no. 1 (July–August 1984), pp. 15–16. **Notes**: Reprinted: item 273.

257. "Sin" in *Evangelical Dictionary of Theology* / edited by Walter A. Elwell.—Grand Rapids, Mich.: Baker, 1984, pp. 1012–16. **Notes**: Reprinted: item 274; abridged: item 330; 2nd edition: item 407. **Headings**: The Biblical Understanding of Sin—Sin and Hubris—Historical Controversy over Sin—Modern Reappraisals of Sin—In Twentieth Century America—Overcoming Sin—Sin in Evangelical and Legalistic Religion.

258. "Sin, Atonement, and Redemption" in *Evangelicals and Jews in an Age of Pluralism* / edited by Marc H. Tanenbaum, Marvin R. Wilson, A. James Rudin.—Grand Rapids, Mich.: Baker, 1984, pp. 163–82. **Notes**: Reprinted: item 315. **Headings**: Interreligious Dialogue—The Meaning of Sin—The Substitutionary Atonement—The Drama of Redemption—Salvation by Grace.

259. [Review] *Eternity*, vol. 35, no. 2 (February 1984), pp. 43–45. **Notes**: Review of: *The Divine Feminine: The Biblical Imagery of God as Female* / Virginia Ramey Mollenkott.—New York: Crossroad, 1983.

260. [Review] *Spirituality Today*, vol. 36, no. 4 (Winter 1984), pp. 366–68. **Notes**: Review of: *Christian Spirituality* / Wolfhart Pannenberg.—1st ed.—Philadelphia: Westminster, 1983.

261. [Review] *TSF Bulletin*, vol. 7, no. 3 (January–February 1984), pp. 32–33. **Notes**: Review of: *An Introduction to Protestant Theology* / Helmut Gollwitzer; translated by David Cairns.—Philadelphia: Westminster, 1982.

1985

262. *The Battle for the Trinity: The Debate over Inclusive God-Language.*—Ann Arbor, Mich.: Vine, Servant, c1985. xix, 143 pp.; 21 cm. **Notes**: Foreword by Elizabeth Achtemeier. Reprinted: item 396; selected adaptation: item 283; excerpted: item 333. **Contents**: THE CURRENT DEBATE. A Growing Controversy. Types of Feminism. Theologians and Philosophers behind Feminism. The Gnostic Connection. Where the Issue Lies.—THE ENIGMA OF GOD-LANGUAGE. Religious Language and the Knowledge of God. Symbols and Revelation.—GOD IN BIBLICAL PERSPECTIVE. God Transcendent and Immanent. Significance of the Biblical Symbols. Goddess Religion.—RESYMBOLIZING THE FAITH. The Grammar of Feminism. Gnostic Resymbolizing. The Problem of Inclusive Language.—THE PROBLEM OF AUTHORITY. Authority in Feminism. The Bible in Feminism. The Language of the Bible. The Return to Theonomy.—PARALLELS WITH THE GER-

MAN CHRISTIANS. Who Were the German Christians? Biblical–Cultural Synthesis in America. Ideology and Theology.—THE GROWING CHURCH CONFLICT. Doctrinal Erosion. Religious and Philosophical Language.

263. "A Christological Hermeneutic: Crisis and Conflict in Hermeneutics" in *The Use of the Bible in Theology: Evangelical Options* / edited by Robert K. Johnston.—Atlanta: John Knox, 1985, pp. 78–102. **Headings**: An Exposition of Some Key Texts—Word and Spirit.

264. "Concerns of the Biblical Witness Fellowship" in *Theological Ferment in the United Church of Christ: Six Essays* / edited by the Consultation on Theology of the Central Atlantic Conference.—[Baltimore, Maryland]: The Conference, 1985, pp. 7–10. **Notes**: Cf. item 311.

265. "Conversion" in *Evangelical Dictionary of Theology* / edited by Walter A. Elwell.—Basingstoke, England: Marshall Pickering, c1985, pp. 272–73. **Notes**: Reprint of item 244.

266. "Descent into Hell (Hades)" in *Evangelical Dictionary of Theology* / edited by Walter A. Elwell.—Basingstoke, England: Marshall Pickering, c1985, pp. 313–15. **Notes**: Reprint of item 246.

267. "Everybody's Favorite Symbol: Why Is Everyone from Falwell to Ortega Being Called a Nazi?" *Christianity Today*, vol. 29, no. 18 (December 13, 1985), pp. 29–32. **Headings**: Where the Parallels Fall Down—Where the Parallels Exist—Revival or Religiosity?

268. "Fate, Fatalism" in *Evangelical Dictionary of Theology* / edited by Walter A. Elwell.—Basingstoke, England: Marshall Pickering, c1985, p. 407. **Notes**: Reprint of item 248.

269. "Forecast '85. Theology." *Eternity*, vol. 36, no. 1 (January 1985), p. 32. **Headings**: Feminist Theology—Debate on Sacraments.

270. "Forsyth, Peter Taylor, 1848–1921" in *Evangelical Dictionary of Theology* / edited by Walter A. Elwell.—Basingstoke, England: Marshall Pickering, c1985, pp. 422–23. **Notes**: Reprint of item 249.

271. "Moral Rearmament" in *Evangelical Dictionary of Theology* / edited by Walter A. Elwell.—Basingstoke, England: Marshall Pickering, c1985, pp. 733–34. **Notes**: Reprint of item 253.

272. "Prayer" in *Evangelical Dictionary of Theology* / edited by Walter A. Elwell.—Basingstoke, England: Marshall Pickering, c1985, pp. 866–67. **Notes**: Reprint of item 255. **Headings**: Heiler's Typology—Hallmarks of Christian Prayer—The Paradox of Prayer.

273. "Sanctity." *Renewal News*, no. 91 (July–August 1985), p. 13. **Notes**: Reprint of item 256.

274. "Sin" in *Evangelical Dictionary of Theology* / edited by Walter A. Elwell.—Basingstoke, England: Marshall Pickering, c1985, pp. 1012–16. **Notes**: Reprint of item 257. **Headings**: The Biblical Understanding of Sin—Sin and Hubris—Historical Controversy over Sin—Modern Reappraisals of Sin—In Twentieth-Century America—Overcoming Sin—Sin in Evangelical and Legalistic Religion.

275. "A Typology of Marriage" in "Voices in the United Church of Christ: Theological Reflections on Family Life," *The Family Album: Resources for Family Life Ministries*.—St. Louis, Mo.: Church Leadership Resources, 1985, pp. 5–8.

1986

276. "America's Catholics: What They Believe." Interview with Avery Dulles. *Christianity Today*, vol. 30, no. 16 (November 7, 1986), pp. 23–27. **Headings**: Papal Infallibility—The Assumption of Mary—The Immaculate Conception—Purgatory—Scripture and Tradition—Justification by Faith.
277. "Be Wise as Serpents." *Eternity*, vol. 37, no. 11 (November 1986), "Doors '87: A Special Section for Graduate and Seminary Students," pp. D12–D15.
278. "Bloesch Replies to Finger." *TSF Bulletin*, vol. 10, no. 1 (September–October 1986), p. 43. **Notes**: A response to Thomas N. Finger's review of *The Battle for the Trinity*.
279. "Christian Faith and Twentieth-Century Ideologies" in *Christianity in Conflict: The Struggle for Christian Integrity and Freedom in Secular Culture* / edited by Peter Williamson and Kevin Perrotta.—Ann Arbor, Mich.: Servant, 1986, pp. 43–61. **Notes**: Reprinted as part of item 287. **Headings**: The Ideological Spell—Faith and Ideology—Types of Ideology—Ideology and Mythology.
280. "An Evangelical Perspective on Authority." *Prism*, vol. 1, no. 1 (Spring 1986), pp. 4–22. **Notes**: Regarding the Bible. **Headings**: The Problem of Authority— The Meaning of Revelation—Inspiration and Infallibility.
281. "Karl Barth: Appreciation and Reservations" in *How Karl Barth Changed My Mind* / edited by Donald K. McKim.—Grand Rapids, Mich.: W. B. Eerdmans, 1986, pp. 126–30.
282. "The Legacy of Karl Barth." *TSF Bulletin*, vol. 9, no. 5 (May–June 1986), pp. 6–9 **Headings**: An Evangelical Theologian—Particularism and Universalism—Christ and Culture—Reservations.
283. "Mere Symbols? The God-Language Debate." *Catalyst*, vol. 12, no. 4 (April 1986), pp. 1, 4. **Notes**: Adapted from *The Battle for the Trinity*, item 262.
284. "Toward the Recovery of Our Evangelical Heritage." *The Reformed Review*, vol. 39, no. 3 (Spring, 1986), pp. 192–98. **Headings**: The Meaning of "Evangelical"—The Battle for the Gospel in Historical Perspective—Distortions of the Gospel Today—Reclaiming the Gospel.
285. [Review] *TSF Bulletin*, vol. 10, no. 2 (November–December 1986), p. 34. **Notes**: A revision of this review forms part of chapter 10 of item 287. Review of: *Ethics from a Theocentric Perspective* / James M. Gustafson.—Chicago: University of Chicago Press, 1981–1984.

1987

286. "Foreword" in *A Hermeneutics of Ultimacy: Peril or Promise?* / James H. Olthuis with Donald G. Bloesch, Clark H. Pinnock, and Gerald T. Sheppard.—Lanham [MD]: University Press of America, c1987, pp. 7–10.
287. *Freedom for Obedience: Evangelical Ethics in Contemporary Times.*—1st ed.—San Francisco: Harper and Row, c1987. xviii, 342 pp.; 25 cm. **Notes**: Reprinted: item 415; selected abridgment: item 299. The chapter entitled "The Ideological Temptation" previously appeared as "Christian Faith and Twentieth-

Century Ideologies," item 279; part of chapter 10, "Alternatives in Ethics Today" is a revision of item 285. **Contents**: LAW AND GRACE IN ETHICS. Beyond Legalism and Relativism. Reinterpreting the Ethical Task. Theological Mentors. The Way of the Cross.—TWO TYPES OF ETHICS. The Radical Character of Christian Ethics. Theological and Philosophical Ethics. General Orientation in Ethics. Criteria in Ethics. Motivations in Ethics. The Tragic Flaw. Goals in Ethics. The Ground for Ethical Action.—PRINCIPLES IN ETHICS. The Contemporary Debate. Need for a Prophetic Casuistry. Toward an Ethics of the Law and Gospel. Principles versus Commandments.—TWO KINDS OF RIGHTEOUSNESS. Two Moralities. The Basis for Natural Goodness. Beyond the Prescriptions of the Law. Sin and Virtue. Social Justice and Kingdom Righteousness.—LOVE AND JUSTICE. The Current Discussion. Definitions. Ultimate and Penultimate Ideals. God's Love and Holiness. The Christian Hope. Appendix on Reinhold Niebuhr.—LAW AND GOSPEL IN HISTORICAL PERSPECTIVE. Roman Catholicism. Luther. Calvin. Anabaptists and Pietists. John Wesley. Niebuhr and Bonhoeffer. Karl Barth. Dispensationalism.—AN ETHICS OF THE LAW AND GOSPEL. A Biblical Alternative. Unity of the Law and Gospel. Lutheran Ethics. The Holiness Corrective. Barth's Contribution. Two Governments. The Whole Counsel of God. Appendix on the Order of Law and Gospel.—CHRISTIAN CARING. Its Christological Basis. The Church's Twofold Mission. Misunderstandings of the Christian Mission. Changing Emphases. Present-Day Temptations.—ALTERNATIVES IN ETHICS TODAY. Situationalism. Historical-Relational Ethics. Natural Law Ethics. Eudaemonism. Enlightened Egoism. Liberationism. Graded Absolutism. Christian Realism. Theocentric Naturalism. Evangelical Contextualism.—DISCERNING THE WILL OF GOD. The Agony of Ethical Decision. Borderline Situations. The Risks of Holiness. The Ideal versus the Actual. Presumption and Humility in Ethical Decision.—GOD THE CIVILIZER. Definitions, Christ and Culture. Patterns of Interaction. Religion and Culture. Conflicting Views on History. Creation and Redemption. Human Culture and the Kingdom of God. The Two Kingdoms. God as Civilizer and Reconciler.—THE IDEOLOGICAL TEMPTATION. The Ideological Spell. Faith and Ideology. Types of Ideology. Ideology and Mythology. Ideology and Heresy. Toward the Recovery of a Prophetic Church. Democracy at the Crossroads.—THE FOLLY OF WAR. Philosophical Perspectives on War. War in the Bible. The Early Church Period. Christian Approaches to War. The Problem of Total War. The Church under the Cross. Appendix on the Warrior God and the God of Peace.

288. "Process Theology and Reformed Theology" in *Process Theology* / edited by Ronald Nash.—Grand Rapids, Mich.: Baker, 1987, pp. 31–56. **Notes**: Reprinted: item 337 and item 381. **Headings**: Two Types of Theology—Authority— Doctrine of God—Christ and Salvation—Ethics and Spirituality—A Biblical— Modern Synthesis.

289. "Promise with Peril: A Response to James Olthuis" in *A Hermeneutics of Ultimacy: Peril or Promise?* / James H. Olthuis with Donald G. Bloesch, Clark H. Pinnock, and Gerald T. Sheppard.—Lanham [MD]: University Press of America, c1987, pp. 61–69. **Notes**: "Papers originally presented in June 1981, at a conference in Toronto called, 'Interpreting an Authoritative Scripture'

cosponsored by the Institute for Christian Studies and Fuller Theological Seminary"–p. 7. Includes a response by Olthuis, pp. 76–90. **Headings**: Points of Convergence and Divergence—The Role of Hermeneutics—Evangelical or Existential Hermeneutics.

290. [Review] *Interpretation*, vol. 41, no. 3 (June–July 1987), pp. 328–29. **Notes**: Review of: *Created in God's Image* / Anthony Hoekema.—Grand Rapids, Mich.: W. B. Eerdmans; Exeter, UK: Paternoster, 1986.

291. [Review] *Theological Education*, vol. 24, no. 1 (Autumn 1987), pp. 140–43. **Notes**: Review of: *The Humiliation of the Word* / Jacques Ellul; translated by Joyce Main Hanks.—Grand Rapids, Mich.: W. B. Eerdmans, 1985.

292. [Review] *TSF Bulletin*, vol. 10, no. 5 (May–June 1987), pp. 36–37. **Notes**: Review of: *Christian Theology: An Eschatological Approach. Vol. 1* / Thomas Finger.—Nashville: Nelson, 1985.

1988

293. *The Crisis of Piety: Essays towards a Theology of the Christian Life.*—2nd ed.—Colorado Springs: Helmers and Howard, c1988. xvii, 159 pp.; 22 cm. **Notes**: This edition contains "Author's Note" (pp. ix–xiii) not present in the previous edition. Cf. item 66 for 1st edition and remainder of contents.

294. *The Future of Evangelical Christianity: A Call for Unity amid Diversity* / [foreword by Mark A. Noll].—1st pbk. ed.—Colorado Springs: Helmers and Howard, c1988. xxii, 202 pp.; 21 cm. **Notes**: Dr. Mark Noll's foreword, "The Surprising Optimism of Donald Bloesch" originally appeared as an article under the same title in *Center Journal* (Summer, 1984)—T.p. verso. Cf. item 228 for remainder of contents and previous edition.

295. "God the Civilizer" in *Christian Faith and Practice in the Modern World: Theology from an Evangelical Point of View* / edited by Mark A. Noll and David F. Wells.—Grand Rapids, Mich.: W. B. Eerdmans, 1988, pp. 176–98. **Notes**: Reprinted: item 350. **Headings**: Definitions—Christ and Culture—Patterns of Interaction—Religion and Culture—Conflicting Views on History—Creation and Redemption—Human Culture and the Kingdom of God—The Two Kingdoms—God as Civilizer and Reconciler—The Church and Society.

296. "No Other Gospel." *Presbyterian Communiqué*, vol. 11, no. 1 (January–February 1988), pp. 8–9. Reprinted in part: item 303, with permission, Servant Publications, cf. item 297. **Headings**: No Other Lord—The Pseudo-Religion, Militarism—No Other Gospel—Process Theology—From Trinitarianism to Unitarianism.

297. "No Other Gospel: 'One Lord, One Faith, One Baptism'" in *Courage in Leadership: A Call to Boldness in Preaching, Teaching, and Pastoral Care* / edited by Kevin Perrotta and John C. Blattner.—Ann Arbor, Mich.: Servant, 1988, pp. 83–94. **Notes**: Cf. item 296 and item 303. **Headings**: No Other Lord—No Other Gospel—Resymbolization—Christian Faith versus Idolatry.

298. *The Struggle of Prayer.*—1st pbk. ed.—Colorado Springs: Helmers and Howard, c1988. ix, 180 pp.; 22 cm. **Notes**: Cf. item 185 for contents, of which this is a reprint.

299. "Two Types of Ethics." *International Christian Digest*, vol. 2, no. 10 (December–January 1988/1989), pp. 1–4. **Notes**: Abridged from *Freedom for Obedience*, item 287. **Headings**: General Orientation in Ethics—Criteria in Ethics—Motivations in Ethics—The Two Understandings of Love—The Tragic Flaw—The Ground for Ethical Action.
300. "What's to Come." *Eternity*, vol. 39, no. 12 (December 1988), pp. 41–42. **Notes**: Review of: *Knowing the Truth about Heaven and Hell: Our Choices and Where They Lead Us* / Harry Blamires.—Ann Arbor, Mich.: Servant, 1988.

1989

301. "All Israel Will Be Saved: Supersessionism and the Biblical Witness." *Interpretation*, vol. 43, no. 2 (April 1989), pp. 130–42. **Headings**: The Supersessionist Controversy—The Mystery of Israel's Election and Rejection—Judaism and Christianity—Missions to Jews.
302. "Changing People, Changing Nations." *Christianity Today*, vol. 33, no. 4 (March 3, 1989), pp. 60–61. **Notes**: Review of: *On the Tail of a Comet: The Life of Frank Buchman* / Garth Lean.—Colorado Springs: Helmers and Howard, 1988. **Headings**: Reaching the Nazi Elite—No Substitute for God.
303. "No Other Gospel." *Channels*, vol. 6, no. 2 (Spring 1989), pp. 6–8. **Notes**: Reprinted from item 296. **Headings**: No Other Lord—The Pseudo-Religion, Militarism.
304. "A Reply to Paul Quackenbush." *On the Way*, vol. 6, no. 2 (Autumn 1989), pp. 41–45. **Notes**: Regarding Quackenbush's article, "Homosexuality and the Church," which appeared in the same issue.
305. "Reply to Randy Maddox." *Christian Scholar's Review*, vol. 18, no. 3 (March 1989), pp. 281–84. **Notes**: Cf. Maddox's article, item 454. "The Necessity of Recognizing Distinctions: Lessons from Evangelical Critiques of Christian Feminist Theology."
306. *Theological Notebook. Vol. 1, 1960–1964.*—Colorado Springs: Helmers and Howard, c1989. xii, 244 pp.; 22 cm.—(The Spiritual Journals of Donald G. Bloesch) **Notes**: Vol. 2 published: item 331; vol. 3 published: item 433.

1990

307. "Beyond Patriarchalism & Feminism." *Touchstone* (Chicago, Ill.), vol. 4, no. 1 (Summer 1990), pp. 9–11.
308. "The DuPage Declaration: A Call to Biblical Fidelity." **Notes**: Signed in 1990. Although issued as a joint statement of "evangelical renewal leaders" as stated in the preamble of the declaration, DGB was responsible for much of the text. The Declaration has been published by The National Association of Evangelicals, as well as many other organizations, and is also available as an electronic resource: www.brfwitness.org/Articles/dupagedec.htm (accessed February 14, 2007).

309. "Ethics/Spiritual Life" in *The Best in Theology, IV* / General editor, J. I. Packer.—Carol Stream, Ill.: *Christianity Today,* 1990. **Notes**: DGB wrote the introduction (pp. 177–80) and edited a section (pp. 181–221).
310. "Evangelicalism" in *Harper's Encyclopedia of Religious Education* / General editors, Iris V. Cully and Kendig Brubaker Cully.—1st ed.—San Francisco: Harper and Row, c1990, pp. 234–36. **Headings**: History—Theology—Strengths and Weaknesses—Education.
311. "A Faithful Church: Concerns of the Biblical Witness Fellowship" in *Theology and Identity: Traditions, Movements, and Polity in the United Church of Christ* / edited by Daniel L. Johnson and Charles Hambrick-Stowe.—New York: Pilgrim, c1990, pp. 132–38. **Notes**: Cf. item 264.
312. "The Father and the Goddess." *Christianity Today,* vol. 34, no. 14 (October 8, 1990), pp. 74–76. **Notes**: Reprinted: item 321. Reviews of: *Women and Early Christianity: A Reappraisal* / Susanne Heine; translated by John Bowden.—1st American ed.—Minneapolis: Augsburg, 1988; and *Matriarchs, Goddesses, and Images of God: A Critique of a Feminist Theology* / Susanne Heine; translated by John Bowden.—1st American ed.—Minneapolis: Augsburg, 1989.
313. "Niebuhr, Karl Paul Reinhold (1892–1971)" in *Dictionary of Christianity in America* / coordinating editor, Daniel G. Reid; consulting editors, Robert D. Linder, Bruce L. Shelley, and Harry S. Stout.—Downers Grove, Ill.: InterVarsity, c1990, pp. 825–26. **Notes**: Abridged: item 362.
314. "A Plan for Unity." *Christianity Today,* vol. 34, no. 3 (February 19, 1990), p. 17 (Evangelical Megashift).
315. "Sin, Atonement, Redemption" in *Evangelicals and Jews in an Age of Pluralism* / edited by Marc H. Tanenbaum, Marvin R. Wilson, and A. James Rudin.—Lanham, MD: University Press of America, 1990, pp. 163–82. **Notes**: Reprint of item 258, q.v. for headings.

1991

316. *The Christian Life and Salvation.*—Colorado Springs: Helmers and Howard, c1991. 164 pp.; 22 cm. **Notes**: Cf. item 57 for contents, of which this is a reprint.
317. "Conversion" in *The Concise Evangelical Dictionary of Theology* / edited by Walter A. Elwell; abridged by Peter Toon.—Grand Rapids, Mich.: Baker, c1991, pp. 117–18. **Notes**: Abridgement of item 244.
318. "Descent into Hell (Hades)" in *The Concise Evangelical Dictionary of Theology* / edited by Walter A. Elwell; abridged by Peter Toon.—Grand Rapids, Mich.: Baker, c1991, pp. 136–37. **Notes**: Abridgement of item 246.
319. "Expiation, Propitiation" in *Holman Bible Dictionary: With Summary Definitions and Explanatory Articles on Every Bible Subject, Introductions and Teaching Outlines for Each Bible Book, In-Depth Theological Articles, Plus Internal Maps, Charts, Illustrations, Scale Reconstruction Drawings, Archaeological Photos, and Atlas* / General editor, Trent C. Butler; Contributing editors, Marsha A. Ellis Smith, Forrest W. Jackson, Phil Logan, and Chris Church.—Nashville: Holman Bible, c1991, pp. 458–60.

320. "Fate, Fatalism" in *The Concise Evangelical Dictionary of Theology* / edited by Walter A. Elwell; abridged by Peter Toon.—Grand Rapids, Mich.: Baker, c1991, p. 178. **Notes**: Abridgement of item 248.

321. "The Father and the Goddess." *Partnership* (Winter 1991), pp. 18–19. **Notes**: The issue of the periodical carries no volume designation. Reprint of item 312, q.v. for additional notes.

322. "The Finality of Christ & Religious Pluralism." *Cross Point*, vol. 4, no. 4 (Winter 1991), pp. 22–28. **Notes**: Reprint of item 323.

323. "The Finality of Christ & Religious Pluralism." *Touchstone (Chicago, Ill.)*, vol. 4, no. 3 (Summer 1991), pp. 5–9. **Notes**: Reprinted: item 322; abridged and revised: item 335 and item 372; expanded as part of item 373.

324. "Forsyth, Peter Taylor" in *The Concise Evangelical Dictionary of Theology* / edited by Walter A. Elwell; abridged by Peter Toon.—Grand Rapids, Mich.: Baker, c1991, p. 184. **Notes**: Abridgement of item 249.

325. "Law and Gospel in Reformed Perspective." *Grace Theological Journal*, vol. 12, no. 2 (Fall 1991), pp. 179–87. **Headings**: Meaning of Reformed—Contrasting Positions—Distinctive Reformed Emphases—Love and Law—Call to Discipleship—The Ultimate Criterion.

326. "The Lordship of Christ in Theological History." *Southwestern Journal of Theology*, vol. 33, no. 2 (Spring 1991), pp. 26–34. **Notes**: Incorporated into item 373. **Headings**: Theological Issues—New Testament Views—Augustine and Aquinas—Luther and Calvin—Liberal Theology—The Contemporary Scene—Jesus as Lord and Victor—Conclusion.

327. "Lost in the Mystical Myths." *Christianity Today*, vol. 35, no. 9 (August 19, 1991), pp. 22–24. **Headings**: When Seminaries Go Spiritual—Earth Mother Mysticism—Grounded in the Promises of God—What Mysticism Can Teach Us.

328. "Moral Re-Armament" in *The Concise Evangelical Dictionary of Theology* / edited by Walter A. Elwell; abridged by Peter Toon.—Grand Rapids, Mich.: Baker, c1991, pp. 322–23. **Notes**: Abridgement of item 253.

329. "Prayer" in *The Concise Evangelical Dictionary of Theology* / edited by Walter A. Elwell; abridged by Peter Toon.—Grand Rapids, Mich.: Baker, c1991, pp. 393–94. **Notes**: Abridgement of item 255. **Headings**: Heiler's Typology—Hallmarks of Christian Prayer—The Paradox of Prayer.

330. "Sin" in *The Concise Evangelical Dictionary of Theology* / edited by Walter A. Elwell; abridged by Peter Toon.—Grand Rapids, Mich.: Baker, c1991, pp. 466–68. **Notes**: Abridgement of item 257. **Headings**: The Biblical Understanding of Sin—Historical Controversy over Sin—Modern Reappraisals of Sin—In 20th-Century America—Overcoming Sin—Sin in Evangelical and Legalistic Religion.

331. *Theological Notebook. Volume 2, 1964–1968.*—Colorado Springs: Helmers and Howard, c1991. x, 214 pp.; 22 cm.—(The Spiritual Journals of Donald G. Bloesch) **Notes**: Vol. 1 published: item 306; vol. 3 published: item 433.

332. "Twenty-five Years Later." *Perspectives*, vol. 6, no. 2 (February 1991), p. 24. **Notes**: Review of: *Vatican II and Its Documents: An American Reappraisal* / edited by Timothy E. O'Connell.—Wilmington, Del.: M. Glazier, 1986. [*also*: Collegeville, Minn.: Liturgical, 1991].

1992

333. "Authority and the Language of the Bible" in *The Politics of Prayer: Feminist Language and the Worship of God* / edited by Helen Hull Hitchcock.—San Francisco: Ignatius, 1992, pp. 195–206. **Notes**: A chapter from *The Battle for the Trinity*, item 262. **Headings**: Authority in Feminism—The Bible in Feminism—The Language of the Bible—The Return to Theonomy.

334. "Evangelicalism" in *A New Handbook of Christian Theology* / edited by Donald W. Musser and Joseph L. Price.—Nashville: Abingdon, c1992, pp. 168–73. Another edition: item 422.

335. "The Finality of Christ and Religious Pluralism." *Mission and Ministry*, vol. 9, no. 2 (Summer 1992), pp. 4–9. **Notes**: Abridgment and revision of item 323. **Headings**: The New Paradigm—Relativism in the Churches—Countering the New Theologies—Biblical and General Revelation—Christianity and World Religions—The Mission of the Church—The Confessional Crisis—The Battle Today.

336. "Our Vocation to Holiness: Our Task Is to Make Visible, Not Ourselves, but the Living God in Christ." *Faith & Renewal*, vol. 17, no. 2 (September–October 1992), pp. 20–25. **Notes**: Revised and enlarged: item 338. **Headings**: The Meaning of Holiness—Separated unto God—True Spirituality—Faith in Action—Works of Piety—Works of Evangelism—Intercession and Instruction—Works of Mercy—Works of Justice—Modern Parables—The Fruit of Faith—Spent for Christ.

337. "Process Theology and Reformed Theology" in *Major Themes in the Reformed Tradition* / edited by Donald K. McKim.—Grand Rapids, Mich.: W. B. Eerdmans, c1992, pp. 386–99. **Notes**: Reprint of item 288, q.v. for headings.

338. "Salt & Light: Our Vocation to Holiness." *Touchstone (Chicago, Ill.)*, vol. 5, no. 4 (Fall 1992), pp. 25–28, 48. **Notes**: Revised and enlarged edition of item 336; incorporated into item 359. **Headings**: The Meaning of Holiness—True Spirituality—Faith in Action—Works of Piety—Works of Evangelism—Works of Mercy—Works of Justice—The Fruit of Faith.

339. "Sanctification" in *Encyclopedia of the Reformed Faith* / edited by Donald K. McKim; David F. Wright, consulting editor.—1st ed.—Louisville, Ky.: Westminster/John Knox; Edinburgh, Scotland: Saint Andrew, 1992, pp. 336–38. **Notes**: Reprinted: item 406. **Headings**: Different Understandings—The Paradox of Sanctification—Errors to Be Avoided.

340. *A Theology of Word & Spirit: Authority & Method in Theology.*—Downers Grove, Ill.: InterVarsity, c1992. 336 pp.; 24 cm.—(Christian Foundations; [1]) **Notes**: Reprinted: item 341 and item 434; extracted: item 387. **Contents**: INTRODUCTION. Reclaiming Dogma. Toward the Recovery of Biblical, Evangelical Theology.—THE THEOLOGICAL MALAISE. The Slide into Relativism. A New Church Conflict?—FAITH AND PHILOSOPHY. Faith and Reason. Theology and Philosophy. Faith and Metaphysics. Faith and Religion. Faith and Ethics. Beyond Fideism and Rationalism. Appendix A, Kierkegaard.—THEOLOGICAL LANGUAGE. The Enigma of Faith-Language. Dialectic and Paradox. The Divine Names. Resymbolizing God. Words and Images. Appendix B, On Meaning.—TOWARD THE RENEWAL OF THEOLOGY. Theology Defined. Dogma and Doctrine. Dimensions of a Renewed Theology. The Two Sides of Theology. The Challenge Today. A Venture in Obedience. Appendix C, Gospel and

Kerygma. Appendix D, Orthodoxy.—NATURAL THEOLOGY. Karl Barth and His Adversaries. The New Catholicism. General Revelation. Natural Morality. A Theology of Creation. Natural Theology Today. Appendix E, Thomas F. Torrance.—RETHINKING THEOLOGICAL AUTHORITY. Loci of Authority. Absolute and Relative Norms. The Paradoxical Nature of Theological Authority. The Ground of Certainty. Mystery and Meaning. Appendix F, The Wesleyan Quadrilateral.—THE COMMUNICATION OF THE GOSPEL. Revelation and Communication. Questionable Methods. A Biblical Alternative. A Reappraisal of Apologetics. Religious Imperialism versus Evangelism.—THEOLOGY AT THE CROSSROADS. Four Options. Theology of Restoration. Theology of Accommodation. Theology of Correlation. Theology of Confrontation. Points of Conflict. Toward a New Kind of Confessional Theology. Discordant Voices.

341. *A Theology of Word & Spirit: Authority & Method in Theology.*—Carlisle, Cumbria, UK: Paternoster, c1992. 336 pp.; 24 cm.—(Christian Foundations; [1]) **Notes**: For contents cf. item 340, of which this is a reprint.

342. [Review] *Interpretation*, vol. 46, no. 1 (January 1992), pp. 106. **Notes**: Review of: *Tracking the Maze: Finding Our Way through Modern Theology from an Evangelical Perspective* / Clark H. Pinnock.—1st ed.—San Francisco: Harper and Row, 1990.

1993

343. *The Ground of Certainty: Toward an Evangelical Theology of Revelation.*—Vancouver, B.C.: Regent College Bookstore, 1993. 212 pp.; 21 cm. **Notes**: Cf. item 100 for contents, of which this is a reprint.

344. "Liberation and Confession." *The Christian Century*, vol. 110, no. 8 (March 10, 1993), pp. 275–76. **Notes**: Review of: *Loyalty to God: The Apostles' Creed in Life and Liturgy* / Theodore W. Jennings Jr.—Nashville: Abingdon, 1992.

345. [Review] *The Christian Century*, vol. 110, no. 27 (October 6, 1993), pp. 950–51. **Notes**: Review of: *No Other Gospel!: Christianity among the World's Religions* / Carl E. Braaten.—Minneapolis: Fortress, 1992.

346. [Review] *Interpretation*, vol. 47, no. 1 (January 1993), pp. 105–6. **Notes**: Review of: *The Variety of American Evangelicalism* / edited by Donald W. Dayton and Robert K. Johnston.—1st ed.—Knoxville: University of Tennessee Press, 1991. [*also*: Downers Grove, Ill.: InterVarsity, 1991].

347. [Review] *Theology Today*, vol. 49, no. 4 (January 1993), pp. 579, 582. **Notes**: Review of: *Doing Theology in Today's World: Essays in Honor of Kenneth S. Kantzer* / edited by John D. Woodbridge and Tom Edward McComisky.—Grand Rapids, Mich.: Zondervan, 1991. Also available as an electronic resource via: theologytoday.ptsem.edu (accessed February 14, 2007)

1994

348. "Counterfeit Spirituality" by Timothy R. Phillips and Donald G. Bloesch in *The Christian Educator's Handbook on Spiritual Formation* / edited by Kenneth

O. Gangel and James C. Wilhoit.—Wheaton, Ill.: Victor, c1994, pp. 60–73.
Notes: Reprinted: item 349 and item 371. **Headings**: Spirituality Is Established by God in Jesus Christ. *The Spiritual Counterfeits of Subjectivism and
Mysticism*—Spirituality Is Dependent upon God's Supernatural Act of Regeneration. *The Spiritual Counterfeit of Pelagianism*—Spirituality Is Based
upon Justification. *The Spiritual Counterfeit of Legalism*—Spirituality Lives
through Faith in Jesus Christ. *The Spiritual Counterfeit of Formalism*—Spirituality Is a Process of Being Sanctified. *The Spiritual Counterfeit of Gnosticism*—
Conclusion.

349. "Counterfeit Spirituality" by Timothy R. Phillips and Donald G. Bloesch in
The Christian Educator's Handbook on Spiritual Formation / edited by Kenneth
O. Gangel and James C. Wilhoit.—Colorado Springs: Cook Communications
Ministries, 1994, pp. 60–73. **Notes**: Reprint of item 348, q.v. for headings.**

350. "God the Civilizer" in *Christian Faith and Practice in the Modern World: Theol-
ogy from an Evangelical Point of View* / edited by Mark A. Noll and David F.
Wells.—Ann Arbor, Mich.: UMI Books on Demand, 1994, pp. 176–98.**
Notes: On-demand reprint of item 295, q.v. for headings.

351. *Holy Scripture: Revelation, Inspiration & Interpretation.*—Downers Grove, Ill.:
InterVarsity, c1994. 384 pp.; 24 cm.—(Christian Foundations; [2]) **Notes**:
Reprinted: item 352 and item 428. **Contents**: INTRODUCTION. The Witness of
Sacred Tradition. Modern Errors. Toward a Theology of Word and Spirit.—
THE CRISIS IN BIBLICAL AUTHORITY. Inerrancy and Infallibility in Historical Per-
spective. Need for Reinterpretation. Models of Scriptural Authority.—THE
MEANING OF REVELATION. Revelation as Truth and Event. Revelation and the
Bible. Truth and Error in Protestant Orthodoxy. Revelation in Nature and
History. Revelation and Reason. Appendix A, Conflict in Theological
Method.—THE INSPIRATION OF SCRIPTURE. The Reformation. Orthodoxy and
Pietism. Fundamentalism. Neo-Orthodoxy. Liberalism. The Question of In-
errancy. The Nature of Inspiration. Inspiration and Revelation. Appendix B,
The Rogers–McKim Proposal.—SCRIPTURE & THE CHURCH. The Problem of the
Canon. The Bible over the Church. The Bible within the Church. The
Supreme Authority for Faith. Appendix C, The Apocrypha.—THE HERMENEU-
TICAL PROBLEM. The Dynamics of Interpretation. Breakthrough into Under-
standing. The Natural and the Spiritual Sense. Guidelines of the Reformers.
Hermeneutical Options Today. Faith and Criticism. Appendix D, Narrative
Theology. Appendix E, Hermeneutical Pluralism and Transcendence.—
RUDOLF BULTMANN, AN ENDURING PRESENCE. Cultural and Theological Back-
ground. Distinctive Emphases. Demythologizing. A New Venture in
Hermeneutics. God Hidden and Revealed. Freedom for Obedience. A Ne-
oliberal Theology—THE BIBLE & MYTH. The Conversion of Myth. Narrative
Forms in the Bible. The Bible as Myth and History—TRUTH IN BIBLICAL &
PHILOSOPHICAL PERSPECTIVE. Biblical Understandings. Faith's Encounter with
Philosophy. Truth in the Technological Society. Models of Truth. The Current
Controversy.

352. *Holy Scripture: Revelation, Inspiration & Interpretation.*—Carlisle, Cumbria,
UK: Paternoster, c1994. 384 pp.; 24 cm.—(Christian Foundations; [2])**
Notes: For contents, cf. item 351, of which this is a reprint.

353. "Is Spirituality Enough?: Differing Models for Living" In *Roman Catholicism: Evangelical Protestants Analyze What Divides and Unites Us* / Alister McGrath, Harold O. J. Brown, Donald Bloesch, Michael Horton, and others; General editor, John Armstrong.—Chicago: Moody, 1994, pp. 142–60. **Headings**: Types of Spirituality—Catholicism and Hellenism—Gains and Losses in the Reformation—Enduring Issues.
354. "An Open Orthodoxy." *Touchstone (Chicago, Ill.)*, vol. 7, no. 1 (Winter 1994), p. 10. **Notes**: At head of title: A Touchstone Symposium. Part of the larger article: "Ecumenical Orthodoxy: What Is It?" Other participants in the symposium (pp. 7–13): S. M. Hutchens, Patrick Henry Reardon, George Austin, Carl E. Braaten, Thomas Howard, Richard John Neuhaus, Andrew Walker, and Jack White.
355. "Theologian Donald Bloesch Speaks on Justice, Morality." *The Presbyterian Layman*, vol. 27, no. 6 (November–December 1994), p. 15. **Notes**: An interview conducted by Kevin McDonald. **Headings**: Human Development, Justice—Homosexuality—Theological View—Most Pressing Moral Issue—"Creeping Moral Anarchy."

1995

356. "Barth, Karl" in *New Dictionary of Christian Ethics & Pastoral Theology* / edited by David J. Atkinson and David H. Field; consulting editors, Arthur F. Holmes and Oliver O'Donovan.—Downers Grove, Ill.; Leicester, England: InterVarsity, c1995, pp. 184–85.
357. "The Demise of Biblical Preaching: Distortions of the Gospel and Its Recovery." *Touchstone (Chicago, Ill.)*, vol. 8, no. 4 (Fall 1995), pp. 13–16. **Headings**: Aberrations after the Reformation—Toward the Recovery of Biblical Preaching.
358. "A Fellowship of Love." *Christianity Today*, vol. 39, no. 2 (February 6, 1995), pp. 64–66. **Notes**: Review of: *Theology for the Community of God* / Stanley J. Grenz.—Nashville: Broadman and Holman, 1994.
359. *God, the Almighty: Power, Wisdom, Holiness, Love.*—Downers Grove, Ill.: InterVarsity, c1995. 329 pp.: ill.; 24 cm.—(Christian Foundations; [3]) **Notes**: Reprinted: item 360 and item 427. The section "Call to Holiness," which forms part of the chapter "Holiness & Love," previously appeared in part as item 338, "Salt & Light." **Contents**: INTRODUCTION. Questionable Alternatives. The Gender Issue. The Theological Task.—THEOLOGY'S ATTEMPT TO DEFINE GOD. Act and Being. Essence and Existence. Essence and Attributes. God and Necessity. Rationalism and Mysticism. Supernaturalism and Naturalism. God's Almightiness in Question.—THE SELF-REVEALING GOD. Natural Knowledge of God. God as Elector and Persuader. The Authority of Holy Scripture.—TRANSCENDENCE & IMMANENCE. Infinity and Spirituality. Immutability and Impassibility. Reinterpretations of Transcendence. Dynamic Transcendence.—POWER & WISDOM. Creator and Redeemer. Lord and Ruler. Wisdom. Glory. The Problem of Evil.—HOLINESS & LOVE. Two Sides of God. Divine and Human Love. Holiness and Justice. The Call to Holiness.—THE MYSTERY OF

THE TRINITY. The Biblical Basis. Historical Development. Contemporary Re-
assessments. Restating the Trinity. Trinitarian Spirituality. Appendix A, Mod-
ern Forms of Unitarianism. Appendix B, Subordination and Equality.—THE
BIBLICAL–CLASSICAL SYNTHESIS. The Living God and the Eternal Now. Provi-
dence and Fate. Truth as Event and Idea. Revelation and Reason. Agape and
Eros. Blessedness and Happiness. Grace and Merit. Sin and Ignorance.
Prayer and Contemplation. Justification and Deification. Reconciliation and
Reunion. Resurrection and Immortality.—THE BIBLICAL–MODERN SYNTHESIS.
Authority and Truth. God, Humanity, and the World. The New Spirituality.
Worldviews in Conflict. God and Futurity. Appendix C, Open-View Theism.

360. *God, the Almighty: Power, Wisdom, Holiness, Love.*—Carlisle, Cumbria, UK: Paternoster, c1995. 329 pp.: ill.; 24 cm.—(Christian Foundations; [3]) **Notes**: For
contents cf. item 359, of which this is a reprint.

361. "A Jesus for Everyone, A Christ for None: Küng's One, True (but Less Than
Christian) Religion." *Christianity Today*, vol. 39, no. 11 (October 2, 1995), pp.
40, 42. **Notes**: Review of: *Christianity: Essence, History, and Future* / Hans
Küng.—New York: Continuum, 1995.

362. "Niebuhr, (Karl Paul) Reinhold (1892–1971)" in *Concise Dictionary of Christianity in America* / coordinating editor, Daniel G. Reid; consulting editors,
Robert D. Linder, Bruce L. Shelley, and Harry S. Stout; abridging editor, Craig
A. Noll.—Downers Grove, Ill.: InterVarsity, c1995, p. 243. **Notes**: Abridged,
unsigned version of item 313.

363. "On Natural Law: Carl F. Henry & Critics." *First Things*, no. 52 (April 1995), pp.
3–4. **Notes**: Letter to the editor. Also available as an electronic resource via:
www.firstthings.com/article.php3?id_article'4026 (accessed February 14, 2007).

364. "A Theology for the Twenty-First Century: Pannenberg Attempts to Reaffirm
Historical Christian Faith." *Christianity Today*, vol. 39, no. 4 (April 3, 1995), p.
106. **Notes**: Review of: *Systematic Theology. Vol. 2* / Wolfhart Pannenberg; translated by Geoffrey W. Bromiley.—Grand Rapids, Mich.: W. B. Eerdmans, 1994.

365. [Review] *Interpretation*, vol. 49, no. 2 (April 1995), pp. 218, 220. **Notes**: Review
of: *Ecumenical Faith in Evangelical Perspective* / Gabriel Fackre.—Grand
Rapids, Mich.: W. B. Eerdmans, 1993.

366. [Review] *The Princeton Seminary Bulletin*, vol. 16, no. 3 (1995), pp. 375–77.
Notes: Review of: *The Scandal of the Evangelical Mind* / Mark A. Noll.—Grand
Rapids, Mich.: W. B. Eerdmans, 1993.

1996

367. "Betraying the Reformation?: An Evangelical Response" [to] *Faith Alone.
Christianity Today*, vol. 40, no. 11 (October 7, 1996), pp. 54–55. **Notes**: Regarding: *Faith Alone: The Evangelical Doctrine of Justification* / R. C. Sproul; foreword by Michael Horton.—Grand Rapids, Mich.: Baker, 1995.

368. "Hymns for the Politically Correct: Hallelujah to the All-Inclusive One."
Christianity Today, vol. 40, no. 8 (July 15, 1996), pp. 49–50. **Notes**: Review of:
The New Century Hymnal.—Cleveland, Ohio: Pilgrim Press, 1995.

369. "A Response to Elmer Colyer." *Journal for Christian Theological Research*, vol. 1, no. 2 (1996). Available as an electronic resource via: www.luthersem.edu/ ctrf/JCTR/Vol01/Bloesch.htm (accessed February 14, 2007).
370. [Review] *The Ellul Forum for the Critique of Technological Civilization*, no. 17 (July 1996), p. 14. **Notes**: Review of: *Resist the Powers with Jacques Ellul* / Charles Ringma.—1st ed.—Sutherland, NSW, Australia; Claremont, Calif.: Albatross, 1995.

1997

371. "Counterfeit Spirituality" by Timothy R. Phillips and Donald G. Bloesch in *The Christian Educator's Handbook on Spiritual Formation* / edited by Kenneth O. Gangel and James C. Wilhoit.—Grand Rapids, Mich.: Baker, 1997, pp. 60–73. **Notes**: Reprint of item 348, q.v. for headings.
372. "The Finality of Christ and Religious Pluralism." *InCourage* [*sic*], vol. 10, no. 2 (Summer 1997), pp. 3–5. Cf. item 335 for headings.
373. *Jesus Christ: Savior & Lord.*– Downers Grove, Ill.: InterVarsity, c1997. 304 pp.: ill.; 24 cm.—(Christian Foundations; [4]) **Notes**: Reprinted: item 374 and item 430. The chapter, "The Lordship of Christ in Theological History" originally appeared as item 326. The chapter, "The Finality of Christ" is an expansion of item 323. **Contents**: CHRIST IN DISPUTE. The Pivotal Issues. Christologies in Conflict. The Road Ahead.—THE PLIGHT OF HUMANITY. Classical and Modern Views. Sin in the Non-Christian Religions. Sin in the History of Theology. A Biblical Perspective. Pitfalls to Avoid.—THE MYSTERY OF THE INCARNATION. True Humanity and True Divinity. Christological Heresies. Tensions between the Churches. Modern Restatements of Christology. A Reaffirmation of Orthodox Christology. Appendix A, Implications of Gender-Inclusive Language for Christology.—THE VIRGIN BIRTH. The Current Controversy. The Traditional Understanding. Valid and Compelling Reasons for Believing. Valid Reasons for Emphasizing. Invalid Reasons for Believing. Invalid Reasons for Not Believing. Epilogue. Appendix B, The Role of Mary. Appendix C, Myth and Reality in the Bible.—THE PREEXISTENCE OF JESUS CHRIST. A Historical Overview. Karl Barth's Position. Epilogue—CHRIST'S ATONING SACRIFICE. The Purpose of the Incarnation. Theories of the Atonement. Christ as Our Substitute. The Two Poles of the Atonement. Limited or Universal Atonement. Appendix D, The Death of God.—SALVATION IN EVANGELICAL PROTESTANTISM. Justification. Sanctification. Continuing Issues. Models of Salvation. Ecumenical Implications.— LAW AND GOSPEL, A REFORMED PERSPECTIVE. Contrasting Positions. Distinctive Reformed Emphases. Love and Law. Call to Discipleship. The Ultimate Criterion—THE LORDSHIP OF CHRIST IN THEOLOGICAL HISTORY. New Testament Views. Augustine and Aquinas. Luther and Calvin. Liberal Theology. The Contemporary Scene. Jesus as Lord and Victor—THE FINALITY OF CHRIST. Christ in the New Theologies. A Reaffirmation of Biblical Christianity. An Emerging Confessional Situation.

374. *Jesus Christ: Savior and Lord.*—Carlisle, Cumbria, UK: Paternoster, 1997. 304 pp.: ill.; 24 cm.—(Christian Foundations; [4]) **Notes**: For contents cf. item 373, of which this is a reprint.
375. "The Paradoxical Love of the Cross." *Reformation & Revival*, vol. 6, no. 4 (Fall 1997), pp. 133–47. **Headings**: The Mystery of Agape—Metaphors for Love—Movements in Love—The Problem of Self-Love—Love and Faith—Love and Hope—Paradoxical Aspects of Love.
376. "Two Patterns of Discipleship." *Cross Point*, vol. 10, no. 4 (Winter 1997), pp. 6–7, 10–11. **Heading**: Life of Faith in the World and the Religious Life in Community.
377. [Review] *The Christian Century*, vol. 114, no. 29 (October 22, 1997), pp. 952–54. **Notes**: Review of: *In the Face of God* / Michael Horton.—Dallas, Tex.: Word, 1996.

1998

378. *Essentials of Evangelical Theology.*—Peabody, Mass.: Prince, 1998. 2 v.; 24 cm. **Notes**: Prince Press is an imprint of Hendrickson Publishers. For contents, cf. item 162 and item 172, of which this is a reprint.
379. "Evangelical Rationalism and Propositional Revelation." *The Reformed Review*, vol. 51, no. 3 (Spring 1998), pp. 169–81. **Headings**: A Legacy Reexamined—Propositional vs. Narrational Theology—Toward a Theology of Word and Spirit—Endnotes.
380. "Knowing Jehovah: What the Old Testament Teaches Us about Spirituality." *Christianity Today*, vol. 42, no. 2 (February 9, 1998), pp. 72–74. **Notes**: Review of: *The Friendship of the Lord* / Deryck Sheriffs.—Carlisle, Cumbria, UK: Paternoster, 1996.
381. "Process Theology and Reformed Theology" in *Major Themes in the Reformed Tradition*, edited by Donald K. McKim.—Eugene, Ore.: Wipf and Stock, 1998, pp. 386–99. **Notes**: Reprint of item 288, q.v. for headings.
382. *The Reform of the Church.*—Eugene, Ore.: Wipf and Stock, 1998. 199 pp.; 21 cm. **Notes**: For contents, cf. item 92, of which this is a reprint.
383. "There's More to Church Than Proclamation: Wolfhart Pannenberg's Sacramental Theology." *Christianity Today*, vol. 42, no. 9 (August 10, 1998), pp. 69–70. **Notes**: Review of: *Systematic Theology. Vol. 3* / Wolfhart Pannenberg; translated by Geoffrey W. Bromiley.—Grand Rapids, Mich.: W. B. Eerdmans, 1998.

1999

384. "Accepting the Cross: A Lenten Meditation." *Cross Point*, vol. 12, no. 1 (Spring 1999), pp. 29–33. **Headings**: The Call to Discipleship—Various Responses—The Call to Decision.
385. "Donald Bloesch Responds" in *Evangelical Theology in Transition: Theologians in Dialogue with Donald Bloesch* / edited by Elmer M. Colyer.—Downers Grove, Ill.: InterVarsity, 1999, pp. 183–208.

386. "Orthodoxy with an Attitude." *Christianity Today*, vol. 43, no. 7 (June 14, 1999), p. 88. **Notes**: Review of: *We Believe: Recovering the Essentials of the Apostles' Creed* / Michael Horton.—Nashville: Word, 1998.
387. "The Renewal of Theology." *Evangelical Review of Theology*, vol. 23, no. 2 (April 1999), pp. 101–19. **Notes**: Extracted from *A Theology of Word and Spirit*, item 340.
388. [Review] *International Bulletin of Missionary Research*, vol. 23, no. 2 (April 1999), pp. 80–81. **Notes**: Review of: *God-Mystery-Diversity: Christian Theology in a Pluralistic World* / Gordon D. Kaufman.—Minneapolis: Fortress, 1996.
389. [Letter to the Editor] *International Bulletin of Missionary Research*, vol. 23, no 4 (October 1999), p. 176. **Notes**: Rejoinder to a response to DGB's review, cf. item 388.
390. [Review] *Interpretation*, vol. 53, no. 3 (July 1999), pp. 323–24. **Notes**: Review of: *Restoring the Center: Essays Evangelical & Ecumenical* / Gabriel Fackre.—Downers Grove, Ill.: InterVarsity, 1998.
391. [Review] *The Princeton Theological Review*, vol. 6, no. 4 (issue 19: Autumn 1999), pp. 30–31. **Notes**: Review of: *Encyclical Letter, Fides et Ratio, of the Supreme Pontiff John Paul II: To the Bishops of the Catholic Church on the Relationship between Faith and Reason.*—Washington, D.C.: U.S. Catholic Conference, 1998.
392. [Review] *Scottish Journal of Theology*, vol. 52, no. 2 (1999), pp. 238–40. **Notes**: Review of: *Justice the True and Only Mercy: Essays on the Life and Theology of Peter Taylor Forsyth* / edited by Trevor Hart.—Edinburgh, Scotland: T and T Clark, 1995.

2000

393. *The Holy Spirit: Works & Gifts.*—Downers Grove, Ill.: InterVarsity, c2000. 415 pp.; 23 cm.—(Christian Foundations; [5]) **Notes**: Reprinted: item 394 and item 429. **Contents**: INTRODUCTION. The Collapse of Modernity. A Theology of the Christian Life. Appendix A, Evangelical Rationalism & Propositional Revelation.—THE CONTEMPORARY DEBATE. The Person of the Spirit. Baptism and Conversion. Baptism and Confirmation. Assurance and Evidence. Aspects of Salvation. Word and Spirit. Spiritual Gifts. Gender of the Spirit. Outreach of the Spirit.—THE DESCENT OF THE SPIRIT IN BIBLICAL UNDERSTANDING. Divergent Views. Transmission of the Spirit. Dimensions of the Spirit's Activity. Eschatological Significance. Complementary Emphases.—FATHERS, ENTHUSIASTS & MYSTICS. The Church Fathers. Later Development in Catholicism. Religious Enthusiasm. Christian Mysticism.—REFORMATION PERSPECTIVES. The Twofold Baptism. A New Kind of Confirmation. The Gifts of the Spirit. Call to Holiness. The Decisive Role of Experience.—POST-REFORMATION RENEWAL MOVEMENTS. Puritanism. Pietism. Evangelicalism. The Holiness Movement.—NEW CHALLENGES TO TRADITIONAL FAITH. Definitions. Quakerism and Kindred Movements. Swedenborgianism. New Light from Russia. The Inspirationists. Mormonism. Restorationist Sects. Seventh-Day

Adventism. Jehovah's Witnesses. The Unification Church. The New Age Movement. Dispensationalism. Postscript.—PENTECOSTALISM. Theological Background. Historical Development. Pentecostal Distinctives. The Phenomenon of Glossolalia. Dangers in Pentecostalism. Enduring Contributions. The Spirit of Self-Criticism. Appendix B, Battling the Demons.—RECENT DEVELOPMENTS IN THEOLOGICAL THOUGHT. H. Wheeler Robinson. Karl Barth. Paul Tillich. Rudolf Bultmann. Jürgen Moltmann. Yves Congar. Regin Prenter. Clark Pinnock. Paul Evdokimov. Other Voices. Postscript.—THE HOLY SPIRIT, PERSON & MISSION. The Spirit in the Trinity. Spirit and Word. Water and Spirit. Works of the Spirit. Charisms and Ministries. Rethinking Pentecost. Appendix C, Some Difficult Texts.—THE HIGHWAY OF HOLINESS. A Life of Battle. Holiness and Justification. Stages on Life's Pilgrimage. The Paradox of Sanctity. Appendix D, A Theology of the Cross.

394. *The Holy Spirit: Works & Gifts.*—Leicester, UK: InterVarsity, 2000. 415 pp.; 23 cm.—(Christian Foundations; [5]) **Notes**: For contents, cf. item 393, of which this is a reprint.**

395. "Toward a Consistent Pro-Life Ethic." *The Princeton Theological Review*, vol. 7, nos. 2 and 3 (issues 21 and 22: Spring/Summer 2000), pp. 40–41.

2001

396. *The Battle for the Trinity: The Debate over Inclusive God-Language.*—Eugene, Ore.: Wipf and Stock, 2001. 143 p.; 22 cm. **Notes**: Reprint of item 262, q.v. for contents.

397. "Conversion" in *Evangelical Dictionary of Theology* / edited by Walter A. Elwell.—2nd ed.—Grand Rapids, Mich.: Baker Academic; Carlisle, Cumbria, UK: Paternoster, c2001, pp. 296–97. **Notes**: 1st edition: item 244.

398. "Descent into Hell (Hades)" in *Evangelical Dictionary of Theology* / edited by Walter A. Elwell.—2nd ed.—Grand Rapids, Mich.: Baker Academic; Carlisle, Cumbria, UK: Paternoster, c2001, pp. 338–40. **Notes**: 1st edition: item 246.

399. "Fate, Fatalism" in *Evangelical Dictionary of Theology* / edited by Walter A. Elwell.—2nd ed.—Grand Rapids, Mich.: Baker Academic; Carlisle, Cumbria, UK: Paternoster, c2001, p. 439. **Notes**: 1st edition: item 248.

400. "Forsyth, Peter Taylor" in *Evangelical Dictionary of Theology* / edited by Walter A. Elwell.—2nd ed.—Grand Rapids, Mich.: Baker Academic; Carlisle, Cumbria, UK: Paternoster, c2001, pp. 462–63. **Notes**: 1st edition: item 249.

401. *Is the Bible Sexist?*—Eugene, Ore.: Wipf and Stock, 2001. 139 pp.; 22 cm. **Notes**: Previously published: Westchester, Ill.: Crossway. For contents, cf. item 217, of which is this a reprint.

402. *Jesus Is Victor!: Karl Barth's Doctrine of Salvation.*—Eugene, Ore.: Wipf and Stock, 2001. 176 pp.; 20 cm. **Notes**: For contents, cf. item 140, of which this is a reprint.

403. "Moral Re-Armament" in *Evangelical Dictionary of Theology* / edited by Walter A. Elwell.—2nd ed.—Grand Rapids, Mich.: Baker Academic; Carlisle, Cumbria, UK: Paternoster, c2001, pp. 790–91. **Notes**: 1st edition: item 253.

404. "Most Gracious Heavenly Father, We Thank Thee" in *In Essentials Unity: Reflections on the Nature and Purpose of the Church: In Honor of Frederick R. Trost* / edited by M. Douglas Meeks and Robert D. Mutton.—Minneapolis: Kirk, c2001, p. 100. **Notes**: Prayer.

405. "Prayer" in *Evangelical Dictionary of Theology* / edited by Walter A. Elwell.—2nd ed.—Grand Rapids, Mich.: Baker Academic; Carlisle, Cumbria, UK: Paternoster, c2001, pp. 946–47. **Notes**: 1st edition: item 255. **Headings**: Heiler's Typology—Hallmarks of Christian Prayer—The Paradox of Prayer.

406. "Sanctification" in *The Westminster Handbook to Reformed Theology* / edited by Donald K. McKim.—1st ed.—Louisville, Ky.: Westminster, John Knox, c2001, pp. 202–4. **Notes**: Reprint of item 339.

407. "Sin" in *Evangelical Dictionary of Theology* / edited by Walter A. Elwell.—2nd ed.—Grand Rapids, Mich.: Baker Academic; Carlisle, Cumbria, UK: Paternoster, c2001, pp. 1103–7. **Notes**: 1st edition: item 257, q.v. for headings.

408. "Spirit and Word" in *The Nature and Use of Scripture.*—Louisville, Ky.: Presbyterians for Renewal, 2001, pp. 23–27. **Notes**: At head of title: PFR Reform. **Headings**: The Early Church on Spirit and Word—The Sixteenth Century Reformers on Spirit and Word—Some Conclusions about the Relationship between Spirit and Word—Does One Take Precedence over the Other?—Why This Topic Is So Important for Today's Church—Some Theological Pitfalls to Avoid.

409. "Taking the Bible Seriously." *The Witness*, vol. 22, no. 1 (Summer 2001), pp. 6–7.

410. "Whatever Happened to God?" *Christianity Today*, vol. 45, no. 2 (February 5, 2001), pp. 54–55. **Notes**: Also available as an electronic resource via: www.christianitytoday.com/ct/2001/002/9.54.html (accessed February 14, 2007). **Headings**: Sentimental Appeal—Sad State of the Sermon—Whatever Happened to Social Holiness?—Need for Discernment.

411. [Review] *Interpretation*, vol. 55, no. 2 (April 2001), p. 220. **Notes**: Review of: *Retrieving the Tradition and Renewing Evangelicalism: A Primer for Suspicious Protestants* / D. H. Williams.—Grand Rapids, Mich.: W. B. Eerdmans, 1999.

2002

412. *The Christian Witness in a Secular Age: An Evaluation of Nine Contemporary Theologians.*—Eugene, Ore.: Wipf and Stock, 2002. 160 pp.; 22 cm. **Notes**: For contents, cf. item 64, of which this is a reprint.

413. *The Church: Sacraments, Worship, Ministry, Mission.*—Downers Grove, Ill.: InterVarsity, c2002. 351 pp.; 24 cm.—(Christian Foundations; [6]) **Notes**: Reprinted: item 414 and item 426. **Contents**: INTRODUCTION. Differing Theological Perspectives. Need for a Theological Balance.—CONTINUING ISSUES IN ECCLESIOLOGY. Authority and Infallibility. Reinterpreting the Church's Mission. Quandary over Worship. Marks and Signs. Christian Unity.—THE CHURCH IN THE PLAN OF SALVATION. Roman Catholic Theology. Martin Luther. John Calvin. Emil Brunner. Karl Barth. Thomas F. Torrance. The Redemptive Community. The Church's Mandate. Mary, A Type of the Church.—THE CHURCH AND THE

KINGDOM. Two Sides of the Church. The Kingdom in the Making. The Kingdom and World History.—AUTHORITY IN THE CHURCH. Papalism versus Conciliarism. Biblicism versus Ecclesiasticism. Experientialism versus Rationalism. The Church Militant and Triumphant.—MARKS OF THE CHURCH. The Catholic Consensus. Practical Marks. Marks of the False Church. Word and Spirit.—WORSHIP IN SPIRIT AND TRUTH. Worship in Biblical Perspective. God Transcendent. Word and Image. The Crisis in Spirituality. True Spirituality. Appendix A, Contemporary Worship. Appendix B, An Evangelical Order of Worship. Appendix C, A Reformed Worship Center.—RETHINKING SACRAMENTS. Sacramental Understanding in Christian History. Holy Baptism. Holy Communion. Confession. Word and Sacrament. Appendix D, An Ecumenical Consensus?—THE DEMISE OF BIBLICAL PREACHING. A Legacy in Peril. Aberrations after the Reformation. Toward the Recovery of Biblical Preaching. Postscript.—A SOCIO-THEOLOGICAL TYPOLOGY. A Typology of Religious Association. A Theological Interpretation. Learning from the Sects. Epilogue. Appendix E, Further Thoughts on Sects and Cults.—THE DIVERSITY OF MINISTRIES. Protestant Religious Orders. Women in Ministry. Marriage and Celibacy—THE GOSPEL IN A SYNCRETISTIC AGE. Troeltsch's Theology of Religious History. Moltmann's Global Theology. The Church's Apostolic Mission—TOWARD THE REUNION OF THE CHURCHES. The Trauma of the Reformation. The Retreat from Ecumenicity. Evangelical–Catholic Unity. The Ecumenical Imperative—A CONFESSING CHURCH. The Meaning of a Confessing Church. Types of Confession. Hallmarks of a True Confession. A Confessing Church versus a Cultural Church. The Work of a Confession. Appendix F, The Voice of Orthodoxy. Appendix G, The Meaning of the Gospel.—APPENDIX 1, THE CAMBRIDGE DECLARATION.—APPENDIX 2, THE GOSPEL OF JESUS CHRIST, AN EVANGELICAL CELEBRATION.

414. *The Church: Sacraments, Worship, Ministry, Mission.*—Nottingham, UK: InterVarsity, 2002. 351 pp.; 24 cm.—(Christian Foundations; [6]) For contents cf. item 413, of which this is a reprint.**

415. *Freedom for Obedience: Evangelical Ethics in Contemporary Times.*—Eugene, Ore.: Wipf and Stock, 2002. xviii, 342 pp.; 25 cm. **Notes**: For contents cf. item 287, of which this is a reprint.

416. *The Ground of Certainty: Toward an Evangelical Theology of Revelation.*—Eugene, Ore.: Wipf and Stock, 2002. 212 pp.; 22 cm. **Notes**: For contents cf. item 100, of which this is a reprint.

417. "Penetrating the World with the Gospel: Three Approaches" in *The Conviction of Things Not Seen: Worship and Ministry in the 21st Century* / [edited by] Todd E. Johnson.—Grand Rapids, Mich.: Brazos, c2002, pp. 183–97. **Headings**: Apologetic Theology—Kerygmatic Theology—Charismatic Theology—The Road Ahead.

418. "Reclaiming the Gospel" in *Story Lines: Chapters on Thought, Word, and Deed: For Gabriel Fackre* / edited by Skye Gibson.—Grand Rapids, Mich.; Cambridge, UK: W. B. Eerdmans, c2002, pp. 12–15.

419. *Reinhold Niebuhr's Apologetics.*—Eugene, Ore.: Wipf and Stock, 2002. vii, 147 pp.; 23 cm. **Notes**: Doctoral dissertation, 1956, University of Chicago, revised version, 2002. Cf. item 11. **Contents**: INTRODUCTION. Two Types of Theology. Statement of Thesis.—NIEBUHR'S BREAK WITH TRADITIONAL APOLOGETICS. Back-

ground of Niebuhr's Polemic. Analysis of Syncretic Theology. Attitude towards Other Kinds of Apologetics.—NIEBUHR'S VINDICATION OF THE APOLOGETIC PRINCIPLE. General Revelation. Dialectical Theology. Existential Disruption.—APOLOGETICS AS A MEANS OF VALIDATING THE FAITH. Negative Validation. Positive Validation. Relation of Apologetics to Commitment.—A CRITIQUE OF NIEBUHR'S METHODOLOGY. The Authority of the Bible. Methodological Principles. Niebuhr's Anthropology. Niebuhr on the Means of Grace. The Apologetic Principle.—A NEW ROLE FOR APOLOGETICS. The Mission of the Church. Faith Seeking Understanding. Apologetics as a Subsidiary of Kerygmatic Theology. Apologetics as an Aid in Witnessing.—EPILOGUE.

420. "A Response to Frank Macchia." *Journal of Pentecostal Theology*, vol. 10, no. 2 (2002), pp. 18–24. **Notes**: Regarding Macchia's review article of *The Holy Spirit*, which appeared in the same issue.

2003

421. "Clark Pinnock's Apologetic Theology" in *Semper Reformandum: Studies in Honour of Clark H. Pinnock* / edited by Stanley E. Porter and Anthony R. Cross.—Carlisle, Cumbria, UK: Paternoster, 2003, pp. 247–60. **Headings**: A New Venture in Apologetics—The Fissure in Theology—The Scripture Principle—Creative Reinterpretation.

422. "Evangelicalism" in *New and Enlarged Handbook of Christian Theology* / edited by Donald W. Musser and Joseph L. Price.—Nashville: Abingdon, c2003, pp. 181–86. **Notes**: Previous edition: item 334.

423. "Prayer, Mysticism, Faith, and Reason" in *Indelible Ink: 22 Prominent Christian Leaders Discuss the Books That Shape Their Faith* / General editor, Scott Larsen.—1st ed.—Colorado Springs: Waterbrook, 2003, pp. 99–109. **Headings**: Søren Kierkegaard on Faith and Reason—Anders Nygren on Love—Friedrich Heiler on Prayer—Epilogue.

2004

424. *The Last Things: Resurrection, Judgment, Glory.*—Downers Grove, Ill.: InterVarsity, 2004. 336 pp.; 24 cm.—(Christian Foundations; [7]) **Notes**: Reprinted: item 431. **Contents**: INTRODUCTION. Troeltsch's Typology. Alternate Pathways. Toward a Renewed Church.—CONTROVERSIAL THEMES IN ESCHATOLOGY. The Coming of the Kingdom. The Return of Jesus Christ. The Life Hereafter. The Invisible Communion. Humanity's Final Destiny. The Mission to Israel.—LIGHT AGAINST DARKNESS. The Angelic Rebellion. The Victory of Jesus Christ. The Banishment of the Evil Powers. An Excursus on Angelology.—THE DAY OF THE LORD. Christ's Visitation to His Church. The Encounter with Christ at Death. The Last Judgment. The Advance of the Kingdom. Signs of His Coming. The Blessed Hope. Appendix A, The Olivet Discourse.—THE MILLENNIAL HOPE. Renewed Interest in the Millennium. Premillennialism. Dispensationalism. Amil-

lennialism. Postmillennialism. Idealist-Symbolic Views. Moltmann's Millennial Explorations. Toward a New Understanding of the Millennium.—THE RESURRECTION OF THE DEAD. The Resurrection of Jesus. Resurrection as Event and Process. The Crisis of Death. The Final Resurrection.—THE INTERIM STATE. The Worlds Beyond. Paradise. The Nether World of Spirits. Purgatory.—THE COMMUNION OF SAINTS. Witness of Sacred Tradition. Testimony of Hymns. Mystic Communion between Earth and Heaven. What This Communion Involves. The Saints in the Work of Redemption.—PREDESTINED TO GLORY. The Unfolding of Predestination. Universalism and Particularism. A Theology of Paradox. Openness and Mystery. Appendix B, Theology's Emancipation from Rationalism.—ISRAEL'S SALVATION—THE SUPERSESSIONIST CONTROVERSY. The Mystery of Israel's Election and Rejection. Judaism and Christianity. Missions to the Jews?—THE TRIUMPH OF GRACE. The Last Judgment. The Meaning of Hell. The Glory of Heaven. Grace Invincible. Epilogue.—THE DAWNING OF HOPE. The Ground and Goal of Hope. Self-Transcending Hope. The Certainty of Hope. Relative and Ultimate Hopes. Providence versus Fate. Faith versus Cynicism. Beyond Optimism and Pessimism. Faith, Hope, and Love.

425. [Review] *The Bulletin of the Institute for Reformed Theology*, vol. 4, no. 2 (Fall 2004), pp. 9–10. **Notes**: Also available as an electronic resource via: www.reformedtheology.org/SiteFiles/Fall2004/Review_Horton.html (accessed February 14, 2007). Review of: *Covenant and Eschatology: The Divine Drama* / Michael S. Horton.—Louisville, Ky.: Westminster, John Knox, c2002.

2005

426. *The Church: Sacraments, Worship, Ministry, Mission.*—Downers Grove, Ill.: InterVarsity, 2005, c2002. 351 pp.; 24 cm.—(Christian Foundations; [6]) **Notes**: Paperback reprint of item 413, q.v. for contents.

427. *God, the Almighty: Power, Wisdom, Holiness, Love.*—Downers Grove, Ill.: InterVarsity Academic, 2005, c1995. 329 pp.: ill.; 24 cm.—(Christian Foundations; [3]) **Notes**: Paperback reprint of item 359, q.v. for contents.

428. *Holy Scripture: Revelation, Inspiration & Interpretation.*—Downers Grove, Ill.: InterVarsity Academic, 2005, c1994. 384 pp.; 24 cm.—(Christian Foundations; [2]) **Notes**: Paperback reprint of item 351, q.v. for contents.

429. *The Holy Spirit: Works & Gifts.*—Downers Grove, Ill.: InterVarsity Academic, 2005, c2000. 415 pp.; 23 cm.—(Christian Foundations; [5]) **Notes**: Paperback reprint of item 393, q.v. for contents.

430. *Jesus Christ: Savior & Lord.*– Downers Grove, Ill.: InterVarsity, 2005, c1997. 304 pp.: ill.; 24 cm.—(Christian Foundations; [4]) **Notes**: Paperback reprint of item 373, q.v. for contents.

431. *The Last Things: Resurrection, Judgment, Glory.*—Downers Grove, Ill.: InterVarsity, 2005, c2004. 336 pp.; 24 cm.—(Christian Foundations; [7]) **Notes**: Paperback reprint of item 424, q.v. for contents.

432. "Scriptural Primacy" in *The Living Theological Heritage of the United Church of Christ* / Series editor, Barbara Brown Zikmund. Vol. 7, *United and Uniting* /

edited by Frederick R. Trost—Berea, Ohio: Pilgrim, 2005, pp. 344–45. **Notes**: Excerpted from vol. 1 of *Essentials of Evangelical Theology* (cf. item 162), pp. 51–87.**

433. *Theological Notebook. Volume 3, 1969–1983.*—Eugene, Ore.: Wipf and Stock, 2005. 348 pp.; 22 cm.—(The Spiritual Journals of Donald G. Bloesch) **Notes**: Vol. 1 published: item 306; vol. 2 published: item 331.

434. *A Theology of Word & Spirit: Authority & Method in Theology.*—Downers Grove, Ill.: InterVarsity, 2005, c1992. 336 pp.; 24 cm.—(Christian Foundations; [1]). **Notes**: Paperback reprint of item 340, q.v. for contents.

435. [Review] *The Christian Century*, vol. 122, no. 11 (May 31, 2005), pp. 39–40. **Notes**: Review of: *Deconstructing Evangelicalism: Conservative Protestantism in the Age of Billy Graham* / D. G. Hart.—Grand Rapids, Mich.: Baker Academic, c2004.

436. [Review] *Journal of the Evangelical Theological Society*, vol. 48, no. 4 (December 2005), pp. 858–59. **Notes**: Review of: *Karl Barth's Theological Exegesis: The Hermeneutical Principles of the Römerbrief Period* / Richard E. Burnett.—Grand Rapids, Mich.: W. B. Eerdmans, 2004.

Chapter 2

Works about
Donald G. Bloesch

BOOK REVIEWS OF WORKS BY BLOESCH
AND TO WHICH BLOESCH HAS CONTRIBUTED

The Battle for the Trinity (1985)

437. Alexander, Julian, Jr. *The Presbyterian Outlook*, vol. 168, no. 6 (February 17, 1986), p. 12.

438. Barber, Cyril J. *Journal of Psychology and Theology*, vol. 15, no. 3 (Fall 1987), p. 258.

439. Belonick, Deborah Malacky. "Is God Bisexual?" *Pastoral Renewal*, vol. 10, no. 6 (January 1986), pp. 95–96.

440. Carse, Mary. "'Battle for the Trinity' Places Feminism within Theology." *Vermont Catholic Tribune*, vol. 30, no. 15 (Tuesday, July 22, 1986), p. 20.

441. Cochrane, Charles C. *Presbyterian Record*, vol. 110, no. 6 (June 1986), p. 33.

442. Colyer, Elmer M. "God-Language: More at Stake Than Women's Rights?" *Good News*, vol. 19, no. 5 (March–April 1986), p. 53.

443. Colyer, Elmer M., Jr. "Joining Battle." *The Reformed Journal*, vol. 36, no. 7 (July 1986), pp. 26–27.

444. Farrell, John J. *Fellowship of Catholic Scholars Newsletter*, vol. 12, no. 1 (December 1988), pp. 22–23. **Notes**: Also available as an electronic resource via: www.catholicscholars.org/resources/quarterly/index.htm (accessed February 14, 2007). The name of the periodical was changed from "Newsletter" to "Quarterly" in 1996.

445. Finger, Reta. *Daughters of Sarah*, vol. 14, no. 1 (January–February 1988), pp. 8–9.

446. Finger, Thomas N. "Donald Bloesch on the Trinity: Right Battle, Wrong Battle Lines." *TSF Bulletin*, vol. 9, no. 3 (January–February 1986), pp. 18–21. **Headings**: Linguistic Imprecision—The Trinitarian Foundation—Conclusions.

447. Foh, Susan. *The Westminster Theological Journal*, vol. 48, no. 2 (Fall 1986), pp. 407–9.

448. Hartgerink, Peter. *Touchstone (Winnipeg, Man.)*, vol. 6, no. 2 (May 1988), p. 56.
449. Heiser, W. Charles. *Theology Digest*, vol. 33, no. 2 (Summer 1986), p. 263. **Notes**: One paragraph.
450. Koedyker, John C. *The Reformed Review*, vol. 40, no. 1 (Autumn 1986), pp. 65–66.
451. Kratz, Paul L. *The Sword and Trumpet*, vol. 54, no.1 (January 1986), pp. 12, 27.
452. Kraus, George. *Concordia Theological Quarterly*, vol. 51, no. 1 (January 1987), p. 65. **Notes**: One paragraph.
453. Loesch, Juli. *New Oxford Review*, vol. 53, no. 6 (July–August 1986), pp. 28–30.
454. Maddox, Randy L. "The Necessity of Recognizing Distinctions: Lessons from Evangelical Critiques of Christian Feminist Theology." *Christian Scholar's Review*, vol. 17, no. 3 (1988), pp. 307–23.
455. McGinn, Sheila E. *Booklist*, vol. 81, no. 21 (July 1985), p. 1478.
456. Meilaender, Gilbert. *Religious Studies Review*, vol. 12, nos. 3/4 (July/October 1986), p. 268.
457. Miller, Glenn T. *Faith and Mission*, vol. 4, no. 2 (Spring 1987), pp. 100–101.
458. Palmer, Gordon R. *Themelios*, vol. 14, no. 1 (October–November 1988), pp. 32–33.
459. Payne, Leanne. *Pastoral Care Ministries Newsletter* (December 4, 1985), pp. 5–6. **Notes**: Newsletter has no volume/number designation. Also reviews Bloesch's *Is the Bible Sexist?*
460. Ruehl, Daniel P. *Christian Bookseller*, vol. 32, no. 1 (January 1986), p. 51. **Notes**: One paragraph.
461. Sauer, James L. *The Christian Librarian*, vol. 29, no. 4 (August 1986), p. 83.
462. Scholer, David M. *Update (Evangelical Women's Caucus)*, vol. 10, no. 2 (Summer 1986), pp. 14–15. **Notes**: Also reviews Bloesch's *Is the Bible Sexist?*
463. Spencer, Aída Besançon. *The Bible Newsletter*, vol. 5, no. 10 (October 1985), p. 4.
464. Van Leeuwen, Mary Stewart. *Christianity Today*, vol. 30, no. 14 (October 3, 1986), p. 16-I. (Women in Leadership) **Notes**: One paragraph.
465. Van Leeuwen, Mary Stewart. *Eternity*, vol. 37, no. 4 (April 1986), pp. 40–41.
466. Witmer, John A. *Bibliotheca Sacra*, vol. 144, no. 573 (January–March 1987), pp. 109–10.
467. Wonders, Lance A. *Living Faith*, vol. 6, no. 1 (Spring 1986), p. 24.
468. Wonders, Lance A. *Presbyterian Communiqué*, [n.s.] vol. 9, no. 1 (Spring 1986), p. 14. **Notes**: Volume, issue number inferred.
469. Zook, Jerry, and Zook, Elizabeth. *Channels*, vol. 2, no. 2 (Spring 1985), pp. 17–18.
470. *Celebration*, vol. 15, no. 5 (May 1986), pp. 179–80.
471. *Epiphany*, vol. 6, no. 3 (Spring 1986), pp. 95–96.

Centers of Christian Renewal (1964)

472. Bechtel, Paul, and Bechtel, Mary. *Christian Life*, vol. 26, no. 5 (September 1964), pp. 59–60, 63.
473. Edge, Findley B. *Review and Expositor*, vol. 62, no. 2 (Spring 1965), pp. 244–45.
474. Gable, Lee J. *International Journal of Religious Education*, vol. 41, no. 5 (January 1965), p. 34.
475. Head, David. *Christian Advocate*, vol. 9, no. 3 (February 11, 1965), pp. 18–19.

476. Koops, Hugh A. "Like a Motherless Child." *Christianity Today*, vol. 9, no. 2 (October 23, 1964), p. 29 (85).
477. Littell, Franklin H. *Religion in Life*, vol. 34, no. 1 (Winter 1964/1965), pp. 153–54.
478. Neuhaus, Richard John. *Una Sancta*, vol. 22, no. 1 (1965), pp. 58–59.
479. Vishnewski, Stanley. *The Catholic Worker*, vol. 31, no. 10 (May 1965), p. 7.
480. *Inner City* (November 1964), Unpaged. "Worth Noting."

The Christian Life and Salvation (1967)

481. Ahlen, A. C. M. *Lutheran Quarterly*, vol. 20, no. 2 (May 1968), p. 211.
482. Barber, Cyril, J. *The Minister's Library*. Grand Rapids, Mich.: Baker, 1974, p. 217. **Notes**: One paragraph.
483. Bloesch Reflects on His Latest Books. *Dubuque Theological Seminary Report*, series 1, no. 1. (Summer 1968) p. [2].
484. Bryant, Robert H. *Religion in Life*, vol. 37, no. 4 (Winter 1986), pp. 632–33. **Notes**: Also reviews *Secular Christ* / John J. Vincent.
485. Casteel, John L. *Kirkus Reviews*, vol. 34, no. 23 (December 1, 1966), p. 1275. (Religious Book Supplement no. 10).
486. Daane, James. *The Reformed Journal*, vol. 18, no. 5 (May–June 1968), p. 32. (Short notices).
487. Evans, William B. *Journal of the Evangelical Theological Society*, vol. 38, no. 1 (March 1995), pp. 119–21.
488. Goss, Glenn R. *Calvary Review*, vol. 6, no. 4 (October–December 1967), p. 11.
489. Hunt, Boyd. *Southwestern Journal of Theology*, vol. 10, no. 2 (Spring 1968), p. 128.
490. Johnson, George M. *Central Baptist Seminary Journal* (February 1968), p. 41. **Notes**: Item does not carry a volume or issue number.
491. Layer, Karl G. *The Living Church*, vol. 155, no. 4 (July 23, 1967), p. 3. **Notes**: One paragraph.
492. Meister, John W. *Theology Today*, vol. 24, no. 4 (January 1968), pp. 515–16. **Notes**: Also reviews *Christian Life* / Paul Hessert.
493. Miller, R. S. *Reformed Theological Review*, vol. 27, no. 2 (May–August 1968), pp. 66. **Notes**: Refers to DGB as Bloetsch.
494. Mueller, Walter. "The Two Cannot Be Separated." *Christianity Today*, vol. 11, no. 23 (September 1, 1976), pp. 29–30 (1149–50).
495. Mumaw, John R. *Provident Book Reviews*, vol. 6, no. 4 (April 1968), p. 61.
496. Nobel, Richard. *Good News*, vol. 1, no. 4 (April 1968), pp. 28–29.
497. Porter, Laurence E. *The Evangelical Quarterly*, vol. 42, no. 1 (January–March 1970), pp. 47–49. **Notes**: Also reviews Bloesch's *The Crisis of Piety*.
498. Rochelle, Jay C. *Pittsburgh Perspective*, vol. 8, no. 4 (December 1967), p. 45.
499. Ryrie, C. C. *Bibliotheca Sacra*, vol. 125, no. 499 (July–September 1968), p. 281.
500. Scaer, David P. *The Springfielder*, vol. 31, no. 3 (Autumn 1967), pp. 69–70.
501. Spitz, L. W., Sr. *Concordia Theological Monthly*, vol. 39, no. 3 (March 1968), p. 215. **Notes**: One paragraph.
502. Summers, R. L. *The Presbyterian Journal*, vol. 26, no. 24 (October 11, 1967), p. 20.
503. Taylor, Willard H. *The Nazarene Preacher*, vol. 44, no. 2 (February 1969), pp. 46–47.

504. Thompson, Fred P., Jr. *United Evangelical Action*, vol. 26, no. 6 (August 1967), p. 23.
505. Throckmorton, Burton H., Jr. "Too Much?" *United Church Herald*, vol. 11, no. 12 (December 1968) pp. 46, 48–49.
506. Trites, Allison A. *The Watchman Examiner*, vol. 56, no. 5 (March 7, 1968), p. 148.
507. *Keeping You Posted*. "Recommended." (June 1, 1967), p. 4 m. **Notes**: Item carries no issue or volume number.
508. United Church of Christ. Iowa Conference. *UCC Reporter*, vol. 4, no. 9 (June–July 1967), p. [6]. **Notes**: One paragraph.

Christian Spirituality East & West (Aumann and Hopko: 1968)

509. Dominic, Mary, O.P. *Review for Religious*, vol. 28 (March 1969), pp. 326–27.
510. Graef, Hilda. *The Clergy Review*, n.s. vol. 55, no. 9 (September 1970), pp. 742–43.
511. Green, Austin. *Cross and Crown*, vol. 21, no. 1 (March 1969), pp. 97–98. **Notes**: Also reviews: *Comfort My People: The Pastoral Presence of the Church* / Eugene C. Kennedy.
512. Heiser, W. Charles. *Theology Digest*, vol. 16, no. 4 (Winter 1968), p. 335. **Notes**: One paragraph.
513. Lechner, Robert. *Worship*, vol. 42, no. 10 (January 1969), pp. 60–62.
514. Mulhern, Philip F. *The Thomist*, vol. 33, no. 2 (April 1969), pp. 399–402.
515. Nelson, John Oliver. *Journal of Ecumenical Studies*, vol. 6, no. 3 (Summer 1969), pp. 435–37.
516. Pennington, M. Basil. *Theological Studies*, vol. 30, no. 2 (June 1969), pp. 380–81.

The Christian Witness in a Secular Age (1968)

517. Dominy, Bert B. *Southwestern Journal of Theology*, vol. 13, no. 1 (Fall 1970), pp. 98–99.
518. Heiser, W. Charles. *Theology Digest*, vol. 16, no. 4 (Winter 1968), p. 338. **Notes**: One paragraph.
519. Poling, David. "A Look at Books." *Christian Herald*, vol. 91, no. 12 (December 1968), pp. 48, 51.
520. Schmidt, Karl T. "Views of Nine Theologians Examined." *Book News Letter of Augsburg Publishing House*, no. 406 (November 1968), p. 3.
521. Starkloff, Carl F. *Review for Religious*, vol. 28, no. 2 (March 1969), pp. 322–23.
522. *Choice*, vol. 6, no. 2 (April 1969), p. 228. **Notes**: One paragraph.
523. *The Christian Century*, vol. 85, no. 45 (November 6, 1968), p. 1408. (*This Week*) **Notes**: One paragraph.
524. *Christianity Today*, vol. 13, no. 4 (November 22, 1968), p. 38 (1861). (Paperbacks). **Notes**: One paragraph.
525. *Dubuque Theological Seminary Report*, series 1, no. 3 (Winter 1969), p. [3].

The Church (2002)

526. Adams, Daniel J. *The Reformed Review*, vol. 56, no. 3 (Spring 2003), pp. 286–87.
527. Brand, Chad Owen. *The Southern Baptist Journal of Theology*, vol. 8, no. 2 (Summer 2004), pp. 102–3.

528. Clifton, Shane. *Religious Studies Review*, vol. 29, no. 3 (July 2003), p. 275.
529. Colyer, Elmer M. *Pro Ecclesia*, vol. 12, no. 3 (Summer 2003), pp. 361–62.
530. Engelsma, David J. *Protestant Reformed Theological Journal*, vol. 37, no. 2 (April 2004), pp. 65–68. **Notes**: Also available as an electronic resource via: www.prca .org/prtj/apr2004.htm#Book%20Reviews (accessed February 14, 2007).
531. Lewis, John Peter. *Reformation & Revival*, vol. 12, no. 2 (Spring 2003), pp. 163–67.
532. Parker, David. *Evangelical Review of Theology*, vol. 29, no. 2 (April 2005), pp. 191–92.
533. Resch, Dustin. *The Canadian Evangelical Review*, (Autumn 2004), pp. 33–35.
534. Stamoolis, James. *Missiology*, vol. 33, no. 2 (April 2005), p. 230.

The Crisis of Piety (1968)

535. Anderson, James A. *Cross and Crown*, vol. 21, no. 1 (March 1969), pp. 111–13.
536. Bechtel, Paul, and Bechtel, Mary. "Merging the Sacred and the Profane." *Christian Life*, vol. 30, no. 4 (August 1968), p. 59.
537. Bender, Thorwald W. "Bloesch Explores the Church's Crisis." *Eternity*, vol. 20, no. 7 (July 1969), p. 44.
538. Bicket, Zenas J. *Advance*, vol. 5, no. 3 (March 1969), p. 11.
539. Bicket, Zenas J. *Paraclete*, vol. 3, no. 3 (Summer 1969), p. 32.
540. Bloesch Reflects on His Latest Books. *Dubuque Theological Seminary Report*, series 1, no. 1 (Summer 1968), p. [2].
541. Buis, Harry. *The Church Herald*, vol. 26, no. 9 (February 28, 1969), p. 14.
542. Clendenin, Daniel B. *Journal of the Evangelical Theological Society*, vol. 33, no. 3 (September 1990), pp. 408–9. **Notes**: Reviews the reprint by Helmers and Howard, Colorado Springs, 1988. Includes a review of *The Future of Evangelical Christianity*.
543. Davis, Richard. *Religion in Life*, vol. 38, no. 4 (Winter 1969), pp. 609–10.
544. Davis, Wayne H. *The Presbyterian Journal*, vol. 27, no. 28 (November 6, 1968), p. 21.
545. Doan, Gilbert E., Jr. *Lutheran Forum*, vol. 2, no. 10 (October 1968), p. 36.
546. Dvorak, Robert. *The Church Herald*, vol. 27, no. 25 (June 19, 1970), pp. 14, 22.
547. Eyster, John W. *Christian Advocate*, vol. 12, no. 20 (October 17, 1968), p. 17 (Books of Interest to Pastors)
548. Goldberg, Daniel. *Calvary Review*, vol. 7, no. 4 (October–December 1968), p. 8.
549. Goldsworthy, Graeme Lister. *The Australian Church Record*, no. 1422 (September 19, 1968), p. 7.
550. Healey, Robert M. *The Presbyterian Outlook*, vol. 151, no. 2 (January 13, 1969), p. 15.
551. Higgins, Howard D. *Episcopal Recorder*, n.s. vol. 49, no. 7 (vol. 146, no. 5625) (July 1968), p. 15. (The Book Shelf) **Notes**: One paragraph.
552. Hohenstein, Lewis C. *The Pastor's Herald* [newsletter] (October 1968), pp. 18–20.
553. Holmer, Paul L. "Pro Piety." *The Christian Century*, vol. 85, no. 45 (November 6, 1968), p. 1407.
554. Homrighausen, E. G. *The Princeton Seminary Bulletin*, vol. 61, no. 3 (Summer 1968), p. 101.

555. Jeschke, Marlin. *Provident Book Reviews*, vol. 7, no. 1 (January 1969), p. 3.

556. Johnston, David C. *Information Letter (Laymen's Study Group)*, no. 49 (December 1970), p. 14–15.

557. Kuyvenhhoven, Andrew. *Calvinist-Contact*, no. 856 (June 7, 1968), pp. 3–4 (From the Bookshelf).

558. Layer, Karl G. *The Living Church*, vol. 157, no. 9 (September 1, 1968), p. 21. **Notes**: One paragraph.

559. Ludlow, William L. *Church Management*, vol. 45, no. 5 (February 1969), p. 35.

560. Matrow, Jack. "Spiritual Disciplines." *The Christian*, vol. 107, no. 4 (January 26, 1969), p. 28 (124).

561. Olbricht, Thomas H. "Devotional." *Restoration Quarterly*, vol. 13, no. 3 (Third Quarter 1970), pp. 188–90.

562. Osterhaven, M. Eugene. *The Reformed Review*, vol. 22, no. 3 (March 1969), pp. 27–28.

563. Peters, P. *Wisconsin Lutheran Quarterly*, vol. 65, no. 4 (October 1968), pp. 298–99.

564. Poling, David. *Christian Herald*, vol. 91, no. 7 (July 1968), pp. 47–48. **Notes**: One paragraph.

565. Porter, Laurence E. *The Evangelical Quarterly*, 42, no. 1 (January–March 1970), pp. 47–49.

566. Richardson, Kurt A. *Perspectives in Religious Studies*, vol. 18, no. 3 (Fall 1991), pp. 267–70.

567. Saucy, Robert L. *Talbot Theological Seminary Bulletin* (Summer 1968), p. 10. **

568. Scaer, David P. *The Springfielder*, vol. 32, no. 3 (Autumn 1968), pp. 51–52.

569. Stone, Arnold M. *Evangelize*, vol. 24, no. 9 (November 1968), p. 15 (From the Bookshelf).

570. Veenstra, Rolf. *Missionary Monthly*, vol. 73, no. 836 (October 1968), p. 274.

571. Wagoner, Walter D. *Journal of Ecumenical Studies*, vol. 7, no. 1 (Winter 1970), pp. 145–46.

572. *Canadian Journal of Theology*, vol. 15, no. 1 (January 1969), pp. 71–72.

573. *The Moravian*, "The Church Today," vol. 113, no. 11 (November 1968), p. 30. **Notes**: Article refers to the book as "The Crisis in Piety."

574. *The New Life News*, vol. 11, no. 1 (1969), p. 4 (The Best in Books).

575. *The Pious Papyrus* (May 1, 1968).

576. *Reformed Theological Review*, vol. 27, no. 3 (September–December 1968), pp. 110–11.

577. *Vox Reformata*, no. 11 (November 1968), p. 26. **Notes**: One paragraph.

578. *The Witness (London)*, vol. 98, no. 1174 (October 1968), p. 390. **Notes**: One paragraph.

Crumbling Foundations (1984)

579. Anderson, Glenn P. *The Covenant Quarterly*, vol. 44, no. 2 (May 1986), pp. 47–50.

580. Breyfogle, Valorie. "'Crumbling Foundations' Prescribes Moral Mortar." *Inner View*, vol. 2, no. 1 (February 1985), p. 7.

581. Buursma, Bruce. "Evangelist Finds Hope in Decay." *Chicago Tribune* (December 8, 1984), section 1, p. 10.

582. Dockery, David S. *Criswell Theological Review*, vol. 1, no. 2 (Spring 1987), p. 449.

583. Groothuis, Doug. *TSF Bulletin*, vol. 10, no. 1 (September–October 1986), p. 36.
584. Kurka, R. C. *Journal of the Evangelical Theological Society*, vol. 29, no. 2 (June 1986), pp. 232–34.
585. Massey, Jonathan. *Good News*, vol. 19, no. 1 (July–August 1985), p. 54.
586. Schmidt, Mark Ray. "Trust Not Technology." *Eternity*, vol. 36, no. 10 (October 1985), p. 57.
587. Smith, Harold. *Christianity Today*, vol. 29, no. 4 (March 1, 1985), p. 62.
588. Wonders, Lance A. *The Reformed Review*, vol. 39, no. 1 (Autumn 1985), p. 62.
589. *Evangelical Newsletter*, vol. 11, no. 17 (September 14, 1984), p. 4. **Notes**: One paragraph.

Essentials of Evangelical Theology (1978–1979)

590. Asher, Richard E. *Library Journal*, vol. 103, no. 13 (July 1978), pp. 1420–21. **Notes**: Discusses vol. 1.
591. Asher, Richard E. *Library Journal*, vol. 104, no. 4 (February 15, 1979), p. 499. **Notes**: Discusses vol. 2.
592. Barber, Cyril J. *The Minister's Library. Periodic Supplement #3*. Grand Rapids, Mich.: Baker, 1980, pp. 25–26. **Notes**: One paragraph.
593. Barber, Cyril J. *The Minister's Library. Periodic Supplement #4*. Grand Rapids, Mich.: Baker, 1982, p. 34. **Notes**: One paragraph.
594. Bazyn, Ken. *The New Review of Books and Religion*, vol. 4, no. 3 (November 1979), pp. 8–9. **Notes**: Discusses vol. 2.
595. Branson, Mark. *Catalyst*, vol. 6, no. 2 (February 1980), p. 4. **Notes**: Discusses both vols.
596. Broadus, Edwin. *Gospel Herald*, vol. 45, no. 5 (May 1979), p. 15. **Notes**: Discusses vol. 1.
597. Bromiley, Geoffrey W. *Anglican Theological Review*, vol. 65, no. 3 (July 1983), pp. 355–57. **Notes**: Discusses both vols.
598. Carter, Robert. "From a Pastor's Bookshelf." *Living Faith*, vol. 1, no. 1 (Spring 1980), pp. 29–31.
599. Climenhaga, Arthur. *United Evangelical Action*, vol. 38, no. 4 (Winter 1979), pp. 34–34, 29 [sic]. **Notes**: Discusses vol. 2.
600. Dockery, David S. *Grace Theological Journal*, vol. 2, no. 1 (Spring 1981), pp. 152–54. **Notes**: Discusses both vols.
601. Feinberg, Paul D. *Christianity Today*, vol. 23, no. 22 (September 21, 1979), pp. 38, 41 (1259, 1262). **Notes**: Discusses vol. 1.
602. Ferm, Deane William. "The New Evangelical Theology." *The Presbyterian Outlook*, vol. 163, no. 5 (February 2, 1981), pp. 5–6. **Notes**: Discusses both vols.
603. Fitt, Frank. *Church Management*, vol. 55, no. 9 (August 1979), p. 35. **Notes**: Discusses vol. 1.
604. Foxgrover, David. "Reconceptions." *The Christian Century*, vol. 96, no. 6 (February 21, 1979), p. 192. **Notes**: Discusses vol. 2.
605. Foxgrover, David. *Christianity Today*, vol. 24, no. 9 (May 2, 1980), pp. 38, 40 (574, 576). **Notes**: Discusses vol. 2.
606. Franklin, Stephen T. *The Japan Christian Quarterly*, vol. 48, no. 4 (Fall 1982), pp. 232–36. **Notes**: Discusses both vols.

607. Godsey, John D. "Keeping Continuity." *The Christian Century*, vol. 95, no. 32 (October 11, 1978), pp. 960–61. **Notes**: Discusses vol. 1.
608. Heiser, W. Charles. *Theology Digest*, vol. 26, no. 2 (Fall 1978), p. 265. **Notes**: Discusses vol. 1.
609. Heiser, W. Charles. *Theology Digest*, vol. 27, no. 1 (Spring 1979), p. 63. **Notes**: Discusses vol. 2.
610. Hoekema, Anthony A. *Calvin Theological Journal*, vol. 14, no. 1 (April 1979), pp. 84–87. **Notes**: Discusses vol. 1.
611. Inch, Morris A. *New Oxford Review*, vol. 46, no. 5 (June 1979), pp. 23–24. **Notes**: Discusses vol. 1.
612. Inch, Morris A. *New Oxford Review*, vol. 47, no. 3 (April 1980), p. 26. **Notes**: Discusses vol. 2.
613. Johnston, Robert K. *Crux*, no. 15, no. 2 (June 1979), pp. 26–28. **Notes**: Discusses both vols. Not the same as the review he wrote for the *Journal of the Evangelical Theological Society*.
614. Johnston, Robert K. *Journal of the Evangelical Theological Society*, vol. 22, no. 3 (September 1979), pp. 281–82. **Notes**: Discusses vol. 2.
615. Klann, Richard. *Concordia Journal*, vol. 6, no. 4 (July 1980), p. 176. **Notes**: Discusses vol. 1.
616. Lightner, R. P. *Bibliotheca Sacra*, vol. 136, no. 542 (April–June 1979), p. 181. **Notes**: Discusses vol. 1.
617. Lightner, R. P. *Bibliotheca Sacra*, vol. 137, no. 547 (July–September 1980), p. 279. **Notes**: Discusses vol. 2.
618. McDonald, H. D. *Journal of the Evangelical Theological Society*, vol. 22, no. 3 (September 1979), pp. 279–81. **Notes**: Discusses vol. 1.
619. McKim, Donald K. "What Is the Best Systematic Theology for a Pastor or Lay Person?" *Christianity Today*, vol. 28, no. 4 (March 2, 1984), pp. 72, 74. **Notes**: Also reviews: *Christian Faith* / Hendrikus Berkhof; and *Doxology* / Geoffrey Wainwright; and *Reasonable Faith* / Anthony and Richard Hanson; and *The Word of Truth* / Dale Moody.
620. Moes, Mark. *The New Review of Books and Religion*, vol. 3, no. 7 (March 1979), pp. 9–10. **Notes**: Discusses vol. 1.
621. Olson, Roger. *Christian Scholar's Review*, vol. 10, no. 1 (1980), pp. 85–86. **Notes**: Discusses both vols.
622. Osterhaven, M. Eugene. *Eternity*, vol. 30, no. 6 (June 1979), p. 47. **Notes**: Discusses vol. 2.
623. Osterhaven, M. Eugene. *The Reformed Review*, vol. 32, no. 2 (Winter 1979), pp. 109–10. **Notes**: Discusses vol. 1.
624. Petersen, Rodney L. *The Princeton Seminary Bulletin*, n.s., vol. 2, no. 3 (1979), pp. 289–91. **Notes**: Discusses both vols.
625. Pinnock, Clark H. "Evangelical Essentials." *Sojourners*, vol. 8, no. 8 (August 1979), pp. 31–33. **Notes**: Discusses both vols. Also reviews *Agenda for Theology* / Thomas C. Oden.
626. Pinnock, Clark H. *Theology Today*, vol. 36, no. 2 (July 1979), pp. 266, 268. **Notes**: Discusses both vols. Slightly different than his *Sojourners* review. Also available as an electronic resource via: theologytoday.ptsem. edu (accessed February 14, 2007).

627. Pinnock, Clark H. *TSF News and Reviews* (October 1978), pp. 15–16. **Notes**: This issue of the periodical carries no volume or issue designation. Discusses vol. 1.
628. Pinnock, Clark H. *TSF News and Reviews* (March 1979), pp. 10–11. **Notes**: This issue of the periodical carries no volume or issue designation. Discusses vol. 2.
629. Price, Bob. *The Drew Gateway*, vol. 50, no. 2 (Winter 1979), pp. 54–58. **Notes**: Discusses both vols.
630. Rambo, Lewis R. *Pacific Theological Review*, vol. 12, no. 1 (Fall 1979), pp. 31–32. **Notes**: Discusses both vols.
631. Rambo, Lewis R. *Restoration Quarterly*, vol. 25, no. 3 (Third Quarter 1982), pp. 179–80. **Notes**: Discusses both vols.
632. Ramm, Bernard. "Pioneering Theology." *Eternity*, vol. 29, no. 10 (October 1978), pp. 46–47. **Notes**: Discusses vol. 1.
633. Rice, Richard. *Religious Studies Review*, vol. 7, no. 2 (April 1981), pp. 107–8, 110–12, 114–15. **Notes**: Discusses both vols. Also reviews: *God, Revelation, and Authority* / Carl F. H. Henry.
634. Saucy, Robert L. *Journal of Psychology and Theology*, vol. 7, no. 3 (Fall 1979), pp. 221–22. **Notes**: Discusses both vols.
635. Smith, Joanmarie. *Religious Education*, vol. 74, no. 2 (March–April 1979), p. 142. (Briefly noted) **Notes**: Discusses vol. 1. One paragraph.
636. Stegall, Carroll R., Jr. *The Presbyterian Journal*, vol. 38, no. 20 (September 12, 1979), p. 22. **Notes**: Discusses both vols.
637. Strauss, James D. *Christian Standard*, vol. 114, no. 22, (June 3, 1979), p. 12 (500). **Notes**: Discusses both vols.
638. Tyson, John. *The Asbury Seminarian*, vol. 34, no. 3 (July 1979), pp. 41–43. **Notes**: Discusses vol. 1.
639. Wells, David F. *Religion in Life*, vol. 49, no. 1 (Spring 1980), pp. 119–20. **Notes**: Discusses both vols. Refers to the book as *Essentials of Evangelical Theory*.
640. Wonders, Lance A. *Presbyterian Communiqué*, vol. 11, no. 1 (January–February 1979), pp. 10–12. **Notes**: Discusses vol. 1.
641. Wonders, Lance. "Fresh Insights, Biblical Balance." *The Reformed Journal*, vol. 29, no. 4 (April 1979), pp. 31–32. **Notes**: Discusses both vols.
642. *ADRIS Newsletter*, vol. 8, no. 3 (April–June 1979), p. 82. **Notes**: Discusses vol. 1. One paragraph.
643. *IFACS [Newsletter]* (1980), p. [2]. **Notes**: One paragraph. This issue of the periodical bears no issue or volume designation.
644. *Kirkus Reviews*, vol. 46, no. 9 (May 1, 1978), p. 519. **Notes**: Discusses vol. 1.
645. *Kirkus Reviews*, vol. 46, no. 24 (December 15, 1978), p. 1390. **Notes**: Discusses vol. 2.
646. *Old Testament Abstracts*, vol. 1, no. 3 (October 1978), p. 284.

Evangelical Renaissance (1973)

647. Andrews, Allan R. *Christian Scholar's Review*, vol. 4, no. 2 (1974), pp. 160–61.
648. Barber, Cyril J. *Journal of Psychology and Theology*, vol. 2, no. 1 (Winter 1974), p. 68.
649. Barber, Cyril J. *The Minister's Library. Periodic Supplement #1.* Grand Rapids, Mich.: Baker, 1978, p. 20.

650. Bechtel, Paul M. *Christian Bookseller*, vol. 19, no. 10 (November 1973), p. 12. **Notes**: One paragraph.
651. Boatman, Donald. *Christian Standard*, vol. 108, no. 50 (December 9, 1973), p. 22 (1126).
652. Bromiley, Geoffrey W. *The Virginia Seminary Journal*, vol. 26, no. 2 (March 1974), p. 38.
653. Cook, Paul E. G. *Banner of Truth*, no. 136 (January 1975), pp. 23–24.
654. Cook, Paul E. G. *Christian News*, vol. 8, no. 9 (March 3, 1975), p. 11.
655. Daane, James. *Theology Today*, vol. 31, no. 2 (July 1974), pp. 174, 176–66. **Notes**: Also available as an electronic resource via: theologytoday.ptsem.edu (accessed February 14, 2007).
656. Dayton, Donald W. "Conservative Christians." *The Christian Century*, vol. 91, no. 6 (February 13, 1974), pp. 184–85. **Notes**: Also reviews: *The Evangelical Heritage* / Bernard Ramm.
657. Dayton, Donald W. *The Covenant Quarterly*, vol. 32, no. 1 (February 1974), pp. 45–46. **Notes**: Not same as his review in *The Christian Century*. Includes reviews of *The Evangelical Heritage* / Bernard Ramm; and *Liberal Christianity at the Crossroads* / John B. Cobb Jr.
658. Drummond, Lewis A. *Review and Expositor*, vol. 71, no. 2 (Spring 1974), pp. 276–77.
659. Dulon, Günter. *Ecumenical Review*, vol. 27, no. 2 (April 1975), p. 179.
660. Eaves, James F. *Southwestern Journal of Theology*, vol. 20, no. 1 (Fall 1977), pp. 123–24.
661. Ficken, Carl F. W. *Lutheran Quarterly*, vol. 26, no. 2 (May 1974), pp. 236–38.
662. Fritz, John D. *The Springfielder*, vol. 37, no. 4 (March 1974), p. 285. **Notes**: One paragraph.
663. Gingerich, Melvin. "Author Sees Evangelical Resurgence." *Mennonite Weekly Review*, vol. 52, no. 14 (April 4, 1974), p. 4.
664. Hanko, Herman. *The Standard Bearer*, vol. 50, no. 9 (February 1, 1974), p. 206. **Notes**: One paragraph.
665. Harman, Allan. *Scottish Journal of Theology*, vol. 28, no. 3 (June 1975), pp. 290–91.
666. Heiser, W. Charles. *Theology Digest*, vol. 21, no. 4 (Winter 1973), p. 363. **Notes**: One paragraph.
667. Hesselink, I. John. *The Reformed Review*, vol. 28, no. 2 (Winter 1975), pp. 94–96.
668. Jackman, Edward J. R. *Cross and Crown*, vol. 26, no. 4 (December 1974), pp. 437–38.
669. Jordahl, Leigh D. *Lutheran Forum*, vol. 7, no. 4 (November 1973), p. 40.
670. Kauffman, Nelson F. *Provident Book Finder*, vol. 4, no. 4 (January 1974), p. 37.
671. Layer, Karl G. *The Living Church*, vol. 167, no. 22 (November 25, 1973), p. 23. **Notes**: One paragraph.
672. Lightner, R. P. *Bibliotheca Sacra*, vol. 131, no. 522 (April–June 1974), p. 187.
673. Lueking, F. Dean. *Dialog*, vol. 13, no. 3 (Summer 1974), pp. 236, 238.
674. Meye, Robert P. *Foundations*, vol. 17, no. 1 (January–March 1974), p. 89.
675. Ockenga, Harold J. "Evangelicalism Past and Present." *The Review of Books and Religion*, vol. 3, no. 4 (Mid-January 1974), p. 1. **Notes**: Also reviews: *The Evangelical Heritage* / Bernard L. Ramm.
676. Pierard, Richard V. *The Banner*, vol. 108, no. 44 (November 16, 1973), p. 24.

677. Porter, Laurence E. *The Evangelical Quarterly*, vol. 46, no. 4 (October–December 1974), pp. 245–47.
678. Ramm, Bernard L. "Evangelicals Getting Respectable." *Eternity*, vol. 24, no. 12 (December 1973), p. 68. **Notes**: At head of title: An Acutely Balanced Defense.
679. Sider, Ronald J. "Qualified Usefulness." *Christianity Today*, vol. 18, no. 20 (July 5, 1974), pp. 34–36 (1161–62).
680. Stanger, Frank Bateman. *Religion in Life*, vol. 44, no. 2 (Summer 1975), pp. 254–56. **Notes**: Also reviews: *The Evangelical Heritage* / Bernard Ramm; and *Quest for Reality* / Carl F. H. Henry, et al.
681. Stewardson, Jerry L. "Expounding Evangelical Faith: From Karl Barth to Carl Henry." *Explor*, vol. 2, no. 2 (Fall 1976), pp. 35–39. **Notes**: Includes reviews of three other books.
682. Vernon, Dodd. *The Augusta Chronicle* (August 30, 1973), p. 9A.**
683. Winter, Ralph. "Who Are the Evangelicals?" *Christianity Today*, vol. 20, no. 14 (April 9, 1976), pp. 35–38 (731–34). **Notes**: Also reviews: *The Evangelical Heritage* / Bernard Ramm; and *The Young Evangelicals* / Richard Quebedeaux; and *The Evangelicals* / edited by David F. Wells and John D. Woodbridge.
684. *Baptist Record*, vol. 92, no. 4 (December 20, 1973), p. 4 (Newest Books).
685. *Choice*, vol. 10, no. 10 (December 1973), p. 1567.
686. *Christian Life*, vol. 35, no. 7 (November 1973), p. 36.
687. *Christianity Today*, vol. 18, no. 2 (October 26, 1973), p. 37 (101) (Newly published).
688. *Christianity Today*, vol. 18, no. 11 (March 1, 1974), p. 13 (605). **Notes**: One paragraph.
689. *The Church Herald*, vol. 30, no. 31 (September 21, 1973), p. 23. **Notes**: One paragraph. Review signed: L. H. B.
690. *The Expository Times*, vol. 85, no. 11 (August 1974), p. 351. **Notes**: One paragraph.
691. *Moody Monthly*, vol. 73, no. 9 (May 1973), p. 52 (Watch for These Books). **Notes**: One paragraph.
692. *The North American Moravian*, vol. 4, no. 10 (November 1973), p. 31. **Notes**: One paragraph.
693. *Reformed Theological Review*, vol. 32, no. 3 (September–December 1973), p. 104.
694. *Restoration Quarterly*, vol. 17, no. 4 (Fourth Quarter 1974), p. 249 (Short Notices).
695. *Review for Religious*, vol. 32 (November 1973), p. 1467 (Book Notices). **Notes**: One paragraph.

Evangelical Theology in Transition (1999)

696. Berghuis, Kent D. *Bibliotheca Sacra*, vol. 158, no. 630 (April–June 2001), pp. 237–38.
697. Mills, Robert P. *The Presbyterian Layman*, vol. 32, no. 5 (November–December 1999), p. 20.

Faith and Its Counterfeits (1981)

698. Bowie, Ian C. *B.C. Regular Baptist*, vol. 33, nos. 9–10 (September–October 1981), p. 5.

699. Buckley, Jack. *Radix*, vol. 13, no. 4 (January–February 1982), p. 30 (Book notes). **Notes**: One paragraph.
700. Buursma, William D. *The Banner*, vol. 116, no. 40 (October 19, 1981), p. 19. **Notes**: One paragraph.
701. Claus, Lucille. "Handbook of Spirituality." *The Church Herald*, vol. 39, no. 8 (April 16, 1982), p. 18.
702. Erlendson, Norman. *Evangelica*, vol. 4, no. 2 (January 1983), pp. 17–18.
703. Faber, Charles H. *Christian Standard*, vol. 117, no. 2 (January 10, 1982), p. 21 (45).
704. Fackre, Gabriel. *TSF Bulletin*, vol. 5, no. 3 (January–February 1982), p. 21.
705. Harthan, Stephen. *The Christian Librarian*, vol. 27, no. 1, (November 1983), p. 30.
706. Hitchcock, James. "Handbook on Heresy." *New Covenant*, vol. 11, no. 7 (January 1982), p. 28.
707. Lightner, R. P. *Bibliotheca Sacra*, vol. 139, no. 553 (January–March 1982), p. 91. **Notes**: One paragraph.
708. Long, James. *Campus Life*, 41, no. 4 (November 1982), p. 92. **Notes**: One paragraph.
709. Martin, Joseph M. *Journal of the American Scientific Affiliation*, vol. 35, no. 2 (June 1983), pp. 117–18.
710. Neufeld, Lois. "Recognizing the False." *Mennonite Brethren Herald*, vol. 21, no. 18 (September 24, 1982), pp. 27–38.
711. Olson, Bob. *The Oak Kin*, vol. 10, no. 5 (March 1983), p. 3.
712. Preston, Steve. *The Youth Leader*, vol. 40, no. 1 (January 1983), p. 7.
713. Roberts, R. Philip. *Review and Expositor*, vol. 82, no. 1 (Winter 1985), p. 165.
714. Sanders, Gerald M. *Living Faith*, vol. 2, no. 3 (Fall 1981), pp. 28–29.
715. Smallman, William H. *The Baptist Bulletin*, vol. 47, no. 8 (February 1982), p. 32.
716. Stahlke, Otto F. *Concordia Theological Quarterly*, vol. 46, no. 1 (January 1982), p. 85. **Notes**: One paragraph.
717. Wiessner, Charles. *The Reformed Review*, vol. 38, no. 3 (Spring 1985), pp. 250–51.
718. *Christian Bookseller*, vol. 27, no. 10 (October 1981), p. 16. **Notes**: One paragraph.
719. *Eternity*, vol. 32, no. 10 (October 1981), p. 46. **Notes**: One paragraph.
720. *Firm Foundation*, vol. 98, no. 31 (August 4, 1981), p. 14 (494). **Notes**: One paragraph.
721. *His*, vol. 42, no. 2, (November 1981), p. 24.
722. *The Herald Telephone*, "Faith Counterfeited." (July 18, 1981). **
723. *Voices*, vol. 9, no. 2 (Winter 1983), p. 14 (Bookshelf & Shopper's Guide). **Notes**: One paragraph.

Freedom for Obedience (1987)

724. Aldwinckle, Russell. *Theodolite*, vol. 8, no. 4 (1989), pp. 45–46.
725. Clendenin, Daniel B. *Journal of the Evangelical Theological Society*, vol. 31, no. 2 (June 1988), pp. 249–50.
726. Clendenin, Daniel B. *The Reformed Review*, vol. 41, no. 1 (Autumn 1987), pp. 64–65. **Notes**: Not the same as above.
727. Greenfield, Guy. *Southwestern Journal of Theology*, vol. 31, no. 2 (Spring 1989), pp. 59–60.

728. Hanson, Lyn. "God Will Decide Right and Wrong." *The Telegraph Herald*, vol. 151, no. 186 (Friday, August 7, 1987), p. 1C.

729. Heiser, W. Charles. *Theology Digest*, vol. 35, no. 3 (Fall 1988), p. 260. **Notes**: One paragraph.

730. Howard, John. *The Journal of Religion*, vol. 69, no. 3 (July 1989), pp. 438–39.

731. Klann, Richard. *Concordia Journal*, 16, no. 4 (October 1990), pp. 416–17.

732. McLelland, Reginald F. "Resolving Tensions." *Eternity*, vol. 39, no. 5 (May 1988), pp. 39–40.

733. Milley, Garry E. *Eastern Journal of Practical Theology*, vol. 2, no. 1 (Spring 1988), p. 51.

734. Niebanck, Richard J. *Lutheran Partners*, vol. 5, no. 2 (March–April 1989), pp. 44–45.

735. Palmer, Russell W. *Interpretation*, vol. 43, no. 2 (April 1989), pp. 208, 210.

736. Rush, Charles. *Religious Studies Review*, vol. 14, no. 4 (October 1988), p. 363.

737. Schuurman, Douglas J. *Calvin Theological Journal*, vol. 24, no. 1 (April 1989), pp. 144–50.

738. Sell, Alan P. F. "Irenic but Determined." *The Reformed Journal*, vol. 37, no. 11 (November 1987), pp. 26–27.

739. Verge, Carl F. *Eastern Journal of Practical Theology*, vol. 3, no. 2 (Fall 1989), pp. 43–44.

740. Verhey, Allen D. "What Makes an Ethic Evangelical?" *Christianity Today*, vol. 32, no. 14 (October 7, 1988), pp. 70–71. **Notes**: Also reviews: *Resurrection and Moral Order* / Oliver O'Donovan.

741. Wilson, Jonathan R. *Perspectives in Religious Studies*, vol. 16, no. 1 (Spring 1989), pp. 82–84.

742. Wilton, Carlos. "Bloesch Publishes 'Freedom for Obedience.'" *Inner View*, vol. 3, no. 4 (December 1987), pp. 6–7.

743. Yoder, John Howard. *The Journal of Religion*, vol. 69, no. 3 (July 1989), pp. 438–39.

744. *Prokopē*, vol. 6, no. 6 (November–December 1989), p. [3]. **Notes**: One paragraph.

The Future of Evangelical Christianity (1983)

745. Clendenin, Daniel B. *Journal of the Evangelical Theological Society*, vol. 33, no. 3 (September 1990), pp. 408–9. **Notes**: Includes review of *Crisis of Piety*, both reprinted by Helmers and Howard, Colorado Springs.

746. Davis, John Jefferson. *Theology Today*, vol. 41, no. 4 (January 1985), pp. 509–10. **Notes**: Also available as an electronic resource via: theologytoday.ptsem.edu (accessed February 14, 2007).

747. Dick, Jack. *National Catholic Reporter*, vol. 20, no. 33 (June 22, 1984), p. 16. **Notes**: One paragraph.

748. Dunkly, James. *The Living Church*, vol.188, no. 4 (January 22, 1984), p. 5. **Notes**: One paragraph.

749. Gros, Jeffrey. *America*, vol. 151, no. 7 (September 22, 1984), pp. 152–53.

750. Henry, Carl F. H. *Eternity*, vol. 34, no. 9 (September 1983), p. 74 (Book Wise).

751. Krupp, Robert Allen. *Library Journal*, vol. 108, no. 13 (July 1983), p. 1369.

752. Lovelace, Richard. "The Evangelical Role in the Church's Future." *Presbyterian Survey*, vol. 74, no. 5 (May 1984), p. 54.

753. Lovelace, Richard. "Where Is Renewal?" *Charisma*, vol. 9, no. 9 (April 1984), p. 18. **Notes**: Refers to the book as *The Future of Evangelicalism*.
754. Lovelace, Richard F. *Christian Scholar's Review*, vol. 14, no. 1 (1984), pp. 74–76.
755. Lovelace, Richard F. *Theology Today*, vol. 41, no. 4 (January 1985), pp. 509–10. **Notes**: Also available as an electronic resource via: theologytoday.ptsem.edu (accessed February 14, 2007).
756. McGinniss, Michael J. *Journal of Ecumenical Studies*, vol. 27, no. 4 (Fall 1990), pp. 810–11.
757. Miller, Glenn T. "Theological, Historical, and Missiological Studies." *Faith and Mission*, vol. 1, no. 2 (Spring 1984), pp. 84–86.
758. Noll, Mark A. "The Surprising Optimism of Donald Bloesch." *Center Journal*, vol. 3, no. 3 (Summer 1984), pp. 95–104. **Notes**: Reprinted: item 769.
759. Noll, Mark. "Foreword—The Surprising Optimism of Donald Bloesch" in *The Future of Evangelical Christianity*.—Colorado Springs: Helmers and Howard, 1988, pp. ix–xvii. **Notes**: Reprint of item 758.
760. Peters, Harold. "Author Builds Bridges to Church Unity." *Charisma*, vol. 9, no. 11 (June 1984), p. 102.
761. Pinnock, Clark H. *Calvin Theological Journal*, vol. 27, no. 2 (November 1992), p. 488.
762. Ramm, Bernard L. *Christianity Today*, vol. 27, no. 18 (November 25, 1983), pp. 54–55.
763. Richardson, Kurt A. *Perspectives in Religious Studies*, vol. 18, no. 3 (Fall 1991), pp. 267–70.
764. Richert, Kevin. "Rev. Bloesch : Evangelicalism Is at the Crossroads." *The Telegraph Herald*, vol. 148, no. 24 (Friday, January 27, 1984), p. 5.
765. Ringenberg, William C. *Fides et Historia*, vol. 18, no. 3 (October 1986), pp. 96–98.
766. Roane, Margaret S. "Title Misleading, But Information's Excellent." *Charisma*, vol. 9, no. 3 (October 1983), pp. 145.
767. Rogers, Jack. *The Presbyterian Outlook*, vol. 166, no. 18 (May 7, 1984), p. 13.
768. Sanders, Dale. *TSF Bulletin*, vol. 9, no. 1 (September–October 1985), p. 31. **Notes**: Reprinted: item 769.
769. Sanders, Dale. *The Reformed Review*, vol. 38 (Autumn 1984), pp. 77–78. **Notes**: Reprint of item 768.
770. Simbro, William. "Evangelicals at Key Turn, Writer Says." *The Des Moines Register* (November 13, 1983), p. 3B.
771. Stark, Paul. *Best Sellers*, vol. 43, no. 8 (November 1983), pp. 305–6.
772. Witham, Larry. "A Look at Evangelicals." *Washington Times* (November 18, 1983), p. C1.
773. Wonders, Lance A. "A Landmark Book." *The Reformed Journal*, vol. 34, no. 3 (March 1984), pp. 27–28.
774. *Booklist*, vol. 80, no. 5 (November 1, 1983), p. 382.
775. *Bookstore Journal*, vol. 17, no. 1 (January 1984), p. 198. **Notes**: Article signed: W. W. B.
776. *Kirkus Reviews*, vol. 51, no. 11 (June 1, 1983), p. 643.
777. *The Publishers Weekly*, vol. 223, no. 25 (June 24, 1983), p. 48.
778. *West Coast Review of Books*, vol. 9, no. 6 (November–December 1983), p. 52. **Notes**: Article signed: C. C.

God, the Almighty (1995)

779. Andersen, Carlton. *Dialog*, vol. 36, no. 4 (Fall 1997), pp. 312–14.
780. Burton, Bryan. *Theology Matters*, vol. 2, no. 3 (May–June 1996), p. 9.
781. Chisholm, Daniel L. *The Theological Educator*, no. 54 (Fall 1996), pp. 160–61. **Notes**: Periodical carries no volume number.
782. Colyer, Elmer. *Reformation & Revival*, vol. 6, no. 2 (Spring 1997), pp. 209–18. **Headings**: A Mounting Controversy—A Viable Doctrine of God—The Basis of Our Knowledge of God—God's Attributes—Transcendence and Immanence—Power and Wisdom—Holiness and Love—The Trinity—Biblical–Classical/ Biblical–Modern Syntheses.
783. Elliott, Mark W. *The Scottish Bulletin of Evangelical Theology*, vol. 15 (Autumn 1997), p. 168–70.
784. Engelsma, David J. *Protestant Reformed Theological Journal*, vol. 30, no. 2 (April 1997), pp. 65–68. **Notes**: Also available as an electronic resource via: www.prca .org/prtj/apr97.html#GodTheAlmighty (accessed February 14, 2007).
785. Engelsma, David J. *The Standard Bearer*, vol. 74, no. 16 (May 15, 1998), pp. 381–82. **Notes**: Also available as an electronic resource via: www.rfpa .org/sb/TheStandardBearer.asp (accessed February 14, 2007).
786. Garrett, James Leo. *Southwestern Journal of Theology*, vol. 40, no. 3 (Summer 1998), pp. 80–81.
787. Gill, David W. "God, in His Own Words." *Christianity Today*, vol. 40, no. 6 (May 20, 1996), pp. 37–40. **Headings**: A User-Friendly Deity—God's Power and Wisdom—A Holy Love—Corrective Measures.
788. Hasel, Frank M. *Andrews University Seminary Studies*, vol. 37, no. 1 (Spring 1999), pp. 91–92.
789. Heim, S. Mark. *Religious Studies Review*, vol. 23, no. 1 (January 1997), p. 46.
790. Heiser, W. Charles. *Theology Digest*, vol. 43, no. 3 (Fall 1996), p. 258.
791. Kreider, Glenn R. *Bibliotheca Sacra*, vol. 154, no. 613 (January–March 1997), pp. 111–12.
792. Leupp, Roderick T. *Journal of the Evangelical Theological Society*. vol. 42, no. 3, (September 1999), pp. 527–28.
793. Parker, David. *Evangelical Review of Theology*, vol. 21, no. 1 (January 1997), pp. 85–87.
794. Saville, Andy. *New Directions*, vol. 1, no. 21 (February 1997), pp. 26–27. **Notes**: Also available as an electronic resource via: www.trushare.com/21FEB97/ FE97BOOK.htm (accessed February 14, 2007).
795. Thompson, Philip E. *Perspectives in Religious Studies*, vol. 24, no. 3 (Fall 1997), pp. 337–41. **Notes**: Also reviews: *The Election of Israel* / David Novak; and *Embodying Forgiveness* / L. Gregory Jones.
796. *The Dallas Morning News* (January 6, 1996), p. 6G.
797. *First Things*, no. 64 (June–July 1996), p. 56. **Notes**: Periodical bears no volume numbering. Also available as an electronic resource via: www.firstthings.com/ article.php3?id_article'3876 (accessed February 14, 2007).
798. *The Publishers Weekly*, vol. 242, no. 46 (November 13, 1995), p. 38. **Notes**: One paragraph. Also available as an electronic resource via: reviews.publisher-sweekly.com/bd.aspx?isbn'0830814132&pub'pw (accessed February 14, 2007).

799. *Sun-Sentinel (Fort Lauderdale, Fla.)* (February 3, 1996), p. 11D.
800. *Wisconsin Bookwatch* (February 1996), p. 9.

The Ground of Certainty (1971)

801. Barber, Cyril J. *The Minister's Library.*—Grand Rapids, Mich.: Baker, 1974, p. 196. **Notes**: One paragraph.
802. Bicket, Zenas J. *Advance*, vol. 8, no. 6 (June 1972), p. 34.
803. Brown, Harold O. J. "Some Significant Books of 1971. Part 6, Theology, Ethics, and Apologetics." *Christianity Today*, vol. 16, no. 12 (March 17, 1972), pp. 12–16 (556–60). **Notes**: DGB p. 13 (557).
804. Cahill, P. Joseph. *The Catholic Biblical Quarterly*, vol. 34, no. 2 (April 1972), pp. 203–4.
805. Gates, John F. "The Christian and Philosophy." *The Alliance Witness*, vol. 107, no. 7 (March 29, 1972), p. 14.
806. Hoekstra, Herman. *The Outlook*, vol. 23, no. 5 (May 1973), p. 19.
807. Huisken, J. *The Standard Bearer*, vol. 49, no. 4 (November 15, 1972), p. 94.
808. Kalland, Lloyd A. "Is There a Place of Apologetics?" *Eternity*, vol. 23, no. 10 (October 1972), p. 69.
809. Lawson, John. *Religion in Life*, vol. 41, no. 2 (Summer 1972), pp. 283–84.
810. Lindahl, Elder M. *The Covenant Quarterly*, vol. 30, no. 2 (May 1972), pp. 34–36.
811. Mitchell, Joseph. *Encounter*, vol. 33, no. 4 (Autumn 1972), pp. 422–23.
812. Polkinghorne, G. J. *The Witness (London, England)*, vol. 102, no. 1220 (August 1972), pp. 307–8.
813. Porter, Laurence E. *The Evangelical Quarterly*, vol. 45, no. 2 (April–June 1973), pp. 119–20.
814. Rian, Edward Harold. *The Princeton Seminary Bulletin*, vol. 66, no. 1 (October 1973), p. 146.
815. Robbins, Jerry. *Journal of the American Academy of Religion*, vol. 40, no. 4 (December 1972), pp. 578–80.
816. Ross, Mary Carman. *The Living Church*, vol. 164, no. 1 (January 2, 1972), pp. 12–13.
817. Schachner-Dionne, Robert J. *Theological Studies*, vol. 33, no. 4 (December 1972), pp. 789–90.
818. Scharlemann, Martin. "Biblical Authority." *Christianity Today*, vol. 17, no. 3 (November 10, 1972), pp. 21–22 (133–34). **Notes**: Four other titles also reviewed.
819. Schneider, A. Michael, III. *The Presbyterian Journal*, vol. 30, no. 42 (February 16, 1972), p. 18.
820. Skibbe, Eugene M. *Lutheran Quarterly*, vol. 24, no. 4 (November 1972), pp. 422–24.
821. Smith, B. L. *Reformed Theological Review*, vol. 31, no. 2 (1972), p. 69 (Shorter notices).
822. Vunderink, Ralph W. *Calvin Theological Journal*, vol. 8, no. 1 (April 1973), pp. 84–89.
823. Walker, Robert T. *Scottish Journal of Theology*, vol. 25, no. 2 (May 1972), p. 237.
824. Young, Warren C. *Foundations*, vol. 16, no. 1 (January–March 1973), p. 91.

825. *Christian Bookseller*, vol. 17, no. 12 (December 1971), p. 22. **Notes**: One paragraph.
826. *Christianity Today*, vol. 16, no. 2 (October 22, 1971), p. 28 (86) (Newly published). **Notes**: One paragraph.

Hermeneutics of Ultimacy (Olthuis: 1987)

827. Cotter, Wendy J. *Toronto Journal of Theology*, vol. 4, no. 1 (Spring 1988), pp. 140–43.
828. Heiser, W. Charles. *Theology Digest*, vol. 35, no. 3 (Fall 1988), p. 282. **Notes**: One paragraph.
829. Vander Goot, Henry. *The Journal of Religion*, vol. 68, no. 2 (April 1988), p. 355.
830. *Themelios*, vol. 14, no. 1 (October–November 1988), p. 32.

Holy Scripture (1994)

831. Bell, Richard H. *The Journal of Religion*, vol. 77, no. 4 (October 1977), pp. 636–38.
832. Braaten, Carl E. "A Harvest of Evangelical Theology." *First Things*, no. 63 (May 1996), pp. 45–48. **Notes**: Also reviews: *Theology for the Community of God* / Stanley J. Grenz; and *Systematic Theology : An Introduction to Biblical Doctrine* / Wayne Grunden; and *Systematic Theology. Vol. II* / James William McClendon Jr.; and *Christian Theology: An Introduction* / Alister E. McGrath; and *Not Every Spirit: A Dogmatics of Christian Disbelief* / Christopher Morse. Also available as an electronic resource via: www.firstthings.com/article.php3?id_article'3869 (accessed February 14, 2007).
833. Burton, Bryan D. "Revealing Words." *Touchstone (Chicago, Ill.)*, vol. 7, no. 4 (Fall 1994), pp. 29–31.
834. Cameron, Charles M. *The Scottish Bulletin of Evangelical Theology*, vol. 13, no. 2 (Autumn 1995), pp. 148–50.
835. Clapp, Rodney. "Letting Scripture Speak for Itself." *Academic Alert*, vol. 3, no. 2 (Spring 1994), pp. 1–2, 4. **Notes**: Interview with DGB.
836. Coggins, Richard J. "How to Interpret the Bible." *The Expository Times*, vol. 106 (November 1994), pp. 53–54. **Notes**: Also reviews: *Is the Bible True?* / D. R. Ord and R. B. Coote; and *Taking the Bible Seriously* / J. Benton White.
837. Cook, Matthew A. *Themelios*, n.s. vol. 20, no. 2 (January 1995), p. 31.
838. Davis, John Jefferson. *Perspectives on Science and Christian Faith*, vol. 46, no. 4 (December 1994), pp. 277–78. **Notes**: Also available as an electronic resource via: www.asa3.org/ASA/book_reviews/12-94.htm#HOLY%20SCRIPTURE:%20Revelation,%20Inspiration%20and%20Interpretation%20by%20Donald%20G.%20Bloesch (accessed February 14, 2007).
839. Engelsma, David J. *Protestant Reformed Theological Journal*, vol. 29, no. 2 (April 1996), pp. 27–75. **Notes**: Also available as electronic resource via: www.prca.org/prtj/apr96e.html#scripture (accessed February 14, 2007).
840. Foulkes, Francis. *Affirm*, vol. 3, no. 2 (Spring 1995), p. 35.
841. Garrett, James Leo, Jr. *Southwestern Journal of Theology*, vol. 38, no. 1 (Fall 1995), p. 52.

842. George, Timothy. "Reshaping Evangelical Theology." *Christianity Today*, vol. 38, no. 7 (June 20, 1994), pp. 37–38. **Notes**: Also reviews Bloesch's *A Theology of Word and Spirit*. **Heading**: A Venture of Daring Love.

843. Grider, J. Kenneth. "My Kind of Evangelical." *Perspectives*, vol. 9, no. 10 (December 1994), pp. 20–22.

844. Hannaford, Robert. *Theological Book Review*, vol. 7, no. 1 (October 1994), p. 18. **Notes**: One paragraph.

845. Heiser, W. Charles. *Theology Digest*, vol. 42, no. 1 (Spring 1995), p. 57. **Notes**: One paragraph.

846. Leahy, Frederick S. *Banner of Truth*, no. 385 (October 1995), pp. 29–30.

847. Lindbeck, George A. *Interpretation*, vol. 50, no. 3 (July 1996), pp. 324, 326.

848. Linney, Barry J. "The Word of God." *Proclaimers Journal*, no. 5 (1996), unpaged. **Notes**: Also reviews Bloesch's *A Theology of Word and Spirit*. **Headings**: Propositional Revelation—Revelation and the Authority of the Scriptures—Letter or Spirit—The Hermeneutical Problem.

849. McDonald, Kevin. *The Presbyterian Layman*, vol. 27, no. 5 (September–October 1994), p. 21. **Notes**: Also reviews Bloesch's *A Theology of Word and Spirit*. **Headings**: Human Tradition Judged by Scripture—Guidance in a Perplexing Time.

850. McKim, Donald K. *McKims' Musings* (March 15, 1994), p. 4.

851. McKim, Donald K. *The Reformed Review*, vol. 48, no. 1 (Autumn 1994), p. 57.

852. Meyers, Jeffrey J. "Evangelical Meltdown: It's the Same Old Song with a Different Beat since Barth Is Gone." *Contra Mundum*, no. 12 (Summer 1994), pp. 51–64. **Notes**: also available as an electronic resource via: www.contra-mundum.org/journals.html#Contra (accessed February 14, 2007). **Headings**: Barthian Epistemological Presuppositions—A Theological Divide—What and Where Is Revelation?—Is the Bible the Word of God?—*Loci Classici Neglecti*—Redefining Crucial Theological Terminology—Conveniently Indirect—To Err Is Human—The Locus of Authority—Myths and Old Wives' Tales—The Enemies of Progressive Evangelical Theology Revealed.

853. Morrison, John D. *Journal of the Evangelical Theological Society*, vol. 39, no. 3 (September 1996), pp. 505–6.

854. Parker, David. *Evangelical Review of Theology*, vol. 19, no. 1 (January–March 1995), pp. 87–89.

855. Parker, David. *Evangelical Review of Theology*, vol. 21, no. 3 (July–September 1997), pp. 270–71. **Notes**: Republication of the review that appeared in vol. 19.

856. Rogers, Jack. *Theology Today*, vol. 52, no. 1 (April 1995), p. 168. **Notes**: Also available as an electronic resource via: theologytoday.ptsem.edu (accessed February 14, 2007).

857. Walker, Larry L. *Mid-America Theological Journal*, vol. 19 (1995).**

858. Warden, Duane. *Restoration Quarterly*, vol. 38, no. 4 (Fourth Quarter 1996), p. 244.

859. Wells, David F. *Religious Studies Review*, vol. 20, no. 4 (October 1994), p. 307.

860. Wonders, Lance A. *The Covenant Quarterly*, vol. 52, no. 3 (August 1994), pp. 46–49.

861. Yates, John C. *The Evangelical Quarterly*, vol. 68, no. 2 (April 1996), pp. 173–76.

862. *New Testament Abstracts*, vol. 39, no. 1 (1995), p. 123. **Notes**: One paragraph.

The Holy Spirit (2000)

863. Bridges, William. *The Communicator*, vol. 15, no 6 (September 2001), p. 2. **Notes**: One paragraph.
864. Colyer, Elmer. *Pro Ecclesia*, vol. 11, no. 2 (Spring 2002), pp. 240–41.
865. Engelsma, David J. *Protestant Reformed Theological Journal*, vol. 34, no. 2 (April 2001), pp. 52–54. **Notes**: Also available as an electronic resource via: www.prca .org/prtj/apr2001.html#HolySpiritWorksGifts (accessed February 14, 2007).
866. Macchia, Frank D. "Toward a Theology of the Third Article in a Post–Barthian Era : A Pentecostal Review of Donald Bloesch's Pneumatology." *Journal of Pentecostal Theology*, vol. 10, no. 2 (2002), pp. 3–17.
867. McManus, Patrick. *Reformation & Revival*, vol. 11, no. 1 (Winter 2002), pp. 180–84.
868. Mohler, Richard Albert, Jr. *Preaching*, vol. 17, no. 4 (January–February 2002), p. 34. **Notes**: One paragraph.
869. Parker, David. *Evangelical Review of Theology*, vol. 26, no. 4 (October 2002), pp. 378–80.
870. Payne, Leanne. *Pastoral Care Ministries Newsletter* (Spring–Summer 2001), p. 6. **Notes**: One paragraph.
871. Smith, James K. A. *Pneuma*, vol. 24, no. 2 (Fall 2002), pp. 271–75.

How Karl Barth Changed My Mind (McKim: 1986)

872. Bolich, Gregory C. "More Influential Than When He Died." *Christianity Today*, vol. 31, no. 16 (November 6, 1987), p. 62.
873. McKim, Donald K. "How Karl Barth Changed Their Minds." *TSF Bulletin*, vol. 10, no. 1 (1986), pp. 5–8. **Notes**: Background on the writing of the book. **Headings**: Dogmatics—God—Jesus Christ—Politics—Divergencies—Barth Today.
874. Rumscheidt, H. Martin. *Religious Studies Review*, vol. 14, no. 1 (January 1988), p. 56.
875. Wallace, Mark I. *The Journal of Religion*, vol. 68, no. 1 (January 1988), pp. 125–26.
876. Wood, Ralph C. *The Christian Century*, vol. 104, no. 4 (February 4–11, 1987), pp. 136–37.
877. Wood, Ralph C. *Books & Religion*, vol. 16, no. 1 (Winter 1989), pp. 5, 26, 29–31. **Notes**: Review includes seven other books.

The Invaded Church (1975)

878. Barber, Cyril J. *The Minister's Library. Periodic Supplement #2.*—Grand Rapids, Mich.: Baker, 1978, p. 43. **Notes**: One paragraph.
879. Barr, Browne. "Offering Guidance." *The Christian Century*, vol. 93, no. 2 (June 23–30, 1976), pp. 603–5. **Notes**: Also reviews: *Handbook for Mission Groups* / Gordon Cosby.
880. Boice, James M. "The Secular Church." *Tenth*, (Spring April 1976), pp. 25–26. **Notes**: Also reviews: *The Trivialization of the United Presbyterian Church* / John R. Fry.

881. Caldwell, Frank H. *The Presbyterian Outlook*, vol. 158, no. 11 (March 15, 1976), p. 15.
882. Coleman, Lucien. *Review and Expositor*, vol. 74, no. 2 (Spring 1977), pp. 266–67.
883. Duhs, Robert C. *The Presbyterian Journal*, vol. 35, no. 3 (May 19, 1976), p. 18.
884. Heiser, W. Charles. *Theology Digest*, vol. 24, no. 1 (Spring 1976), pp. 78–79. **Notes**: One paragraph.
885. McIntosh, Duncan. *Foundations*, vol. 20, no. 2 (April–June 1977), pp. 181–83. **Notes**: Also reviews: *The Problem of Wine Skins : Church Structure in a Technological Age* / Howard A. Snyder.
886. Perrotta, Kevin F. *Pastoral Renewal*, vol. 3, no. 8 (February 1979), p. 67. **Notes**: One paragraph.
887. Sprinkle, Robert. *Good News*, vol. 9, no. 2 (January–February 1976), pp. 50–52.
888. White, Hugh L. *Eternity*, vol. 27, no. 11 (November 1976), pp. 66, 68.
889. Williams, Arthur. *Presbyterian Survey*, vol. 66, no. 9 (September 1976), p. 13.
890. *Christian Life*, vol. 37, no. 10 (February 1976), p. 30.
891. *His*, vol. 36, no. 5 (February 1976), p. 21. **Notes**: One paragraph.
892. *Religious Book Review*, vol. 7, no. 2 (Summer 1976), p. 61. **Notes**: One paragraph.
893. *Santa Cruz Sentinel (Santa Cruz, Calif.: 1956)*, vol. 120, no. 25 (January 30, 1976), p. 17.

Is the Bible Sexist? (1982)

894. De Vries, Michael. *Calvin Theological Journal*, vol. 18, no. 2 (November 1983), p. 281. **Notes**: Two paragraphs.
895. Freeman, Martha. *The Oak Kin*, vol. 10, no. 7 (March 30, 1983), p. 1.
896. Gabe, Catherine. "Dubuque Theologian Disputes Claims Bible Is Sexist." *The Telegraph Herald*, vol. 146, no. 233 (Friday, October 1, 1982), p. 7.
897. Gerhart, Mary. *Commonweal*, vol. 110, no. 19 (November 4, 1983), pp. 598–99.
898. Greenfield, Guy. *Southwestern Journal of Theology*, vol. 27, no. 1 (Fall 1984), p. 70.
899. Greenfield, Guy. *Light* (March 1985), p. 6.**
900. Hall, Michael. *United Evangelical Action*, vol. 41, no. 3 (Fall 1982), pp. 36–37.
901. Heiser, W. Charles. *Theology Digest*, vol. 31, no. 2 (Summer 1984), pp. 157–58.
902. Jeambey, Bob. "Dubuque Theologian Refutes Claims of Biblical Sexism." *Presbyterian Life and Times*, vol. 1, no. 9 (December 1982), pp. 4–5. **Notes**: Interview with DGB.
903. Knick, W. Clay. *TSF Bulletin*, vol. 7, no. 2 (November–December 1983), p. 22.
904. Leigh, David L. "Beyond Name Calling." *Brigade Leader*, vol. 24, no. 2 (Winter 1983–1984), pp. 26, 30, 25 [*sic*].
905. Lutz, Ann. *Living Faith*, vol. 3, no. 3 (Fall 1982), pp. 29–31.
906. Maddox, Randy L. *The Christian Century*, vol. 99, no. 36 (November 17, 1982), pp. 1179–80.
907. Maddox, Randy L. "The Necessity of Recognizing Distinctions: Lessons from Evangelical Critiques of Christian Feminist Theology." *Christian Scholar's Review*, vol. 17, no. 3 (1988), pp. 307–23.
908. Pamp, Barbara. "One Step Forward, Two Steps Back." *Daughters of Sarah*, vol. 10, no. 4 (July–August 1984), pp. 11–12.

909. Payne, Leanne. *Pastoral Care Ministries [Newsletter]* (December 4, 1985), pp. 5–6. **Notes**: The Newsletter does not carry a volume or issue designation. Also reviews *The Battle for the Trinity*.
910. Reimers, Adrian. *New Heaven/New Earth*, vol. 1, no. 4 (April 1983), pp. 10–11.
911. Schmid, Donna. *Christian Standard*, vol. 117, no. 44 (October 31, 1982), p. 22 (1014).
912. Scholer, David M. *Update (Evangelical Women's Caucus)*, vol. 10, no. 2 (Summer 1986), pp. 14–15. **Notes**: Also reviews *The Battle for the Trinity*.
913. Sims, Jim. *Mission Journal*, vol. 18, no. 5 (November 1984), pp. 26–27.
914. Smallman, William H. *The Baptist Bulletin*, vol. 48, no. 6 (December 1982), p. 31. **Notes**: One paragraph.
915. Soley, Ginny. "Circular Word Games and Myopic Worldviews: Sexism and Scripture." *Sojourners*, vol. 12, no. 3 (March 1983), pp. 41–42. **Notes**: Also reviews: *The Language of Canaan and the Grammar of Feminism* / Vernard Eller.
916. Spring, Beth. *Today's Christian Woman*, vol. 4, no. 4 (Winter 1982–1983), pp. 24, 27, 30.
917. Wiebe, Katie Funk. "A God of 'Power, Initiative, Superordination.'" *Provident Book Finder*, vol. 13, no. 4 (January–February 1982), p. 31.
918. Wiebe, Katie Funk. *The Other Side*, vol. 19, no. 11, issue 146 (November 1983), pp. 28, 30–31. **Notes**: Also reviews: *The Language of Canaan and the Grammar of Feminism* / Vernard Eller.
919. Wimbish, Dave. "Sexist Angle Gets Rebuttal." *Charisma*, vol. 8, no. 7 (March 1983), p. 94.
920. Yarbrough, Robert. *Journal of the Evangelical Theological Society*, vol. 26, no. 4 (December 1983), pp. 474–76.
921. *Bookstore Journal*, vol. 15, no. 9 (September 1982), p. 160. **Notes**: Article signed: L. K. T.
922. *Christian Life*, vol. 44, no. 4 (August 1982), p. 62. **Notes**: One paragraph.
923. *Eternity*, vol. 33, no. 7–8 (July–August 1982), p. 40. **Notes**: One paragraph.
924. *Good News (Dubuque, Iowa)* (September 13, 1982), p. 2. **Notes**: Item carries no volume or issue designation.
925. *Miami Herald (Miami, Fla.)* (October 22, 1983), p. 20A.
926. *New Testament Abstracts*, vol. 27, no. 1 (1983) p. 107. **Notes**: One paragraph.
927. *The Times (San Mateo, Calif.)*, vol. 82, no. 116 (May 15, 1982), p. 15.

Jesus Christ (1997)

928. Brug, John F. *Wisconsin Lutheran Quarterly*, vol. 96, no. 2 (Spring 1999), p. 157.
929. Daniels, David S. *CBA Marketplace*, vol. 31, no. 1 (January 1998), p. 96.
930. Engelsma, David J. *Protestant Reformed Theological Journal*, vol. 32, no. 1 (November 1998), pp. 85–87. **Notes**: Also available as an electronic resource via: www.prca.org/prtj/nov98.html#AAJEsusChrist (accessed February 14, 2007).
931. Garrett, James Leo, Jr. *Southwestern Journal of Theology*, vol. 42, no. 1 (Fall 1999), pp. 92–93.
932. Heiser, W. Charles. *Theology Digest*, vol. 45, no. 4 (Winter 1998), p. 357.

933. Hogg, Edward E. *Global Journal of Classical Theology*, vol. 1, no. 1 (September 1998), www.trinitysem.edu/journal/hoggrevu.html (accesed February 14, 2007). **Notes**: Available as an electronic resource only.
934. Kennington, John. *Fellowship Today* (April 1998), p. 14. **Notes**: One paragraph.
935. Kovach, Stephen D. *Faith and Mission*, vol. 16, no. 2 (Spring 1999), pp. 121–24. **Notes**: Also reviews: *The Person of Christ* / Donald Macleod; and *Christology* / Hans Schwarz.
936. Lewis, Gordon R. *Themelios*, vol. 23, no. 3 (June 1998), pp. 100–102.
937. Parker, David C. *Evangelical Review of Theology*, vol. 23, no. 2 (April 1999), pp. 184–87.
938. Petersen, F. Scott. *The Reformed Review*, vol. 53, no. 1 (Autumn 1999), pp. 76–77.
939. Wonders, Lance A. M. *The Reformed Review*, vol. 52, no. 1 (Autumn 1998), pp. 65–66.

Jesus Is Victor (1976)

940. Begley, John J. *Review for Religious*, vol. 36, no. 6 (November 1977), p. 963.
941. Dripps, Philip M. *Circuit Rider*, vol. 1, no. 3 (December 1976–January 1977), p. 17.
942. Grider, J. Kenneth. *The Seminary Tower* (Spring 1977), p. 10. **Notes**: The periodical carries no issue or volume number.
943. Guder, Darrell L. *Christian Scholar's Review*, vol. 8, no. 2 (Fall 1978), pp. 165–67. **Notes**: Also reviews: *Karl Barth, His Life from Letters and Autobiographical Texts* / Eberhard Busch; and *Fragments Grave and Gay* / Karl Barth; and *Karl Barth and Radical Politics* / edited and translated by George Hunsinger.
944. Heiser, W. Charles. *Theology Digest*, vol. 25, no. 1 (Spring 1977), p. 74.
945. Lawler, Michael G. *Cross and Crown*, vol. 29, no. 3 (September 1977), pp. 302–4.
946. Lemmon, Eric. "Karl Barth's Continuing Relevance." *Christianity Today*, vol. 21, no. 3 (September 9, 1977), pp. 57–58 (1285–86).
947. McIlhiney, David B. *The New Review of Books and Religion*, vol. 1, no. 5 (January 1977), pp. 9–10.
948. Mueller, David L. *Review and Expositor*, vol. 74, no. 4 (Fall 1977), pp. 575–76.
949. Nelson, James S. *The Covenant Quarterly*, vol. 35, no. 4 (November 1977), pp. 35–38. **Notes**: Also reviews: *The Doctrine of the Trinity* / Eberhard Jungel.
950. Osterhaven, M. Eugene. *The Reformed Review*, vol. 30, no. 2 (Winter 1977), pp. 151–52.
951. Pennington, Chester A. *Iliff Review*, vol. 34, no. 1 (Winter 1977), p. 65.
952. Rogers, Jack. *Religious Studies Review*, vol. 3, no. 4 (October 1977), p. 259.
953. Rossow, Francis C. *Concordia Journal*, vol. 3, no. 5 (September 1977), pp. 231–32.
954. Scaer, David P. *Concordia Theological Quarterly*, vol. 41, no. 2 (April 1977), pp. 102–3.
955. Short, Robert. *Religion in Life*, vol. 47, no. 1 (Spring 1978), pp. 121–22.
956. Trost, Frederick. "A Pointer to Barth." *The Reformed Journal*, vol. 28, no. 8 (August 1978), pp. 23–24.
957. Tuttle, Robert G., Jr. *Anglican Theological Review*, vol. 60, no. 2 (April 1978), pp. 226–28. **Notes**: Also reviews: *Karl Barth, His Life from Letters and Autobi-*

ographical Texts / Eberhard Busch; and *Karl Barth and Radical Politics* / George Hunsinger.

958. Webber, Robert E. "Karl Barth's Capitulation to Culture." *New Oxford Review*, vol. 44, no. 10 (December 1977), pp. 20–21.

959. Wells, David Falconer. *Trinity Journal*, vol. 6, no. 1 (Spring 1977), pp. 110–12.

960. Wood, Charles M. *Perkins Journal*, vol. 31, no. 2 (Winter 1978), pp. 42–43.

961. *Baptist Standard*, vol. 89, no. 2 (January 12, 1977), p. 13. **Notes**: One paragraph. Article signed: W. J. N.

962. *Books for Pastors* (Spring 1977).**

The Last Things (2004)

963. Colyer, Elmer M. *Pro Ecclesia*, vol. 14, no. 3 (Summer 2005), pp. 372–73.

964. Deddo, Gary. "*The Last Things* Completes Donald G. Bloesch's Christian Foundations." *Academic Alert*, vol. 13, no. 2 (Spring 2004), pp. 1, 3. **Notes**: Interview with DGB.

965. Kushiner, James M. *Touchstone*, vol. 18, no. 5 (June 2005), p. 47.**

966. Lewis, John P. *Reformation & Revival*, vol. 14, no. 1 (2005), p. 195–203. **Headings**: Appreciations—Reservations—Conclusion.

967. Parker, David. *Evangelical Review of Theology*, vol. 29, no. 3 (July 2005), pp. 284–88.

968. Resch, Dustin. *The Canadian Evangelical Review*, no. 29 (Spring 2005), pp. 72–75.**

The Orthodox Evangelicals (Webber: 1978)

969. Bechtel, Paul. "Worth Watching." *Christian Bookseller*, vol. 25, no. 5 (May 1979), pp. 23.

970. Daane, James. "An Unheard Summons?" *The Reformed Journal*, vol. 29, no. 11 (November 1979), pp. 28–29.

971. Dayton, Donald. W. *Eternity*, vol. 30, no. 7 (July 1979), pp. 30–31.

972. Doulos, Bill Lane. "Opening Closed Doors." *Sojourners*, vol. 8, no. 5 (May 1979), pp. 32–33, 35.

973. Heiser, W. Charles. *Theology Digest*, vol. 27, no. 3 (Fall 1979), p. 285. **Notes**: One paragraph.

974. Hunt, Boyd. *Southwestern Journal of Theology*, vol. 23, no. 2 (Spring 1981), pp. 121–22.

975. Kuhnle, Howard A. *Church Management*, vol. 55, no. 6 (April 1979), p. 25 (New Books).

976. Matzek, Richard. *The New Review of Books and Religion*, vol. 3, no. 10 (June 1979), p. 20.

977. Mouw, Richard J. *Calvin Theological Journal*, vol. 16, no. 1 (April 1981), p. 133. **Notes**: One paragraph.

978. Oliver, John W. *Christian Scholar's Review*, vol. 10, no. 2 (1981), pp. 167–68.

979. Rice, Richard. *Religious Studies Review*, vol. 7, no. 3 (July 1981), pp. 248–49.

980. Rutler, George William "Elaborating the Chicago Call." *New Oxford Review*, vol. 46, no. 6, (July–August 1979), pp. 22–24.

981. Twombly, Charles. *Christianity Today*, vol. 23, no. 23 (October 5, 1979), pp. 48, 50 (1337, 1339).
982. Walvoord, J. F. *Bibliotheca Sacra*, vol. 136, no. 544 (October–December 1979), pp. 359–60.

Reform of the Church (1970)

983. Barber, Cyril J. *The Minister's Library.*—Grand Rapids, Mich.: Baker, 1974, p. 290. **Notes**: One paragraph.
984. Bassett, Paul Merritt. *The Seminary Tower* (Fall 1970), pp. 6–7. **Notes**: Periodical bears no volume or issue numbers.
985. Edge, Findley B. *Review and Expositor*, vol. 67, no. 4 (Fall 1970), pp. 520–21.
986. Ernsberger, David J. "Concerned Conservative." *The Christian Century*, vol. 88, no. 16 (April 21, 1971), pp. 507–8.
987. Ernsberger, David J. *Trends*, vol. 3, no. 3 (November 1970), pp. 24–25.
988. Gaebelein, Frank E. "Forthright Views on Reform." *Eternity*, vol. 22, no. 1 (January 1971), p. 40.
989. Gerstner, John H. "A Changing Church." *Christianity Today*, vol. 14, no. 19 (June 19, 1970), p. 25 (865).
990. Grimes, Howard. *Perkins Journal*, vol. 28, no. 1 (Fall 1974), pp. 48–49. **Notes**: Also reviews Bloesch's *Wellsprings of Renewal*.
991. Groen, J., Rev. *Calvinist-Contact*, nos. 963–64 (July 30–August 6, 1970), p. 10 (From the Bookshelf).
992. Hanko, Herman. *The Standard Bearer*, vol. 46, no. 14 (April 15, 1970), pp. 332–33.
993. Harris, George R. *The Wesleyan Advocate*, vol. 128, no. 20 (October 5, 1970), p. 18 (398).
994. Hellwig, Monika. *Theological Studies*, vol. 32, no. 1 (March 1971), pp. 155–56.
995. Hill, John Eddie. *The Presbyterian Journal*, vol. 29, nos. 10–11 (July 8, 1970), p. 28.
996. Holbrook, Joseph C., Jr. *The Reformed Review*, vol. 24, no. 1 (Autumn 1970), pp. 31–33.
997. Johnson, Gilbert H. "Solutions to Current Church Problems." *The Alliance Witness*, vol. 105, no. 14 (July 8, 1970), p. 14.
997a. Konrad, George G. "A Review of Books on Church Renewal," *Direction*, vol. 1, no. 2 (April 1972), pp. 58–68. **Notes**: Discusses several books. Also available as an electronic resource via: www.directionjournal.org/article/?16 (accessed February 14, 2007)
998. Magnuson, Norris. *Bethel Seminary Journal*, vol. 20, no. 2 (Winter 1972), p. 25. **Notes**: Also reviews: *Set the Church Afire!* / Wayne Dehoney.
999. Margerie, Bertrand de. Science et Esprit, vol. 23 (1971), pp. 269–72.
1000. Margerie, Bertrand de. *Journal of Ecumenical Studies*, 8, no. 3 (Summer 1971), pp. 649–50.
1001. McBrien, Richard P. *Commonweal*, vol. 93, no. 16 (January 22, 1971), p. 404.
1002. Myers, Albert E. *Lutheran Quarterly*, vol. 24, no. 4 (November 1972), pp. 444–45.

1003. Perkins, James C. *Church Management*, vol. 46, no. 10 (July 1970), pp. 45–46.
1004. Ramsey, John R. *The Living Church*, vol. 160, no. 21 (May 24, 1970), p. 14.
1005. Rosendall, Brendan. *Worship*, vol. 44, no. 8 (October 1970), pp. 506–7.
1006. Scaer, David P. *The Springfielder*, vol. 34, no. 2 (September 1970), pp. 159–61. **Notes**: Cover of issue identifies this as vol. 35 but date, etc., confirms this as vol. 34.
1007. Schakelaar, Eva. *Bookstore Journal*, vol. 3, no. 5 (May 1970), p. 41. **Notes**: One paragraph.
1008. Stalter, Edwin. *Provident Book Finder*, vol. 1, no. 1 (September 1970), p. 25.
1009. Stanger, Frank Bateman. *The Asbury Seminarian*, vol. 24, no. 4 (October 1970), pp. 24–25.
1010. Stuenkel, Omar. *Lutheran Witness Reporter*, vol. 6, no. 12 (June 21, 1970), p. 10. **Notes**: One paragraph.
1011. Tamminga, Edward J. *The Banner*, vol. 106, no. 18 (April 30, 1971), p. 25.
1012. Walvoord, John F. *Bibliotheca Sacra*, vol. 128, no. 510 (April–June 1971), p. 159.
1013. *Book Review Digest*, vol. 67 (1971), p. 129. **Notes**: Synopsis of Ernsberger (item 986) and McBrien (item 1000).
1014. *Christian Heritage*, vol. 31, no. 5 (May 1970), p. 31.
1015. *Christian Life*, vol. 32, no. 2 (June 1970), pp. 84–85. **Notes**: "Call to Unity."
1016. *Evening Reporter (Galt, Ontario)* (May 16, 1970), p. 22.
1017. *Good News*, vol. 4, no. 3 (January–March 1971), p. 54.
1018. *Harvester*, vol. 49 (old series, vol. 70), no. 6 (June 1970), p. 91. **Notes**: One paragraph.
1019. *The Moravian*, vol. 115, no. 6 (June 1970), p. 32. "The Church."
1020. *The New Life News*, vol. 12, no. 2 (March–April 1970), p. 6. **Notes**: One paragraph.
1021. *The Publishers Weekly*, vol. 196, no. 12 (September 22, 1969), p. 45. **Notes**: One paragraph.
1022. United Church of Christ. Iowa Conference. *UCC Reporter*, vol. 7, no. 6 (March 1970), p. 7.

Roman Catholicism (Armstrong: 1994)

1023. Garrett, James Leo, Jr. *Southwestern Journal of Theology*, vol. 41, no. 1 (Fall 1998), pp. 125–26.

Servants of Christ (1971)

1024. Andrews, Mary M. "Deaconesses Today." *The Australian Church Record*, no. 1509 (March 23, 1972), p. 7.
1025. Heiser, W. Charles. *Theology Digest*, vol. 20, no. 2 (Summer 1972), pp. 164–65.
1026. Schelp, A. W. *The Lutheran Witness, Part 1*, vol. 91, no. 10 (July 23, 1972), p. 28 (324).
1027. *Christianity Today*, vol. 16, no. 11 (March 3, 1972), p. 23 (515). **Notes**: One paragraph.

The Struggle of Prayer (1980)

1028. Anderson, Dan. *Good News (Dubuque, Iowa)* (September 30, 1980), p. 7. **Notes**: Periodical bears no volume or issue number.
1029. Ayers, James. *Ministry*, vol. 63, no. 7 (July 1990), p. 26 (Biblio file).
1030. Barber, Cyril J. *The Minister's Library. Periodic Supplement #4.*—Grand Rapids, Mich.: Baker, 1982, p. 34. **Notes**: One paragraph.
1031. Chumbley, Ken. "Neither Rapture nor Ritual." *Sojourners*, 10, no. 6 (June 1981), pp. 34–35.
1032. Crupper, John. *The Theological Educator*, vol. 12, no. 1 (Fall 1981), pp. 77–78.
1033. Donnelly, Doris. *Theology Today*, vol. 38, no. 2 (July 1981), p. 279. **Notes**: Also available as an electronic resource via: theologytoday.ptsem.edu (accessed February 14, 2007).
1034. Friberg, Nils C. *The Bethel Seminarian*, vol. 30, no. 3 (Fall 1982), p. 2.
1035. Heiser, W. Charles. *Theology Digest*, vol. 28, no. 4 (Winter 1980), p. 371.
1036. Hosmer, Rachel. *Spirituality Today*, vol. 33, no. 3 (September 1981), pp. 273–74.
1037. Johnston, Robert K. "An Evangelical Weathervane." *The Reformed Journal*, vol. 31, no. 10 (October 1981), pp. 27–28.
1038. Marsh, Douglas S. *Library Journal*, vol. 105, no. 18 (October 15, 1980), p. 2216.
1039. Maxwell, Kent D. "An Evangelical Theology of Prayer." *Christianity Today*, vol. 25, no. 21 (December 11, 1981), pp. 76–77 (1717–18).
1040. Oglesby, William B., Jr. *TSF Bulletin*, vol. 5, no. 3 (January–February 1982), p. 25.
1041. Paul, William E., Jr. *Military Chaplains' Review*, vol. DA Pam 165-131 (Fall 1981), p. 132. **Notes**: Federal document.
1042. Phelan, John E., Jr. "Reviving Evangelical Spirituality." *New Oxford Review*, vol. 49, no. 5 (June 1982), pp. 26, 28.
1043. Schwar, Kathy. "Author Focuses on 'Struggle for Prayer'" *The Telegraph Herald*, vol. 144, no. 297 (Sunday, December 14, 1980), p. 26.
1044. Schwarzer, Anneliese. "Timeless & Timely: A Selection of Noteworthy and/or Useful Religious Titles Published in the Last Year." *Library Journal*, vol. 106, no. 18 (October 15, 1981), pp. 1993–96. **Notes**: One paragraph on DGB: p. 1994.
1045. Stillman, James A. "Touched by Grace." *The Christian Century*, vol. 97, no. 37 (November 19, 1980), p. 1134.
1046. *Kirkus Reviews*, vol. 48 (July 15, 1980), p. 948.

Theological Notebook: Vol. 1, 1960–1964; Vol. 2, 1964–1968

1047. Buis, Harry. *The Reformed Review*, vol. 44, no. 3 (Spring 1991), p. 265.
1048. Clendenin, Daniel B. *Journal of the Evangelical Theological Society*, vol. 34, no. 2 (June 1991), pp. 269–70.
1049. Farrell, John J. "A Spiritual Journal." *The Homiletic and Pastoral Review*, vol. 92, no. 10 (July 1992), pp. 78–79.
1050. Richardson, Kurt A. *Perspectives in Religious Studies*, vol. 18, no. 3 (Fall 1991), pp. 267–70.
1051. Taylor, Lillian McCulloch. *The Presbyterian Outlook*, vol. 173, no. 40 (November 18, 1991), pp. 16, 18.
1052. *Touchstone (Chicago, Ill.)*, vol. 3, no. 4 (Winter 1990), pp. 42–43.

A Theology of Word and Spirit (1992)

1053. Buis, Harry. *The Reformed Review*, vol. 46, no. 3 (Spring 1993), p. 254.

1054. Clapp, Rodney. "A Theology for Confronting the Cultural Captivity of Evangelicalism." *Academic Alert*, vol. 2, no. 1 (Winter 1993), pp. 1–2, 4. **Notes**: Interview with DGB.

1055. Colyer, Elmer M. *Journal for Christian Theological Research*, vol. 1 (1996). **Notes**: Available as an electronic resource via: www.luthersem.edu/ctrf/JCTR/Vol01/Colyer.htm (accessed February 14, 2007).

1056. Ellingsen, Mark. *Dialog*, vol. 32, no. 3 (Summer 1993), pp. 238–39.

1057. Engelsma, David J. *Protestant Reformed Theological Journal*, vol. 27, no. 2 (April 1994), pp. 69–70.

1058. Franke, John R. *Journal of the Evangelical Theological Society*, vol. 40, no. 3 (September 1997), pp. 491–493.

1059. Garrett, James Leo, Jr. *Southwestern Journal of Theology*, vol. 37, no. 3 (Summer 1995), p. 50.

1060. George, Timothy. "Reshaping Evangelical Theology." *Christianity Today*, vol. 38, no. 7 (June 20, 1994), pp. 37–38. **Notes**: Also reviews: Bloesch's *Holy Scripture*. **Heading**: A Venture of Daring Love.

1061. Hart, Trevor A. *The Evangelical Quarterly*, vol. 68, no. 2 (April 1996), pp. 171–73.

1062. Heim, S. Mark. *Religious Studies Review*, vol. 19, no. 3 (July 1993), p. 239.

1063. Heiser, W. Charles. *Theology Digest*, vol. 41, no. 1 (Spring 1994), p. 57 (TD Book Survey).

1064. Hutchens, S. M. *Touchstone (Chicago, Ill.)*, vol. 6, no. 1 (Winter 1993), pp. 32–33.

1065. Johnson, Wendell G. *The Christian Librarian*, vol. 38, no. 3 (September 1995), p. 109.

1066. Krapfl, Mike. "The Word & the Spirit : Author Writes Series on Theological Principles." *The Telegraph Herald*, vol. 157, no. 2 (Saturday, January 2, 1993), p. 10A.

1067. Linney, Barry J. "The Word of God." *Proclaimers Journal*, no. 5 (1996). **Notes**: Unpaged. Also reviews: Bloesch's *Holy Scripture*. **Headings**: Propositional Revelation—Revelation and the Authority of the Scriptures—Letter or Spirit—The Hermeneutical Problem.

1068. Mar, Gary. "What Evangelicalism Needs." *New Oxford Review*, vol. 61, no. 5, (June, 1994), pp. 28–29. **Notes**: Also reviews: *No Place for Truth* / David F. Wells; and *Revisioning Evangelical Theology* / Stanley J. Grenz.

1069. McDonald, Kevin. *The Presbyterian Layman*, vol. 27, no. 5 (September–October 1994), p. 21. **Notes**: Also reviews Bloesch's *Holy Scripture*. **Headings**: Human Tradition Judged by Scripture—Guidance for a Perplexing Time.

1070. McKim, Don. *McKims' Musings*, vol. 1, no. 14 (December 15, 1992), pp. 2–3.

1071. Muller, Richard A. *Calvin Theological Journal*, vol. 29, no. 1 (April 1994), p. 307.

1072. Parker, David. *Evangelical Review of Theology*, vol. 17, no. 4 (October–December 1993), pp. 509–12.

1073. Wonders, Lance A. *The Covenant Quarterly*, vol. 51, no. 2 (May 1993), pp. 48–50.

1074. *First Things*, no. 30 (February 1993), p. 60 (Briefly noted). **Notes**: Also reviews: *Life in the Spirit* / Thomas C. Oden. Also available as an electronic resource via: www.firstthings.com/ftissues/ft9302/reviews/briefly.html# Theology (accessed February 14, 2007).

1075. *Preaching*, vol. 8, no. 5 (March–April 1993), p. 54. **Notes**: Article signed: J. M. D.

Wellsprings of Renewal (1974)

1076. Barber, Cyril J. *The Minister's Library. Periodic Supplement #1.*—Grand Rapids, Mich.: Baker, 1975, p. 28. **Notes**: One paragraph.
1077. Campbell, Jerry D. *Library Journal*, vol. 99, no. 16 (September 15, 1974), p. 2164.
1078. Cousins, Peter. *The Witness (London, England)*, vol. 105, no. 1249 (January 1975), p. 31.
1079. Durnbaugh, Donald. F. *Encounter*, vol. 37, no. 3 (Summer 1976), pp. 311–12.
1080. Green, Harold Frederic. *The Times (Gainesville, Ga.)*, vol. 29, no. 148 (July 16, 1975), p. 13A. **Notes**: One paragraph.
1081. Grimes, Howard. *Perkins Journal*, vol. 28, no. 1 (Fall 1974), pp. 48–59. **Notes**: Also reviews Bloesch's *The Reform of the Church*.
1082. Heiser, W. Charles. *Theology Digest*, vol. 22, no. 3 (Autumn 1974), p. 263. **Notes**: One paragraph.
1083. Kiewiet, John J. *Southwestern Journal of Theology*, vol. 18, no. 1 (Fall 1975), p. 117.
1084. Logan, John B. *Scottish Journal of Theology*, vol. 29, no. 1 (February 1976), p. 95.
1085. Mills, Watson E. *Lutheran Quarterly*, vol. 27, no. 1 (February 1975), pp. 81–82.
1086. Mulica, Olive Mae. "Community Renewal." *The Review of Books and Religion*, vol. 4, no. 1 (September 1974), p. 7.
1087. Noble, Lowell. "Community Life and Renewal." *Eternity*, vol. 26, no. 2 (February 1975), pp. 40–41. **Notes**: Also reviews: *Living Together in a World Falling Apart* / Dave and Neta Jackson.
1088. Payne, Harold W. *The Virginia Seminary Journal*, vol. 27, no. 1 (January 1975), pp. 37–38.
1089. Porter, Laurence E. *The Evangelical Quarterly*, vol. 48, no. 1 (January–March 1976), pp. 53–54.
1090. Studer, Gerald C. *Mennonite Weekly Review*, vol. 54, no. 5 (January 29, 1976), p. [4]. **Notes**: Also published: *Provident Book Finder*, September–October 1975.
1091. Studer, Gerald C. *Provident Book Finder*, vol. 6, no. 2 (September–October 1975), p. 17. **Notes**: Also published: *Mennonite Weekly Review* (January 29, 1976).
1092. Tinder, Donald. "History of Christianity." *Christianity Today*, vol. 19, no. 12 (May 14, 1975), pp. 33–40 (589–94) (Significant Books of '74). **Notes**: DGB one paragraph, p. 35 (591).
1093. Weiser, Frederick S. *Lutheran Forum*, vol. 8, no. 3 (August 1974), p. 24.
1094. *The Christian Century*, vol. 91, no. 16 (April 24, 1974), p. 458 (Section: *This Week's Arrivals*).
1095. *Christianity Today*, vol. 18, no. 18 (June 7, 1974), p. 34 (1062). **Notes**: One paragraph.
1096. *The Prophetic Witness*, vol. 58, no. 2 (February 1975), p. 51 (The Bookshelf). **Notes**: One paragraph.

1097. *Reformed Theological Review*, vol. 33, no. 3 (September–December 1974), p. 92. **Notes**: One paragraph.
1098. *Transformation, United Christian Ashram Quarterly*, vol. 15, no. 2 (Summer 1974), p. 21.

RESPONSES TO SPECIFIC ARTICLES

"Betraying the Reformation" (1996)

1099. Neal, Marshall. *Biblical Viewpoint*, vol. 31, no. 1 (April 1997), pp. 106–8.

"Beyond Patriarchalism & Feminism" (1990)

1100. Jensen, Kenneth S. "Anti-Nicene Speculation." *Touchstone (Chicago, Ill.)*, vol. 4, no. 2 (March 1991), p. 2.

"Penetrating the World with the Gospel" (2002)

1101. Boydston, Brad. *The Ooze : Conversation for the Journey*. **Notes**: Available as an electronic resource via: www.theooze.com/articles/article.cfm?id'483 (accessed February 14, 2007).

"The Renewal of Theology" (1999)

1102. Webster, Jefferson P. *Bibliotheca Sacra*, vol. 156, no. 624 (October–December 1999), pp. 488–89.

"Whatever Became of Neo-Orthodoxy?"

1103. Witmer, John A. *Bibliotheca Sacra*, vol. 132, no. 526 (April–June 1975), pp. 178–79. **Notes**: Also reviews: "An American Revival of Karl Barth?" / Donald W. Dayton in *The Reformed Journal* (October–November, 1974).

CRITIQUES

1104. Allen, David L. "A Tale of Two Roads: Homiletics and Biblical Authority." *Journal of the Evangelical Theological Society*, vol. 43, no. 3 (September 2000), pp. 489–515. **Notes**: Cf. esp. pp. 493–97.
1105. Allen, Martha Sawyer, "Finding the Bible's 'Silent Voices.'" *Star Tribune (Minneapolis)* (September 19, 1993), p. 8A.
1106. Bolich, Gregory G. "Bloesch, Invaluable Ally and Useful Foil" in Bolich's *Karl Barth & Evangelicalism.*—Downers Grove, Ill. : InterVarsity, c1980, pp. 89–91. **Notes**: The title refers to Bloesch's assessment of Barth, not Bolich's asssessment of Bloesch.

1107. Briggs, Kenneth A. *New York Times* (November 18, 1984), p. SM106.
1108. Burton, Bryan D. "Renewing Our Minds: An Interview with Donald G. Bloesch." *reNews*, vol. 4, no. 4 (November 1993), pp. 3–4.
1109. Callahan, James. "Bloesch, Donald G." *Evangelical Dictionary of Theology.*— 2nd ed.—Grand Rapids, Mich.: Baker, 2001, p. 175.
1110. Colyer, Elmer M., Jr. "Donald G. Bloesch & His Career" in *Evangelical Theology in Transition : Theologians in Dialogue with Donald Bloesch* / edited by Elmer M. Colyer.—Downers Grove, Ill. : InterVarsity, 1999, pp. 11–17, 212–15. **Headings**: Early Years—Theological Education—Teaching Career— Publications—The Man behind the Persona.
1111. Colyer, Elmer M., Jr. "A Theology of Word and Spirit: Donald Bloesch's Theological Method." *Journal for Christian Theological Research*, vol. 1, no. 1 (1996). Also available as an electronic resource via: www.luthersem.edu/ ctrf/JCTR/Vol01/Colyer.htm (accessed February 14, 2007). **Notes**: Response by DGB available as an online resource via: www.luthersem.edu/ ctrf/JCTR/Vol01/Bloesch.htm (accessed February 14, 2007).
1112. Conn, Harvie M. "Evangelical Feminism: Reflections on the State of the 'Union,' part 2." *TSF Bulletin*, vol. 8, no. 3 (January–February 1985), pp. 18–21. **Notes**: Part 1 appeared in *TSF Bulletin*, vol. 8, no. 2, but did not discuss DGB per se. **Headings**: Where Do We Go from Here?—A Third Evangelical Option—A Study Agenda for the Future.
1113. Crampton, W. Gary, "The Neo-Orthodoxy of Donald Bloesch," *The Trinity Review*, no. 126 (August 1995), pp. 1–4. **Notes**: Also available as electronic resource via: www.trinityfoundation.org/PDF/126a-TheNeo-Orthodoxyof-DonaldBloesch.pdf (accessed February 14, 2007).
1114. Dayton, Donald W. "Karl Barth and Evangelicalism: The Varieties of a Sibling Rivalry." *TSF Bulletin*, vol. 8, no. 5 (1985), pp. 18–23. **Headings**: Evangelicalism as Fidelity to Reformation Themes—Evangelicalism as Expressed in the Pietist Traditions—Evangelicalism as the Defense of Orthodoxy.
1115. Deddo, Gary W. "Shapers of Modern Evangelical Thought: Donald Bloesch," *Religious and Theological Studies Fellowship Bulletin*, no. 6 (January–February 1995), pp. 17–19.
1116. Dorrien, Gary. *The Remaking of Evangelical Theology.*—1st ed.—Louisville, Ky.: Westminster, John Knox, c1998. **Notes**: Cf. especially "Evangelicalism beyond Modernity: Donald Bloesch's Catholic (Neo)Orthodoxy" pp. 189–93.
1117. Dulles, Avery Robert. "Donald Bloesch on Revelation" in *Evangelical Theology in Transition: Theologians in Dialogue with Donald Bloesch* / edited by Elmer M. Colyer.—Downers Grove, Ill. : InterVarsity, 1999, pp. 61–76, 219–21. **Headings**: Five Models—Revelation and History—Revelation and Doctrine—Revelation and Experience—Revelation and New Awareness—Revelation and Personal Encounter—Summary Evaluation—The Bible, Church, and Tradition—Faith and Reason—Implicit Faith—Revelation and Symbol—Conclusion.
1118. Edwards, James R. "Does God Really Want to Be Called 'Father'?" *Christianity Today*, vol. 30, no. 3 (February 21, 1986), pp. 27–30. **Notes**: Reference to DGB, two paragraphs.
1119. Erickson, Millard J. "Donald Bloesch's Doctrine of Scripture" in *Evangelical Theology in Transition: Theologians in Dialogue with Donald Bloesch* / edited by

Elmer M. Colyer.—Downers Grove, Ill.: InterVarsity, 1999, pp. 77–97, 221–24. **Headings**: His Theological Orientation—The Crisis in Biblical Authority—Revelation—The Inspiration of Scripture—Inerrancy—Interpretation of the Bible—The Role of Rationalism—Bloesch's Presuppositions—Evaluation of Bloesch's View.

1120. *Evangelical Theology in Transition: Theologians in Dialogue with Donald Bloesch* / edited by Elmer M. Colyer.—Downers Grove, Ill.: InterVarsity, 1999. **Notes**: For a more detailed description of the contents, cf. the citations in this section for each of the contributors. **Contents**: DONALD G. BLOESCH & HIS CAREER / Elmer M. Colyer—LOCATING DONALD G. BLOESCH IN THE EVANGELICAL LANDSCAPE / Roger E. Olson—"FIDEISTIC REVELATIONALISM": DONALD BLOESCH'S ANTIRATIONALIST THEOLOGICAL METHOD / Stanley J. Grenz—DONALD BLOESCH ON REVELATION / Avery Dulles—DONALD BLOESCH'S DOCTRINE OF SCRIPTURE / Millard J. Erickson—JESUS CHRIST IN BLOESCH'S THEOLOGY / Gabriel Fackre—THE HOLY SPIRIT IN THE THEOLOGY OF DONALD G. BLOESCH / Clark H. Pinnock—BLOESCH'S DOCTRINE OF GOD / Thomas F. Torrance—BLOESCH'S DOCTRINE OF THE CHRISTIAN LIFE / John Weborg and Elmer M. Colyer—DONALD BLOESCH AS A SOCIAL PROPHET / James R. Rohrer—DONALD BLOESCH RESPONDS / Donald G. Bloesch—SELECTED BIBLIOGRAPHY OF DONALD G. BLOESCH'S MAJOR PUBLICATIONS.

1121. Fackre, Gabriel J. "Jesus Christ in Bloesch's Theology" in *Evangelical Theology in Transition: Theologians in Dialogue with Donald Bloesch* / edited by Elmer M. Colyer.—Downers Grove, Ill.: InterVarsity, 1999, pp. 98–118, 224–27. **Headings**: Formative Factors—Christology and Its Contexts—The Person of Christ—The Work of Christ—The Application of the Benefits of Christ—Commentary on Bloesch's Christology—Conclusion.

1122. Flinn, P. Richard. "Theological Double Talk." *The Journal of Christian Reconstruction*, vol. 7, no. 2 (Winter 1981), pp. 187–95. **Notes**: Excoriates DGB's view of Scripture.

1123. *From East to West: Essays in Honor of Donald G. Bloesch* / edited by Daniel J. Adams.—Lanham, Md.: University Press of America, c1997.

1124. Gier, Nicholas F. *God, Reason, and the Evangelicals: The Case against Evangelical Rationalism.*—Lanham, Md.; New York; London: University Press of America, 1987. **Notes**: DGB discussed passim; cf. index.

1125. Glasser, Arthur F. "Biblical Revelation & Missions: Another Evangelical View." *Touchstone (Chicago, Ill.)*, vol. 4, no. 4 (Fall 1991), pp. 29–31. **Notes**: A reply to DGB and Carl E Braaten's articles that appeared in *Touchstone*, vol. 4, no. 3 (Summer 1991), pp. 5–13.

1126. Grenz, Stanley J. "'Fideistic Revelationalism': Donald Bloesch's Antirationalist Theological Method" in *Evangelical Theology in Transition: Theologians in Dialogue with Donald Bloesch* / edited by Elmer M. Colyer.—Downers Grove, Ill.: InterVarsity, 1999, pp. 35–60, 216–19. **Headings**: The "Standard" Evangelical Paradigm—The Nature of Revelation—The Role of Theology—The Sources for Theology—Theology and Culture—Bloesch's Program in Contemporary Perspective—Conclusion.

1127. Harvey, Bob. "Battle over Bible Still Rages in the Church." *Ottawa Citizen* (July 6, 1991), Religion Section, p. 17.

1128. Hasel, Frank M. *Scripture in the Theologies of W. Pannenberg and D. G. Bloesch: An Investigation and Assessment of Its Origin, Nature, and Use.*—Frankfurt; New York: Peter Lang, 1995. **Notes**: Reprinted: item 1114. Reviewed: items 1129–1133.

1129. Cameron, Charles M. *The Scottish Bulletin of Evangelical Theology*, vol. 18, no. 2 (Autumn 2000), p. 216.

1130. Harris, James. *European Journal of Theology*, vol. 8, no. 1 (1999), pp. 105–6.

1131. Norman, Bruce. *Andrews University Seminary Studies*, vol. 36, no. 1 (Spring 1998), pp. 127–28.

1132. Williams, Stephen. *Themelios*, vol. 22, no. 2 (January 1997), p. 78.

1133. Wonders, Lance. *Reformation & Revival*, vol. 9, no. 1 (Winter 2000), pp. 163–66.

1134. Hasel, Frank M. *Scripture in the Theologies of W. Pannenberg and D. G. Bloesch: An Investigation and Assessment of Its Origin, Nature, and Use.*—Eugene, Ore.: Wipf and Stock, 2004.** **Notes**: Reprint of item 1128.

1135. Herzog, Frederick. *God-Walk: Liberation Shaping Dogmatics.*—Maryknoll, N.Y.: Orbis, 1988, p. 252, note 19, and pp. 255–56, note 35. **Notes**: The latter note is a discussion of DGB's views on liberation theology.

1136. Houts, Margo G. "Is God Also Our Mother?" *Perspectives*, vol. 12, no. 6 (June/July 1997), pp. 8–12. **Headings**: Achtemeier, Bloesch, and Frye—Form, Function, and Meaning—Establishing Limits on Language for God—God, Gender, and Accommodation—Conclusion.

1137. Husbands, Mark. "Donald G. Bloesch" in *Biographical Dictionary of Evangelicals* / edited by Timothy Larsen; Consulting editors, D. W. Bebbington and Mark A. Noll; Organizing editor, Steve Carter.—Leicester, England; Downers Grove, Ill.: InterVarsity, 2003.

1138. Isaac, Shirley. "God-Language and Gender: Some Trinitarian Reflections." *Direction*, vol. 29, no. 2 (Fall 2000), pp. 169–84. **Notes**: Also available as an electronic resource via: www.directionjournal.org/article/?1056 (accessed February, 2007). **Headings**: The Argument against Inclusive God-Language—Limitations on Female God-Language—A Challenge to This Trinitarian Argument—The Unknown God in Bloesch's Trinitarian Theology—The Revelation of God in Scripture—Sophia and Shekinah—The Suffering of God in Christ—Subordination versus Trinitarianism—Moving beyond the Baptismal Formula—Implications for Male–Female Relations—Implications for God-Language.

1139. Keylock, Leslie R. "Evangelical Leaders You Should Know: Meet Donald G. Bloesch." *Moody Monthly* vol. 88, no. 7 (March 1988), pp. 61–63.

1140. Lovelace, Richard. "Renewal and the Future of Evangelicalism." *Renewal*, vol. 3, no. 3 (November 1983), pp. [1]–12.

1141. Maddox, Randy L. "Reply to Donald Bloesch." *Christian Scholar's Review*, vol. 18, no. 3 (1989), pp. 285–88.

1142. McCurdy, Leslie. *Attributes and Atonement: The Holy Love of God in the Theology of P. T. Forsyth.*—Carlisle, Cumbria, UK: Paternoster, 1999, pp. 257–59. **Notes**: Originally presented as the author's thesis—University of Aberdeen. DGB discussed passim.

1143. McDonald, Jeff. "Bloesch Criticizes 'Penetration of Secularism' in Protestant Churches." *The Layman Online* (November 29, 2005). Available as an electronic resource only via: www.layman.org (accessed February 14, 2007).

1144. McDonald, Kevin. "Theologian Donald Bloesch Speaks on Justice, Morality." *The Presbyterian Layman*, vol. 27, no. 6 (November–December 1994), p. 15. **Notes**: Interview with DGB. **Headings**: Human Development, Justice—Homosexuality: Theological View—Most Pressing Moral Issue—"Creeping Moral Anarchy."

1145. McKim, Donald K. "Donald G. Bloesch" in *Handbook of Evangelical Theologians* / edited by Walter A. Elwell.—Grand Rapids, Mich.: Baker, 1993, pp. 388–400.

1146. Morrison, John D. "Scripture as the Word of God: Evangelical Assumption or Evangelical Question?" *Trinity Journal*, vol. 20, no. 2 (Fall 1999), pp. 165–90.

1147. Murphy, Nancey C. *Beyond Liberalism and Fundamentalism: How Modern and Postmodern Philosophy Set the Theological Agenda.*—Valley Forge, Pa.: Trinity, 1996. **Notes**: DGB discussed passim; cf. index.

1148. Nash, Ronald H. *The Word of God and the Mind of Man.*—Grand Rapids, Mich.: Zondervan, 1982. **Notes**: Cf., pp. 95–96, 124–32, et passim. Subtitle on cover: *The Crisis of Revealed Truth in Contemporary Theology.* **Notes**: Reprinted: item 1149.

1149. Nash, Ronald H. *The Word of God and the Mind of Man.*—Phillipsburg, N.J.: P and R, 1991. **Notes**: Reprint of 1148.

1150. Nessan, Craig L. *Orthopraxis or Heresy: The North American Theological Response to Latin American Liberation Theology.*—Atlanta, Ga.: Scholars, 1989. **Notes**: Chapter 4 is titled, "Critical Issues"; Section F of that chapter, "Evangelical Critiques," section 3, "Donald G. Bloesch," pp. 302–7.

1151. Oden, Thomas C. *Turning around the Mainline: How Renewal Movements Are Changing the Church.*—Grand Rapids, Mich.: Baker, 2006. **Notes**: DGB, the Dubuque Declaration and the Dupage Declaration discussed passim.

1152. Olson, Roger. "Donald Bloesch" in *A New Handbook of Christian Theologians* / edited by Donald W. Musser and Joseph L. Price.—Nashville: Abingdon, 1996, pp. 67–73.

1153. Olson, Roger. "Donald G. Bloesch" in Olson's *The Westminster Handbook to Evangelical Theology.*—1st ed.—Louisville, Ky.: Westminster, John Knox, c2004, pp. 105–6.

1154. Olson, Roger E. "Locating Donald G. Bloesch in the Evangelical Landscape" in *Evangelical Theology in Transition: Theologians in Dialogue with Donald Bloesch* / edited by Elmer M. Colyer.—Downers Grove, Ill.: InterVarsity, 1999, pp. 18–34, 215–16. **Headings**: The Evangelical Landscape—Bloesch's Location in the Evangelical Landscape—Bloesch's Theological Mentors—Mediating Theologian—Discerning Alternatives—Progressive Evangelical?—Bloesch's Influence.

1155. Parker, David. "Donald Bloesch, Evangelical Theologian of Word and Spirit" in *From East to West: Essays in Honor of Donald G. Bloesch* / edited by Daniel J. Adams.—Lanham, Md.: University Press of America, c1997, pp. 1–22.

1156. Parker, David. "Original Sin: A Fresh Approach." *Evangelical Review of Theology*, vol. 13, no. 3 (July 1989), pp. 228–45. **Headings**: History—Issues Involved—Reformed Theology—Arminian Theology—Contemporary Solutions [DGB et al.]—Conclusions.

1157. Parker, David. "Original Sin: A Study in Evangelical Theory." *The Evangelical Quarterly*, vol. 61, no. 1 (January 1989), pp. 51–69. **Headings**: Introduction—History—Issues—Reformed Theology—Arminian Theology—Contemporary Solutions: Donald G. Bloesch. Millard J. Erickson—Conclusions.

1158. Pinnock, Clark H. "The Holy Spirit in the Theology of Donald G. Bloesch" in *Evangelical Theology in Transition: Theologians in Dialogue with Donald Bloesch* / edited by Elmer M. Colyer.—Downers Grove, Ill.: InterVarsity, 1999, pp. 119–34, 227–29. **Headings**: Spirit and the Word—Spirit of Inspiration and Interpretation—Spirit and Trinity—Spirit and Creation—Spirit and Jesus Christ—Spirit and Conversion—Spirit and Christian Existence—Conclusion.

1159. Rohrer, James R. "Donald Bloesch as a Social Prophet" in *Evangelical Theology in Transition: Theologians in Dialogue with Donald Bloesch* / edited by Elmer M. Colyer.—Downers Grove, Ill.: InterVarsity, 1999, pp. 169–82, 234–36. **Headings**: Bloesch's Theology of Culture—Bloesch as a Social Prophet, 1950s–1980—Bloesch's Engagement with Feminism—Critical Assessment of Bloesch's Accomplishment.

1160. Rohrer, James R. "The Theologian as Prophet: Donald Bloesch and the Crisis of the Modern Church" in *From East to West: Essays in Honor of Donald G. Bloesch* / edited by Daniel J. Adams.—Lanham, Md.: University Press of America, c1997, pp. 211–32.

1161. Schwar, Kathleen. "Evangelical Scholar Sees Growing Polarization in Nation's Churches." *St. Petersburg Times (St. Petersburg, Fla.)* (October 6, 1990), p. 6E.

1162. Scriven, Charles. "The Bible as Benchmark: Hauerwas, Bloesch, and Yoder." *The Transformation of Culture: Christian Social Ethics after H. Richard Niebuhr.*—Scottdale, Pa.: Herald, 1988, pp. 126–58. **Notes**: Cf. especially pp. 136–46.

1163. Smith, David L. *All God's People: A Theology of the Church.*—Wheaton, Ill.: Victor, 1996. **Notes**: Cf. especially "Donald Bloesch," pp. 170–73. **Headings**: The Church—The Unity of the Church—The Sacrament of Preaching—The Priesthood of Believers—Conclusion.

1164. Stevens, Nancy. "Force of Nature, Imminent [*sic*] Mother? Theologian Sees Harm in Tinkering with References to God." *The Gazette (Cedar Rapids, Iowa)*, vol. 105, no. 1 (January 10, 1987), pp. 1, 12A.

1165. Thorne, Phillip R. "Donald Bloesch: Converging Mainline Evangelical" in Thorne's *Evangelicalism and Karl Barth: His Reception and Influence in North American Evangelical Theology.*—Allison Park, Pa.: Pickwick, c1995, pp. 133–47, et passim.

1166. Toon, Peter. *The End of Liberal Theology: Contemporary Challenges to Evangelical Orthodoxy.*—Wheaton, Ill.: Crossway, 1995. **Notes**: DGB discussed pp. 156–60, et passim; cf. index.

1167. Torrance, Thomas F. "Bloesch's Doctrine of God" in *Evangelical Theology in Transition: Theologians in Dialogue with Donald Bloesch* / edited by Elmer M. Colyer.—Downers Grove, Ill.: InterVarsity, 1999, pp. 136–48, 229–30.

1167a. Ungar, Walter. "Focusing the Evangelical Vision." *Direction*, vol. 20, no. 1, p.317. **Notes**: DGB discussed passim. Also available as an electronic resource via: www.directionjournal.org/article?692 (accessed February 14, 2007).

1168. Van Essen, Rob. "A Theological Portrait: Dr. Donald G. Bloesch." / translated by Daniel W. Bloesch. *Soteria: Evangelical Theological Reflections*, vol. 3, no. 3 (September 1986).**

1169. Weborg, John, and Colyer, Elmer M. "Bloesch's Doctrine of the Christian Life" in *Evangelical Theology in Transition: Theologians in Dialogue with Donald Bloesch* / edited by Elmer M. Colyer.—Downers Grove, Ill.: InterVarsity, 1999, pp. 149–68, 230–34. **Headings**: Part One, The Autobiographic and Architectonic Dimensions of Bloesch's Doctrine of the Christian Life—Part Two, "A Pious Erudition" and an "Erudite Piety": Stewards and Safeguards of the Christian Life.

1170. White, James Emery. *What Is Truth: A Comparative Study of the Positions of Cornelius Van Til, Francis Schaeffer, Carl F. H. Henry, Donald Bloesch, and Millard Erickson.*—Nashville: Broadman and Holman, 1994. viii, 240 pp.; 23 cm. **Contents**: THE QUESTION OF TRUTH—AMERICAN EVANGELICALISM—EVANGELICALS AND THE QUESTION OF TRUTH—TRUTH AND PRESUPPOSITION, CORNELIUS VAN TIL—TRUTH AND APOLOGETIC, FRANCIS A. SCHAEFFER—TRUTH AND REASON, CARL F. H. HENRY—TRUTH AND GOD'S TRUTHFULNESS, MILLARD J. ERICKSON—TRUTH AND THEOLOGY, DONALD G. BLOESCH—SUMMARY OF THE CONCEPT OF TRUTH IN CONTEMPORARY AMERICAN EVANGELICAL THEOLOGY—NON-EVANGELICAL REACTIONS TO THE EVANGELICAL CONCEPT OF TRUTH—DEFENSE OF THE EVANGELICAL CONCEPT OF TRUTH—PROPOSALS FOR THE EVANGELICAL CONCEPT OF TRUTH. **Headings in the chapter on Bloesch**: Biographical Background—Description of Bloesch's Concept of Truth—Philosophy and Truth—Theology and Truth—Truth and Scripture—Bloesch's Criteria of Truth—Critique of Bloesch's Concept of Truth—Summary. Reviewed: items 1171–1174.

1171. Beckwith, Francis J. *Journal of Psychology and Christianity*, vol. 14, no. 1 (Spring 1995), p. 87.

1172. Oliphint, K. Scott. *The Westminster Theological Journal*, vol. 57, no. 2 (Fall 1995), pp. 495–97.

1173. Parrish, Stephen E. *Criswell Theological Review*, vol. 7, no. 1 (Fall 1993), pp. 140–41.

1174. Vunderink, Ralph W. *Calvin Theological Journal*, vol. 30, no. 1 (April 1995), p. 318.

1175. Yurs, Mark E. "The Evangelical Homiletics of Donald G. Bloesch," *Journal of the American Academy of Ministry*, vol. 7, no. 1 (Winter/Spring 2001), pp. 31–37.

1176. "Keys for Leadership, Spiritual Conflicts Studied by Scholars." *Southwestern News*, vol. 47, no. 7 (March 1989), p. 7.

1177. "Bloesch Completes Landmark Systematic Theology." *The Witness*, vol. 26, no. 1 (Winter 2005), pp. 1, 22.

THESES DISCUSSING THE WORK OF DONALD G. BLOESCH

1178. Baxter, S. Edward, Jr. *A Historical Study of the Doctrine of 'Apokatastasis.'* iv, 309 leaves; 28 cm. **Notes**: Thesis (ThD)—Mid-America Baptist Theological Seminary, Memphis, Tenn., 1988. Cf. especially, "Donald Bloesch," leaves 232–34 under the heading "Evangelicalism" in chapter 4, "The Twentieth Century."

1179. Brand, Chad Owen. *Donald George Bloesch's Contribution to Theological Method.* v, 305 pp.; 28 cm. **Notes**: Thesis (PhD)—Southwestern Baptist Theological Seminary, Fort Worth Tex., 1998. **Contents**: A HISTORY OF THE THEOLOGICAL

ISSUES RELATED TO METHOD TO THE 1960S. Faith and Reason in Christian Tradition. Hermeneutics and History and the Nature of Religious Language. The Nature and Task of Theology.—AN EXAMINATION OF THE CURRENT CONVERSATION: FROM GILKEY TO LINDBECK. PARADIGMS OF METHODOLOGY IN CONTEMPORARY THEOLOGY. David Tracy. George Lindbeck. Hans Frei. Correlating the Typologies: Paramount Issues in Theological Methodology. Conclusion.—FAITH AND PHILOSOPHY. The Role of Reason. Defining the Terms. Reason and Faith in the Church. A Place for Metaphysics. Theology and Its Relation to Metaphysics. A Metaphysical Resting Place for Faith? Beyond Fideism and Rationalism.—HERMENEUTICS AND THE POSSIBILITY OF COMMUNICATING THE GOSPEL TODAY. The Reconstruction of Textuality. Theological Exegesis. Hermeneutics of Word and Spirit. The Possibility of God-Talk. Is Language an Adequate Vehicle? A Possible Solution. Narrative and the Grammar of Faith. Communicating the Gospel: Beyond Imperialism and Silence. Conclusion.—THE TASK AND DEFINITION OF THEOLOGY. The Task of Theology. Theology as Polemics. Theology as Apologetics. Theology as Dogmatics. The Definition of Theology. The Future of Theology. Conclusion.

1180. Corts, Stephen David Charles. *Particularism as an Evangelical Response to Religious Plurality.* xxi, 412 leaves; 28 cm. **Notes**: Thesis (PhD)—The Southern Baptist Theological Seminary, Louisville, Ky., 1991. **Notes**: Cf. especially "Donald G. Bloesch," leaves 69–98 in chapter 3, "Representative Evangelical Responses to the Challenge of Religious Plurality." This section has the subheadings: Bloesch and Evangelicalism. Bloesch and Religious Plurality. The Universal Human Dilemma. Salvation. *Sola Gratia. Solus Christus.* Conclusions.

1181. Hall, Christopher Alan. *The Source and Significance of Paradoxical Elements in the Thought of Donald Bloesch.* viii, 244 leaves; 29 cm. **Notes**: Thesis (ThM)—Regent College, Vancouver, B.C., 1987. **Contents**: THE QUESTION OF PARADOX. DONALD BLOESCH, HIS BACKGROUND AND CONTRIBUTION. Bloesch's Dialectical Methodology. The Key Question. The Concept of Paradox. Methodological Guidelines for Paradox. Bloesch and Paradox. Paradox, Obedience, and the Knowledge of God. Calvin and Bloesch on the Same Wavelength? Bloesch versus Hodge.—THE FOUNDATIONAL PARADOXES AND THE SPIRITUAL LIFE. The Two Primary Paradoxes. Implications of the Primary Paradoxes. The Key Problem. A Continuing Error. The Question of Irresistible Grace. Salvation and the Christian Life. The Tenses of Salvation. The Expansion of the Paradox. The Nature of the Christian Life. The *Theologia Crucis* and *Theologia Gloriae.* Signs and the Pilgrimage of Faith. Importunity, Prayer, and Paradox.—PARADOXICAL ELEMENTS IN THE *ESSENTIALS,* VOL. 1. Introduction to the *Essentials.* The Meaning of "Evangelical." Paradox and the Sovereignty of God. Paradox and the Paradoxical Language. Paradox and the Primacy of Scripture. Infallibility, Inerrancy, and Paradox. The Noetic Consequences of Sin. The Source of Christological Error. An Unnecessary Dichotomy. Paradoxical Elements in the Atonement. Paradox and Salvation by Grace. The Dynamics of Faith. The Paradoxical Structure of Assurance.—PARADOXICAL ELEMENTS IN THE *ESSENTIALS,* VOL. 2. Paradox and the New Birth. Holiness as Both Gift and Task. The Paradox of Perfection. Prayer as Gift and Command. The Paradox of

Fulfillment. The Paradox of Preaching. Present and Still Future. Paradoxical Elements in the Mission of the Church. Eschatological Paradoxes. Fundamental Issues.—CONCLUDING THOUGHTS. The Fundamental Paradoxes and the Spiritual Life. The Struggle to Persevere. The Contribution of Bloesch. Areas of Disagreement. The Influence of Kierkegaard. Two Critical Errors.

1182. Hasel, Frank Michael. *Scripture in the Theologies of W. Pannenberg and D. G. Bloesch: An Investigation and Assessment of Its Origin, Nature, and Use.* xix, 363 leaves; 28 cm. **Notes**: Thesis (PhD)—Seventh-Day Adventist Theological Seminary of Andrews University, Berrien Springs, Mich., 1995. **Notes**: Published as item 1128 and item 1134.

1183. Inman, Michael R. *The Existentialism of John Macquarrie: Its Implications for Modern Theology and Ecclesiology.* viii, 303 leaves.; 28 cm. **Notes**: Thesis (PhD)—Duquesne University, Pittsburgh, Pa., 1997. **Partial Contents**: CHAPTER 5. BLOESCH'S PROTESTANT EVANGELICAL ECCLESIOLOGY. I. The Protestant Evangelical Church. A. Doctrine of Salvation. B. The Proclamation Model. II. Existential Implications. A. Philosophical Problems. B. Doctrinal Problems. C. Ecclesial Problems—CHAPTER 6. CONCLUSION. III. Evaluation of Bloesch. A. Bloesch's Strengths. B. Bloesch's Weaknesses.

1184. Kuczynski, Edward Clark. *"But Who Do You Say That I Am?": A Comparative Analysis of the Christologies of Donald G. Bloesch, David Ray Griffin and Jürgen Moltmann.* viii, 189 leaves; 29 cm. **Notes**: Thesis (ThM)—Southeastern Baptist Theological Seminary, Wake Forest, N.C., 1986. **Partial Contents**: INTRODUCTION. Scope and Purpose. Method and Issues. Christology Prior to Chalcedon. The Shape of Christology Today—THE CHRISTOLOGY OF DONALD G. BLOESCH. Preliminary Remarks. The Starting Point of Christology. The Deity of Jesus Christ. *Jesus Christ, Truly Divine and Truly Human. The Pre-Existence and Virgin Birth of Jesus Christ.* Two Types of Christological Heresy. Kenotic Christology. The Work of Jesus Christ. *The Atonement. Different Theories of the Atonement. Bloesch's Theory of the Atonement. Objective and Subjective Atonement. Particular and Universal Atonement.* An Evaluation of Bloesch's Christology—THE CHRISTOLOGY OF DAVID R. GRIFFIN. Preliminary Remarks. Revelation and Christology. Beginnings of a Process Christology. The Relationship of God to Jesus. Christology and the Historical Jesus. Jesus as God's Supreme Act of Self-Expression. An Evaluation of Griffin's Christology—THE CHRISTOLOGY OF JÜRGEN MOLTMANN. Preliminary Remarks. Moltmann's Justification for His Method. Christ as the Center of Christian Theology. The Resurrection of Jesus. Some Questions Regarding Jesus. Moltmann's Christological Method. The Crucified God. An Evaluation of Moltmann's Christology—BUT WHO DO YOU SAY THAT I AM? Preliminary Remarks. An Analysis of the Three Christologies Presented. *Donald G. Bloesch. David R. Griffin. Jürgen Moltmann.* Some Comparative Reflections. Implications Drawn from This Study. Point a Way Forward. Conclusion.

1185. Lewis, John. *Discovering a Means to an End: Influence, Source, and Agenda in the Theology of Donald Bloesch.* ii, 115 leaves; 30 cm. **Notes**: Thesis (MA)—University of South Australia, Adelaide, 2001. **Contents**: INTRODUCTION—THE THEOLOGY OF DONALD BLOESCH: CONTEXT AND AGENDA—BLOESCH'S THEOLOGY OF REVELATION—BLOESCH'S DOCTRINE OF GOD—BLOESCH'S CHRISTOLOGY—BLOESCH'S SOTERIOLOGY I—BLOESCH'S SOTERIOLOGY II—CONCLUSION—BIBLIOGRAPHY.

1186. Malone, Kelly Scott. *The Kingdom of God and the Mission of the Church in Con-temporary Evangelical Thought: George Eldon Ladd, Donald George Bloesch, and Howard Albert Snyder.* vi, 271 leaves; 29 cm. **Notes**: Thesis (PhD)—Southwest-ern Baptist Theological Seminary, Fort Worth, Tex., 1995. Cf. especially chap-ter 3, "Donald G. Bloesch: Spiritual Mission and the Future Kingdom," and chapter 5, "Ladd, Bloesch, and Snyder: Contrast and Comparison." Chapter 3 has the headings: Bloesch's Context: Modernism and Secularism in Christian-ity—Bloesch's Contributors: The Reformers, Pietism, Barth, and Bonhoeffer—Bloesch's Theological Method—The Two Kingdoms: The Present Struggle be-tween God and the Demonic—The Church: Present Colony of the Future Kingdom—The Church's Spiritual Mission: Evangelism, Social Service, and Social Action—Strengths and Weaknesses of Bloesch's Presentation. Chapter 5 has the headings: The Kingdom of God as the Presence of the Future—The Church as Kingdom Community—An Evangelical Consensus.

1187. Maxwell, Ronald Keith. *Newer Evangelicalism: Two Approaches to Social Re-sponsibility.* iii, 189 leaves; 28 cm. **Notes**: Thesis (ThM)—Vancouver School of Theology, B.C., 1980. Cf. especially the section "Donald Bloesch, A Con-ventional Style" in chapter 4, "Models for Social Change," leaves 97 & ff.

1188. McElhattan, Martha J. *The Role of the Holy Spirit in the Soteriologies of John Calvin and Donald Bloesch: A Look at the Ordo Salutis.* vi, 105 leaves; 28 cm. **Notes**: The-sis (MA)—Pittsburgh Theological Seminary, Pa., 2004. **Contents**: INTRODUC-TION—THE OPERATION OF THE HOLY SPIRIT. The Work of the Holy Spirit in Re-demption. The *Ordo Salutis.*—JOHN CALVIN. Biography and Theological Overview. Deity of the Holy Spirit. Titles of the Holy Spirit. Union with Christ. Word and Faith. Election. Calvin's Understanding of Romans 8:28–30. The *Ordo Salutis* According to Calvin.—DONALD G. BLOESCH. Theological Overview. Renewed Interest in the Holy Spirit. The Salvific Role of the Holy Spirit. Word and Spirit. Works of the Holy Spirit. Four Stages of Salvation. The Paradox of Salvation. The Responsibility of the Believer. The *Ordo Salutis* Ac-cording to Bloesch. The Human Perspective of Salvation. The Divine Per-spective of Salvation. Three Tenses of Salvation.—A COMPARISON OF THE SOTE-RIOLOGIES OF CALVIN AND BLOESCH. Points of Agreement. Points of Contrast.—WHAT WOULD CALVIN AND BLOESCH SAY TO THE CHURCH TODAY? In-troduction. John Calvin's Concerns. Donald Bloesch's Concerns. Conclusion.

1189. McManus, Patrick Michael. *Donald G. Bloesch and Hans W. Frei on Theology, Authority, and Scripture: A Contribution to the Evangelical–Post-Liberal Dia-logue.* ii, 97 leaves; 29 cm. **Notes**: Thesis (MA)—University of St. Michael's College, Toronto, Ont., 2004. **Contents**: INTRODUCTION: DONALD BLOESCH, HANS FREI AND THE EVANGELICAL–POSTLIBERAL CONVERSATION. By Way of Jus-tification: Why Bloesch and Frei? The Legacy of Apologetical Theology.—ON GETTING STARTED: BLOESCH AND FREI IN CONVERSATION ON METHOD AND AUTHORITY IN THEOLOGICAL DISCOURSE. Donald Bloesch and Hans Frei as Anselmian Theologians: On Continuity. Donald Bloesch, Hans Frei & the In-fluence of Karl Barth. Donald Bloesch's Dialectic of Word and Spirit. Hans Frei and the Presence and Identity of Jesus Christ.—CONCERNS AND EM-PHASES: ON DISCONTINUITY? Bloesch's Concerns: On Ontology and Truth. Bloesch's Reading of "Narrative Theology": Frei and the Question of Onto-

logical Reference.—METHOD & AUTHORITY: TOWARD AN EVANGELICAL AC-
COUNT OF SCRIPTURE—THE NATURE OF HOLY SCRIPTURE: EVANGELICAL AND
POST-LIBERAL CONSIDERATIONS. Scripture & Theology. Hans Frei, Sola Scriptura, and the Sufficiency of Scripture. The Later Frei and the 'Cultural-Lin-
guistic' Turn. Bloesch's Doctrine of Scripture. Bloesch's 'Sacramental' Bibliology: The Being of Scripture Is in Its Becoming.—THEOLOGY, SCRIPTURE, AND
METHOD: EVANGELICAL & POST-LIBERAL.

1190. Mohler, Richard Albert, Jr. *Evangelical Theology and Karl Barth: Representative
Models.* x, 340 leaves; 28 cm. **Notes**: Thesis (PhD)—Southern Baptist Theo-
logical Seminary, Louisville, Ky., 1989. **Contents, Chapter 3**: Evangelicals in
Critical Dialogue with Barth. Klaas Runia. Colin Brown. Clark H. Pinnock.
Donald Bloesch: Karl Barth as Evangelical Church Father. Bloesch and the
Problem of Evangelical Definition. Bloesch's Encounter with Karl Barth.
Karl Barth's Doctrine of Salvation. Freedom for Obedience: Barth and an
Evangelical Ethic. Barth and the Shape of Bloesch's Theology. Karl Barth
and the Evangelical Heritage. Gerrit C. Berkouwer: Karl Barth and the Tri-
umph of Grace. Berkouwer and American Evangelicalism. Berkouwer and
the Theology of Karl Barth. The Triumph of Grace and the Faith of the
Church. Jesus Is Victor!: Barth's Response to Berkouwer. Barth and the
Hope of an Evangelical Theology.

1191. Nyquist, John Paul. *An Evaluation of the Inroads of Process Theology into Contemporary Evangelicalism.* iv, 272, [20] leaves; 28 cm. **Notes**: Thesis (ThD)—
Dallas Theological Seminary, Tex., 1984. DGB discussed p. 180 & ff. passim.

1192. Perry, Ronald Mark. *A Holistic Model of Church Renewal in Light of a Critical
Evaluation of the Contributions of D. Elton Trueblood, Donald G. Bloesch and
Leonardo Boff.* v, 260 leaves; 28 cm. **Notes**: Thesis (PhD)—New Orleans Bap-
tist Theological Seminary, La., 1992. Cf. especially chapter 3, "The Renewal
Thought of Donald G. Bloesch," pp. 106–53. Chapter 3 has the headings: A
Biographical Sketch—The Need for Renewal—The Theological Bases for
Renewal: An Understanding of the Bible; An Understanding of Disciple-
ship; An Understanding of the Church—The Application of Renewal to
Ministry: A Spiritual Dimension; A Social Dimension; A Communal Dimen-
sion—Summary.

1193. Price, Robert McNair. *The Crisis of Biblical Authority: The Setting and Range of
the Current Evangelical Crisis.* ii, 287 leaves; 28 cm. **Notes**: Thesis (PhD)—
Drew University, Madison, N.J., 1981. DGB discussed in passing in chapters
4 and 6. **Contents**: INERRANT THE WIND—PRODIGAL FUNDAMENTALISTS—"IN-
ERRANCY, LTD."—ENIGMA AND KERYGMA—THROUGH A KALEIDOSCOPE
DARKLY—"IT AIN'T NECESSARILY SO"—THE ORTHODOXFORD OPTION.

1194. Resch, Dustin G. *"Finitum (Non) Capax Infiniti: The Sacramental Character of
Scripture in the Theology of Donald G. Bloesch,"* vii, 138 leaves; 28 cm. **Notes**:
Thesis (MA)—Briercrest Seminary, Caronport, Sask., 2004. **Contents**: TO-
WARD A CATHOLIC EVANGELICALISM. Evangelicals and Contemporary Views of
Scripture. Bloesch's Career. Views of Bloesch's Work and Theology. Toward
Bloesch's Pastoral Theology of Scripture.—THE SACRAMENTAL CHARACTER OF
THE DOCTRINE OF SCRIPTURE. Sacramental Character. The Bible and the Word
of God. Christological Analogies. Word, Spirit, and Bible. God-language

and the Biblical Text. Conclusion.—HEARING THE SPIRIT IN THE TEXT. Scripture and Tradition. A Christological, Pneumatic Hermeneutic. Bultmann's Enduring Presence. Scripture, the Virgin Birth, and Mary. Conclusion.—THE PROCLAIMED WORD OF GOD. The Church Invaded by Ideology. The Renewal of the Church. Preaching the Word of God in Scripture. A Sacramental Sermon.—CONCLUSION.

1195. Rosser, William Ray. *The Cross as the Hermeneutical Norm for Scriptural Interpretation in the Theology of Peter Taylor Forsyth.* viii, 259 leaves; 28 cm. **Notes**: Thesis (PhD)—Southern Baptist Theological Seminary, Louisville, Ky., 1990. Cf. especially "Donald Bloesch," leaves 156–69 in chapter 4, "Forsyth in Dialogue with Current Hermeneutical Approaches."

1196. Rowlett, Martha Graybeal. *A Process Theology of Prayer.* vii, 156 leaves; 28 cm. **Notes**: Thesis (DMin)—School of Theology at Claremont, Claremont, Calif., 1981. **Partial Contents**: Part 3. A Reflective Postscript. Heiler Typology. Contemporary Examples. Bloesch—Prophetic Prayer. Merton—Mystical Prayer. Process Theology of Prayer: A Both/and Alternative.

1197. Scriven, Charles Wayne. *The Transformation of Culture: Christian Social Ethics after H. Richard Niebuhr.* iv, 348 leaves; 28 cm. **Notes**: Thesis (PhD)—Graduate Theological Union, Berkeley, Calif., 1985. Cf. item 1140. DGB discussed, pp. 230–49: **Partial Contents**: Chapter 5. The Bible as Benchmark: Hauerwas, Bloesch, and Yoder. Introduction. Stanley Hauerwas. Donald Bloesch. John Howard Yoder.

1198. Smith, Michael T. *Theology as a Resource in Faith Translation for the Local Church.* 90 leaves; 28 cm. **Notes**: Thesis (DMin)—Northern Baptist Theological Seminary, Lombard, Ill., 1986. **Partial Contents**: Chapter 2: The Theology and Theological Constructs of Donald Bloesch, Douglas Wingeier, and John Macquarrie. Introduction. Donald Bloesch's Method. Douglas Wingeier's Method. John Macquarrie's Method. The Theological Constructs of Donald Bloesch, Douglas Wingeier, and John Macquarrie and Their Evaluation. The Participant's Theological Construct.

1199. Sorge, Sheldon Warren. *Karl Barth's Reception in North America: Ecclesiology as a Case Study.* viii, 288 p.; 28 cm. **Notes**: Thesis (PhD)—Duke University, Durham, N.C., 1987. Cf. especially pp. 139–63: chapter 3. American Reception of Barth's Ecclesiology : Three Case Studies. Barth and American Evangelicalism. Paradigm 1: Donald G. Bloesch. Bloesch and "Evangelicalism." Bloesch's General Response to Barth. On Barth and Church Unity. On Barth and Church Mission.

1200. Turner, Jeffrey A. *Inerrancy: A Comparison between the Theological Views of Norman Geisler and Donald Bloesch.* 47 leaves; 28 cm. **Notes**: Thesis (MA)—North American Baptist Seminary, Sioux Falls, S.D., 2000. **Contents**: DONALD BLOESCH'S VIEW OF INERRANCY. EVALUATION—NORMAN GEISLER'S VIEW OF INERRANCY. EVALUATION—CRITICAL COMPARISON. CONCLUSION.

1201. Waser, David Harold. *A Study of the Theology of Donald G. Bloesch.* vi, 111 leaves; 28 cm. **Notes**: Thesis (MDiv)—Lexington Theological Seminary, Ky., 1980. **Contents**: THE NEW EVANGELICALISM AND DONALD G. BLOESCH. Background and Development of the Movement. The Chicago Call. Donald G. Bloesch: Neo-Evangelical Theologian. Summarization and Personal Reflection.—THE ATTEMPT TO RELATE CATHOLIC AND EVANGELICAL EMPHASES IN BLOESCH'S EARLY WRITINGS. What Is Meant by Catholic and Evangelical Emphases? Centers of Christian Renewal. The Crisis of Piety. The Reform of the Church. The Evangelical Renaissance. Wellsprings of Renewal. His Other Books.—THE ATTEMPT TO DEVELOP A CATHOLIC EVAN-GELICAL THEOLOGY IN BLOESCH'S RECENT MAJOR WORKS. Review of What Is Meant by Catholic and Evangelical Emphases. Catholic and Evangelical Emphases in "The Meaning of Evangelical." Catholic and Evangelical Emphases in "The Primacy of Scripture." Catholic and Evangelical Emphases in "The Deity of Jesus Christ." Catholic and Evangelical Emphases in "The Substitutionary Atonement of Christ." Catholic and Evangelical Emphases in "Salvation by Grace." Catholic and Evangelical Emphases in "The New Birth." Catholic and Evangelical Emphases in "The Priesthood of All Believers." Catholic and Evangelical Emphases in "The Church's Spiritual Mission." Catholic and Evangelical Emphases in "Toward the Recovery of the Biblical Faith."—CRITICISMS OF BLOESCH'S ES-SENTIALS OF EVANGELICAL THEOLOGY. Criticisms of the Catholic and Evan-gelical Emphases. Criticism That It Is Difficult to Read. Criticism That It Is Not a Systematic Theology. Criticism That It Is Only Presenting the Re-formed Point of View. Criticism That Bloesch Is Vague in His Acceptance of Biblical Criticism.—THE VALUES OF A CATHOLIC EVANGELICAL THEOLOGY. Contact with the Whole of Christian Tradition. A Contribution to the Ec-umenical Spirit. Summation.

1202. White, James Emery. *The Concept of Truth in Contemporary American Evangel-ical Theology*. PhD Dissertation, Southern Baptist Theological Seminary, 1991. **Notes**: Cf. item 1148 for a published edition of this dissertation. Cf. es-pecially chapter 6, "The Concept of Truth in the Theology of Donald G. Bloesch," pp. 215–53. Chapter 6 has the headings: Biographical Back-ground—Description of Bloesch's Concept of "Truth": Philosophy and Truth. Correspondence Theory of Truth, Coherence Theory of Truth, Prag-matic Theory of Truth, Mystical Theory of Truth; Theology and Truth. Bib-lical Terms for Truth, Existential Truth; Truth and Scripture. Nature of Scrip-ture, Biblical Inerrancy, Christological Hermeneutic—Bloesch's Criteria of "Truth"—Summary.

BIOGRAPHICAL AND BIO-BIBLIOGRAPHICAL WORKS

1203. *Directory of American Scholars*. Lancaster, Pa.: Science; New York: R. R. Bowker; Farmington, Mich.: Gale.

5th ed., 1969
6th ed., 1974
7th ed., 1978
8th ed., 1982
9th ed., 1999
10th ed., 2002

1204. *Indiana Authors and Their Books, 1917–1966.* Compiled by Donald E. Thompson. Crawfordsville, Ind.: Wabash College, 1974.
1205. *The International Authors and Writers Who's Who.* Cambridge, England: International Biographical Centre.

   9th ed., 1982
   11th ed., 1989

1206. *Who's Who in America.* New Providence, N.J.: Marquis Who's Who.

   54th ed., 2000
   55th ed., 2001
   56th ed., 2002
   57th ed., 2003
   58th ed., 2004

1207. *Who's Who in Religion.* Chicago, Ill.: Marquis Who's Who.

   1st ed., 1975–1976
   2nd ed., 1977

1208. *Who's Who in the Midwest: United States of America and Canada.* Chicago, Ill.: Marquis Who's Who.

   19th ed., 1984–1985
   26th ed., 1998–1999

1209. *The Writers Directory.* London: St. James; New York: St. Martin's.

   1st ed., 1971–1973
   2nd ed., 1974–1976
   3rd ed., 1976–1978
   4th ed., 1980–1982
   5th ed., 1982–1984
   6th ed., 1984–1986
   7th ed., 1986–1988
   8th ed., 1988–1990
   9th ed., 1990–1992
   10th ed., 1992–1994
   11th ed., 1994–1996
   12th ed., 1996–1998
   13th ed., 1998–2000
   14th ed., 1999
   15th ed., 2000
   16th ed., 2001
   17th ed., 2002
   18th ed., 2003
   19th ed., 2004
   20th ed., 2005

Chapter 3

Indexes

THE WRITINGS OF DONALD G. BLOESCH—CHECKLISTS

Note: For a fuller description of each item, see the entry given in the main body of the bibliography. The number given at the end of each description here refers to the citation in the bibliography.

*The Christian Life in the Plan of Salvation. See The Theological
Seminary of the University of Dubuque Presents the Inaugural
Address of Donald Bloesch . . .*

*The Christian Witness in a Secular Age: An Evaluation of Nine
Contemporary Theologians.*—Minneapolis: Augsburg, c1968.
160 pp.; 22 cm.   64

*The Christian Witness in a Secular Age: An Evaluation of Nine
Contemporary Theologians.*—Eugene, Ore,: Wipf and Stock,
2002. 160 pp.; 22 cm.   412

The Church: Sacraments, Worship, Ministry, Mission.
—Downers Grove, Ill.: InterVarsity, c2002. 351 pp.; 24 cm.
—(Christian Foundations; [6])   413

The Church: Sacraments, Worship, Ministry, Mission.—
Nottingham, UK: InterVarsity, 2002. 351 pp.; 24 cm.—
(Christian Foundations; [6])   414

The Church: Sacraments, Worship, Ministry, Mission.—
Downers Grove, Ill.: InterVarsity, 2005, c2002. 351 pp.; 24 cm.—
(Christian Foundations; [6])   426

The Crisis of Piety: Essays towards a Theology of the Christian Life.—
Grand Rapids, Mich.: W. B. Eerdmans, c1968. 168 pp.; 23 cm.   66

The Crisis of Piety: Essays Towards a Theology of the Christian Life.—
2nd ed.—Colorado Springs: Helmers and Howard, c1988.
xvii, 159 pp.; 22 cm.   293

Crumbling Foundations: Death and Rebirth in an Age of Upheaval.—
Grand Rapids, Mich.: Academie, Zondervan, c1984.
168 pp.; 21 cm.   245

Emil Brunner's Approach to Non-Christian Religions.—ii, 74 leaves;
28 cm. Thesis (BD)—Federated Theological Faculty in
cooperation with the Chicago Theological Seminary, 1953.   8

Essentials of Evangelical Theology. Vol. 1, God, Authority, Salvation.—
1st ed.—San Francisco: Harper and Row, c1978. xii, 265 pp.;
25 cm.   162

Essentials of Evangelical Theology. Vol. 2, Life, Ministry, and Hope.—
1st ed.—San Francisco: Harper and Row, c1979. xii, 315 pp.;
25 cm.   172

Essentials of Evangelical Theology.—1st HarperCollins pbk. ed.—
[San Francisco]: HarperSanFrancisco, 1982. 2 v.; 24 cm.   214

Essentials of Evangelical Theology.—1st Harper and Row
paperback ed.—San Francisco: Harper and Row, 1982. 2 v.;
24 cm.   215

Essentials of Evangelical Theology.—Peabody, Mass.: Prince, 1998.
2 v.; 24 cm.   378

A Theology of Word & Spirit: Authority & Method in Theology.—
Downers Grove, Ill.: InterVarsity, 2005, c1992. 336 pp.; 24 cm.
—(Christian Foundations; [1])   434
This Immoral War.—[Dubuque, Iowa: University of Dubuque,
1968] 11 pp. pamphlet.   73

Wellsprings of Renewal: Promise in Christian Communal Life.—
Grand Rapids, Mich.: W. B. Eerdmans, c1974. 124 pp.: ill.; 21 cm.   125

BOOKS TO WHICH DONALD G. BLOESCH HAS CONTRIBUTED

The Authoritative Word: Essays on the Nature of Scripture / edited
by Donald K. McKim.—Grand Rapids, Mich.: W. B. Eerdmans,
1983, pp. 117–53, "The Primacy of Scripture"   231

Beacon Dictionary of Theology / edited by Richard S. Taylor;
Associate editors, J. Kenneth Grider and Willard H. Taylor.—
Kansas City, Mo.: Beacon Hill, 1983, pp. 400–02, "Pietism"   230

Christ Is Victor / edited by W. Glyn Evans.—Valley Forge, Pa.:
Judson, 1977, pp. 27–30, "The Basic Issue"   150
The Christian Educator's Handbook on Spiritual Formation / edited
by Kenneth O. Gangel and James C. Wilhoit.—Wheaton, Ill.:
Victor, c1994, pp. 60–73, "Counterfeit Spirituality"   348
The Christian Educator's Handbook on Spiritual Formation / edited
by Kenneth O. Gangel and James C. Wilhoit.—Colorado
Springs: Cook Communications Ministries, 1994, pp. 60–73,
"Counterfeit Spirituality"   349
The Christian Educator's Handbook on Spiritual Formation / edited
by Kenneth O. Gangel and James C. Wilhoit.—Grand Rapids,
Mich.: Baker, 1997, pp. 60–73, "Counterfeit Spirituality"   371
*Christian Faith and Practice in the Modern World: Theology from an
Evangelical Point of View* / edited by Mark A. Noll and
David F. Wells.—Grand Rapids, Mich.: W. B. Eerdmans, 1988,
pp. 176–98, "God the Civilizer"   295
*Christian Faith and Practice in the Modern World: Theology from an
Evangelical Point of View* / edited by Mark A. Noll and David F.
Wells.—Ann Arbor, Mich.: UMI Books on Demand, 1994,
pp. 176–98, "God the Civilizer"   350
Christian Spirituality East & West / Jordan Aumann, Thomas
Hopko, and Donald G. Bloesch.—Chicago: Priory, c1968,
pp. 165–202, "Evangelical Spirituality"   68

BOOKS REVIEWED BY DONALD G. BLOESCH

Note: For a fuller description of each item, see the entry given in the main body of the bibliography. For access by author, cf. the index of names. The number given at the end of each description here refers to the citation in the bibliography.

INDEX OF TITLES, CHAPTERS, AND HEADINGS

Note: Titles of books are given in *italics*, chapter titles of books are given in SMALL CAPS, titles of articles are given "within quotation marks," and headings appearing on parts of an article or parts of a book chapter are in normal text. In the rare event that an even smaller part is given a title, it appears in *italics*. Smaller parts are always given with the title of the larger part following. Thus, in the first line of the title index, "Aberrations after the Reformation" refers to a heading used within an article entitled "The Demise of Biblical Preaching," which is described in detail as item 357. In the second line of the title index, "Aberrations after the Reformation" refers to a heading within the chapter entitled THE DEMISE OF BIBLICAL PREACHING contained in the book *The Church* and is described in detail as item 413.

INDEX OF NAMES

NOTE, The names here, of course, refer to names appearing in this bibliography rather than to names appearing in Bloesch's works. For the latter, cf. the Index of Names appearing in each of Bloesch's books.

Ramsey, John R., 1004
Read, Francis W., 171
Reardon, Patrick Henry, 354
Reid, Daniel G., 313, 362
Reimers, Adrian, 910
Resch, Dustin, 533, 968, 1194
Reuilly Sisters. *See* Sisters of Reuilly
Rian, Edward Harold, 814
Rice, Richard, 633, 979
Richardson, Kurt A., 566, 763, 1050
Richert, Kevin, 764
Ringenberg, William C., 765
Ringma, Charles, 370
Roane, Margaret S., 766
Robbins, Jerry, 815
Roberts, R. Philip, 713
Robertson, Edwin H., 63
Robinson, H. Wheeler, 393
Robinson, John, 64
Rochelle, Jay C., 498
Rogers, Jack, 351, 767, 856, 952
Rohrer, James R., 1120, 1159–60
Rosendall, Brendan, 1005
Ross, Mary Carman, 816
Rosser, William Ray, 1195
Rossow, Francis C., 953
Rowland, Christopher, 223
Rowlett, Martha Graybeal, 1196
Rudin, A. James, 258, 315
Ruehl, Daniel P., 460
Ruether, Rosemary Radford, 252
Rumscheidt, H. Martin, 874
Runia, Klaas, 1190
Rush, Charles, 736
Rutler, George William, 980
Ryrie, C. C., 499

Sanders, Dale, 768–69
Sanders, Gerald M., 176, 714
Saucy, Robert L., 567, 634
Sauer, James L., 461
Saville, Andy, 794
Scaer, David P., 500, 568, 954, 1006
Schachner-Dionne, Robert J., 817
Schaeffer, Francis, 1170–74
Schakelaar, Eva, 1007
Scharlemann, Martin, 818

Schelp, A. W., 1026
Schmid, Donna, 911
Schmidt, Karl T., 520
Schmidt, Mark Ray, 586
Schmiechen, Peter, 189
Schneider, A. Michael, III, 819
Scholer, David M., 462, 912
Schuurman, Douglas J., 737
Schwar, Kathleen, 1161
Schwar, Kathy, 1043
Schwarz, Hans, 935
Schwarzer, Anneliese, 1044
Schweitzer, Albert, 98
Scriven, Charles, 1162, 1197
Sell, Alan P. F., 738
Shelley, Bruce L., 313, 362
Sheppard, Gerald T., 286, 289
Sheriffs, Deryck, 380
Short, Robert, 955
Sider, Ronald J., 679
Simbro, William, 770
Sims, Jim, 913
Sisters of Reuilly, 104
Skibbe, Eugene M., 820
Smallman, William H., 715, 914
Smedes, Lewis B., 86
Smith, B. L., 821
Smith, David L., 1163
Smith, George H., 132
Smith, Harold, 587
Smith, James K. A., 871
Smith, Joanmarie, 635
Smith, Marsha A. Ellis, 319
Smith, Michael T., 1198
Smith, Ronald G., 88
Snyder, Howard Albert, 885, 1186
Soley, Ginny, 915
Sorge, Sheldon Warren, 1199
Souttar, Elizabeth, 104
Sowers, Sidney G., 62
Spencer, Aída Besançon, 463
Spitz, L. W., Sr., 501
Spring, Beth, 916
Sprinkle, Robert, 887
Sproul, R. C., 367
St. Julian's Community, 39
Stagg, Frank, 76

INDEX OF PERIODICALS

Kin; *Pastoral Care Ministries Newsletter; The Pastor's Herald; Renewal; Tenth*
NEWSPAPERS. *See The Augusta Chronicle; Chicago Tribune; The Dallas Morning News; The Des Moines Register; Evening Reporter (Galt, Ont.); The Gazette (Cedar Rapids, Ia.); The Herald Telephone; Miami Herald (Miami, Fla.); New York Times; Ottawa Citizen; Santa Cruz Sentinel (Santa Cruz, Calif.); St. Petersburg Times (Saint Petersburg, Fla.); Star Tribune (Minneapolis, Minn.); Sun-Sentinel (Fort Lauderdale, Fla.); The Telegraph Herald; The Times (Gainesville, Ga.); The Times (San Mateo, Calif.); The Washington Times*
The North American Moravian (Bethlehem, Pa.: Moravian Church in America, Northern Province), 692

The Oak Kin, 1st Covenant Newsletter (Omaha, Neb.: First Covenant Church), 711, 895
Old Testament Abstracts (ISSN 0364-8591), 646
On the Way: Occasional Papers of the Wisconsin Conference of the United Church of Christ (De Forest, Wisc. : United Church of Christ), 304
The Ooze: Conversation for the Journey (www.theooze.com/main.cfm [accessed February 14, 2007]), 1101
The Other Side (ISSN 0145-7675), 918
Ottawa Citizen (ISSN 0839-3222), 1127
The Outlook (ISSN 8750-5754), 806
The Owl of Minerva (Elmhurst, Ill.: Elmhurst College), 4

Pacific Theological Review (ISSN 0360-1897), 630
Paraclete (ISSN 0190-4639), 539
Partnership (Grand Rapids, Mich.: Committee for Women in the Christian Reformed Church), 321

Pastoral Care Ministries Newsletter (Wheaton, Ill.: Pastoral Care Ministries), 459, 870, 909
Pastoral Renewal (ISSN 0744-8279), 181, 188, 241, 251, 256, 439, 886
The Pastor's Herald [newsletter] (S.l.: s.n.), 552
Perkins Journal (ISSN 0730-2142), 960, 990, 1081
Perspectives (ISSN 0888-5281), 332, 843, 1136
Perspectives in Religious Studies (ISSN 0093-531X), 566, 741, 763, 795, 1050
Perspectives on Science and Christian Faith (ISSN 0892-2675), 838
The Pious Papyrus (Dubuque, Iowa: Dubuque Theological Seminary), 575
Pittsburgh Perspective (Pittsburgh: Pittsburgh Theological Seminary), 498
Pneuma (ISSN 0272-0965), 871
Preaching (ISSN 0882-7036), 868, 1075
Presbyterian Communiqué (ISSN 0194-4436), 220, 296, 468, 640
The Presbyterian Journal (ISSN 0032-7549), 111, 152, 502, 544, 636, 819, 883, 995
The Presbyterian Layman (ISSN 0555-0572), 218, 355, 697, 849, 1069, 1144
Presbyterian Life (ISSN 0032-7557), 80
Presbyterian Life and Times (Bloomington, Minn.: Synod of Lakes and Prairies), 902
The Presbyterian Outlook (ISSN 0032-7565), 25, 33, 37, 44, 55, 63, 87, 236, 437, 550, 602, 767, 881, 1051
Presbyterian Record (ISSN 0032-7573), 441
Presbyterian Survey (ISSN 0032-759X), 752, 889
The Princeton Seminary Bulletin (ISSN 0032-8413), 366, 554, 624, 814
The Princeton Theological Review (1994) (Princeton, N.J.: Princeton Theological Seminary), 391, 395
Prism (ISSN 0887-5049), 280

INDEX OF URLS

Note: All websites were last accessed on February 14, 2007.

About the Author

Paul E. Maher received an A.B. from Marion College (now Indiana Wesleyan University) in 1972, an M.A.R. from the University of Dubuque Theological Seminary in 1974, and an M.A. in Middle Eastern Studies from the University of Michigan in 1976.

In 2002, Mr. Maher retired from the Library of Congress, in Washington, D.C., where he had worked as a senior Hebrew cataloger for several years and later as automated operations coordinator for non-Roman languages.

Among his other books is *Hebraica Cataloging: A Guide to ALA/LC Romanization and Descriptive Cataloging*, which was published by the Library of Congress in 1987. Mr. Maher currently makes his home in Aledo, Illinois, where he was born in 1951.